T0354115

This is a memoir; my memories as perceived and articulated through my individual experience. Though they are in truth what I experienced; they may not coincide with what others depicted in the story experienced or remember. Some dramatic effect might occur to better illustrate the influence the events had on those involved. Therefore, in consideration of that fact and in the interest of protecting identities and privacy, I have changed relationships, names, cities, states, and other locations. Any resemblance to actual persons, living or dead, events, or locales is entirely coincidental.

The Evil Within

True Story
By
Imogene Angel

iUniverse, Inc.
Bloomington

THE EVIL WITHIN

iUniverse books may be ordered through booksellers or by contacting:

iUniverse
1663 Liberty Drive
Bloomington, IN 47403
www.iuniverse.com
1-800-Authors (1-800-288-4677)

ISBN: 978-1-4759-5727-3 (sc)
ISBN: 978-1-4759-5729-7 (hc)
ISBN: 978-1-4759-5728-0 (ebk)

Printed in the United States of America

iUniverse rev. date: 11/21/2012

This book is dedicated to my three sons.
The constant and continuous love I have for all of you
is what helped me get through these hard times.
I will love you all till the end of time. Now I can add my
grandchildren and daughters-in-law to that list.
God Bless and Protect You All!

The Evil Within

I was raised on a ten acre farm on the border of Indiana and Illinois, not far from Chicago. My parents raised thirteen children in a one bedroom, one bathroom home. I have hundreds of relatives, mostly in Alabama where I was born.

We were very poor, but we knew lots of love was always there. My father's family is Swedish, and my mother's family is Irish. I mention this because later in my story I will tell you I thank God for the calm Swedish side or I thank God for the fighting Irish side. Depending on the circumstances.

My two oldest sons were born in Indiana. The oldest is named Adam, and his brother is named Brian. My youngest son Christopher was born in California. There is only fours years age difference in my two oldest sons. There is twelve years between the oldest and the youngest.

After my first two sons were born, I went to visit a cousin that had moved to California. My cousin gave me his car while he was at work so I could see California. My first day there I stopped at a park to let my kids play, somewhere down town Los Angeles.

Two men walked up to me to shake my hand. I said my name is Imogene. The name is pronounced "I'm a gene." They replied laughing, "I'm a David and I'm a Paul." It was David Soul and Paul Michael Glaser a.k.a. Starsky and Hutch. They spent that day talking to me and playing with my sons between scenes.

When I told David I lived near Chicago, he said that is where he was from, and I gave him my phone number. My cousin was a little pissed.

He said he lived in California for years and never even saw an actor. I always said I had an angel on my shoulder because I always seem to be in the right place at the right time. Later I moved to California.

I continued to be friends with David, Paul and all the crew. At first, I was just friends with David because I was not yet divorced. After my divorce I spent a lot of my time with David. I even went to his concert in Griffith Park with him. His song "Don't give up on us baby" had hit the charts.

David gave me a copy of his third album that he was working on at the time. It was never released, so I have a one of a kind tape of the album. I'm not sure why it was never released because it is a good album.

I met hundreds of famous actors and actresses of that era.(70's & 80's) I met producers, writers and crew members from many different sets we went on too. My sons and I went to many studios over the next ten years. We were there so much a lot of people thought I worked there.

I even took my mother and brother and a few other family and friends with me over the years. We went on Starsky and Hutch, Charlie's Angels, Love Boat, Quincy, Mash, Air Wolf, Battlestar Gallactica, C.H.I.P.S, B J and the Bear, Buck Rodgers, Dukes of Hazard, Switch and The Yellow Rose, just to name a few.

We also went on a few movie sets where I met John Travolta, Lilly Tomlin, George Segal, Natalie Wood, Robert Wagner and James Garner. By the way, James Garner was one of the most polite, nicest men I ever had the pleasure to meet. He would always pat me on top of the head and ask if I had a note from my mother to be there. That was his own personal joke for me because he is so tall, and I was so tiny.

My sons and I were greeted with kindness and treated like royalty everywhere we went. Some very famous actors would drive me around the lot in limo's to try to impress me. It was a lot of fun but I never dated much. Out of all the actors that tried to pick me up I only dated David Soul and Gil Gerard a.k.a. Buck Rodgers. But not at the same time.

David tried to talk me into going into acting many times. I was doing fine with my modeling, so I just said thanks, but no thanks.

David had to walk through the lobby of the Bonaventure Hotel for a scene one day. He took my arm and asked me to walk with him. As soon as the red light on the camera came on, I froze in my tracks and he walked through by himself.

I did modeling work in front of a camera and had no problem walking up to anyone to talk to them no matter who they were. I could not walk in front of a movie camera though. I still can't figure that one out.

People told me I was on a billboard down in Huntington Beach for one of the ads I did when I was modeling. I never got down there to see it. I would go someplace and people would say, "So you are the Infamous Imogene, huh."

Everywhere you go in California there is a band. Every little dive and nice restaurant had anywhere from a one piece to a seventeen piece band. There was literally music everywhere. I really liked that. As I said, we really were treated like royalty everywhere we went. That all came to a screeching halt when I met a truly evil man named Isaac Richards.

Chapter 1

My parents raised my mother's half brothers and sisters after her father died. I have one uncle that's younger than me. All together my mom had twenty six bothers and sisters. Mom's father was seventy four when my younger uncle was born.

My mom told me once, that back when she was little, people had lots of kids because they lived on big farms. The more kids you had, the more free labor you had for your farm. She also said that I was almost born in a cotton field. She said I popped out before she even hit the bed at home. They estimated that I weighed about ten pounds.

My biggest child was eight pounds and I only labored an hour and a half and thought I was going to die from it. I can't even imagine hours or even days of labor or a child that weighs more. My hat's off to you if you went through it.

When I brought Chris home from the hospital, Adam and Brian sat in the corner whispering to each other. I asked them what they were whispering about. Brian said, "We were just trying to think of a D name." I told them to save that for the grandchildren. Although it wasn't intentional, they were called my A,B,C boys for years after that.

When I was with David, a lot of people would ask for my autograph too. At first I said that I wasn't an actress, but David said, "Aw come on, they are kids. Give them a thrill. It makes them happy." So I signed a few autographs. I hope they weren't too disappointed when they couldn't figure out who I was later.

I think the biggest reason that I didn't go into acting, other than the obvious stage fright, was because of all the people that hounded them all the time. David and I would be in his motor home and people would crawl all over it trying to get a peek at him through the windows. I didn't want to put my sons through that. Fame equals no privacy EVER.

People always gave me a lot of attention, but to be honest, I was more of a stand in the background to watch everyone kind of person.

One example was the one time I was at Universal. I decided to go on the tour around the lot one day. As the tour tram passed by a big group of people filming on the back lot, all the guys started chanting my name as they saw me go by on the tram. I thought it was sweet, so I just smiled and waved to them. When I turn around, everyone on the tram was staring at me and smiling and snapping pictures. It was a little embarrassing to me, but I smiled and waved for the pictures.

I used to have all the pictures and autographs I had collected from everyone I hung out with from the studios. I put them all on this big bulletin board in my house. Adam and Brian decided to use them for a dartboard. I had to throw most of them away when I discovered what they had been doing.

One day we were at a mansion in Beverly Hills to visit Greg Evigan. It was a beautiful home with plush white carpet all through the house. They had a white tiger with them that day and of course B J the chimp was there.

I rarely lose sight of any of my sons even in a big crowd, but somehow Adam got away from me. He was locked in the mansion while they were filming and no one was allowed in or out until they were done.

Adam was a very hyper child. He got into everything all the time just to see how it worked.

When we visited family when he was little, they would jokingly say, "Hide everything here comes Adam Bomb."

I was in a panic. I just knew I was going to have to spend a fortune to replace everything in this house. When they opened the doors, Adam was sitting on the couch talking to Greg. Greg looked up and smiled and said, "I love this kid, he is so bright. You guys come back anytime." So we went back many times and always had a lot of fun.

My roommate Maureen had a huge crush on Greg, and the guy Thom that played the birdman on Buck Rogers. She went with me a lot. On every movie set even if the scene only has two people in it, there are a hundred people there taking care of lights, cameras, etc.

Maureen loved going with me because she said she felt like a kid in a candy store looking at all these good looking guys all in one place. Being from a huge family I looked at most men like I would my uncles or cousins. I told her that it was better to look and not touch. When you touch, that's when the trouble begins.

Every set I went on everyone took up a lot of time with my sons. On Starsky and Hutch, David spent a lot of time with me and Brian. Adam hung out around Paul. A lot of people thought Brian was David's son. He did look a lot like him and David loved spending time with him. On The Incredible Hulk, Adam would talk to Bill Bixby and Lou Ferrigno would walk around with Brian.

Lou played with Brian a lot. I think it was because his wife was pregnant. Maybe this was practice. Brian was about two then. The first few times we were there, Lou wasn't in costume.

When we watched The Incredible Hulk on TV, Brian was scared to death of The Hulk. He would go screaming through the hall, and I would find him shaking under his covers every time he saw him. He was fine with Lou, so I didn't think anything of it.

We were down at Marina Del Rey for the one where Lou throws a boat. Charles Nelson Reilly was a guest that week. My brother and I were standing with the boys when Brian's eyes got as big as saucers and he literally started climbing up the front of me. He did this so fast that I barely caught him by the heels as he was going over my shoulder.

I looked up to see Lou walking up in all his green makeup. Lou saw all this happen as he walked up, so he came over to Brian and started talking to him to calm him down. Lou smeared a little of the green makeup on Brian's hand from what looked like a bar of soap. Brian said, "Yuck" and wiped off the makeup. Then he recognized Lou's voice and was never afraid of the Hulk again.

Adam spent a lot of time with Bill Bixby. I didn't know at the time but Bill had a son Adam's age.

I believe his name was Adam also. Bill's son had just died. I guess that's why Bill liked talking to Adam so much. I felt really bad later that these people were my friends, and I didn't know this had happened to him.

I met one other person with a son named Adam. That was Tony Danza. Adam and his son played together at L.A.X. They were just about the same age too.

When Chris was first born, my room mate Hal started looking at him one day and said, "Oh my God he is sitting there watching us and thinking." Chris was barely a day old. Hal then said, "Most kids his age still have that blank stare on their face. This kid is actually watching us."

I guess he was right because at three months of age Chris was trying to walk, not crawl. We had to start crawling through the living room to get him to do it. It worked. He was walking by seven months. He was so excited he would run around in circles laughing.

When they brought Chris to me at the hospital, I asked how they keep from getting the babies confused because it was a huge hospital. So many babies were born that week that I didn't even get a room. I was put in a bed in the hall. They laughed and said that Chris was the only boy born that entire week so they were sure they wouldn't get him confused.

With both my other sons, I had to stay in the hospital a week. Chris was born just after midnight, and I was sent home before noon that next day. That way turned out to be much better for us. With two boys at home

I couldn't afford to stay a week. Hal was watching them, and he had to work.

I want to say a special thank you to Hal. He stayed my friend even after he moved. He would come back and take all the boys out to the park or movies or dinner, just to give me a break on mother's day and other days too.

I was told by my doctors that all three of my children were going to be girls. They said they had fast heart beats. I remember the doctor sitting at my feet when Chris was born saying, "Here she comes, here she comes." He wiped him off and said, "Here he is."

Chris was laying on my chest, and I raised one finger and said, "Wait a minute." Chris grabbed a hold of my finger with a very tight grip and smiled at me with these deep beautiful little dimples. I said, "Never mind."

I only took dresses to the hospital when Chris was born. I had to send someone to the gift shop to get a tee shirt to take him home in.

One day in downtown L A, I got bored waiting for the scene changes, so I walked off and sat down on the curb to talk to this one guy. David walked up and had a surprised look on his face. He leaned over to whisper, "This guy isn't a regular from the show." I said, "I know." He leaned over again and said, "You don't understand. He is a real skid row bum. He was passed out on the side walk when we got here this morning."

I introduced him to David and explained to him that this guy was a college professor. His wife and children had been killed in a car wreck a few years before this. He started drinking until he passed out everyday just to cope with the loss and never quit.

David's father was a preacher, so David sat down and tried to council the man for a while. It really seemed to help the man. As we walked away, David thanked me. He said he really enjoyed talking to the guy. You never know where the day will take you.

One time at a bar out in the desert, it was supposed to be a bar in Alabama on the show, a guy asked me for my autograph. David told me to go ahead and sign it. The guy sent over a card from one of those old nude women card decks. He asked me to sign it to the preacher.

The drawing on the card was a redhead. Some people used to call me David's redhead. David found this very funny at the time.

When I went with David to his concert the woman that sings "Midnight at the Oasis" was his opening act. Every time I think about that day I get that song stuck in my head. Is it stuck in your head yet?

David sent a limo to bring Paul to the concert but Paul didn't show. They had a little argument over me a few days earlier. I really hope that isn't what ended their friendship. David and Paul were both almost bashful around me. I found this very sweet.

David always treated me with kindness and respect, even when I went off drinking with the crew when I was bored. There were very few actors that weren't very nice people. Most of the mean ones didn't last very long in the business.

David said that his bashfulness was why he didn't do talk shows. He did Merv Griffin's show a few times because he got him started. He did Carson one time but only because his friend Kenny Rogers was guest host, so he did it as a favor to him.

I hope David doesn't mind me saying this, but he was so bashful that he put a bag over his head to sing and tell jokes. He said that is how he put himself through college. He was known as the Unknown Comic. He was around long before anyone knew it.

He laughed and told me that the first time was a real disaster because he had forgotten to put holes in the bag first to see thru. He fell off the stage.

One time when they were filming on Rodeo Drive, David walked into one of the stores I was in. I was looking at this gorgeous pair of multi-colored, sequined high heels. He wanted to buy them for me, but I wouldn't let him.

I just thought of how much milk that $800 would buy my sons. When you grow up poor, you never get over thinking like this. Now I wish I had let him buy them. That would have been a nice keepsake. Don't you think?

I just finished watching the Dancing with the Stars finale. Do any of you follow that show? It made me think back to when I was dating David. I was training to be a ballroom dance instructor. I didn't have the discipline it takes to be an instructor, but it was a lot of fun. When I was dancing, I didn't have to work out with weights. It gives your whole body a great work out.

When I was a teenager, the neighborhood used to have block parties every weekend. If you want to find something to keep the kids in your neighborhood active, maybe you should bring back the old block parties. It will keep people of all ages busy, and they're a lot of fun.

One time I was going onto the set, and all the guys on the crew were very quickly leaving. They said Paul was upset and told everyone to get out. I said I would wave to David to let him know I was there, and I would be right out.

As I walked up, Paul was yelling and throwing things and picked up a fire poker to throw. He saw me and said, "Hello Imogene" and just casually dropped the poker over his shoulder behind his back and walked away.

The people that saw this kept asking me what I had on Paul. They said he had never treated anyone the way he does me. I told them I had no idea why he was always so nice to me. I assumed it was because we are friends.

One day when I walked up to an outdoor shoot, David got upset and asked me why Paul was always staring at me. I told him I didn't know he was. Then David said, "Right in the middle of a scene Paul will lean over and say, "Here comes Imogene. You are usually still so far away that

I have to go put on my glasses to even see you. Why does he spot you so far away all the time?"

I didn't want to argue and I don't like jealousy so I just walked away and partied with the crew.

I hugged everyone goodbye later and said Happy New Year and left. I didn't see them again.

David moved to a new house during the holidays. While they were on hiatus, the show was cancelled. My younger brother had met all of them, and my mother came out and wanted to meet David. Since he had moved I couldn't find him. She never met him. She did meet some of my friends at Universal though.

That is when I started seeing Gil. I only dated Gil a few months. It was all over the news that Connie Selleca had divorced him. She was engaged to John Tesh. John had just started as a radio host. He used to host Entertainment Tonight.

I lost contact with David until I saw him on The Yellow Rose. I went by the studio one day when I was in town. I stopped at the guard shack and just asked them to tell David that I said hi. The guard said, "Excuse my language ma'am, but he said to tell you to get your ass in there."

David was a little upset that he hadn't heard from me for five years. I had just had my last son. David loves babies. He took Chris' picture all over the set showing it to everyone. That life is such a contrast to where my story leads next.

On the set of Yellow Rose was where I met Cybil Shepherd, Eddie Albert Jr. and Sam Elliot. Cybil and I laughed so much they threatened to kicked us off the set. She is from Tennessee.

On one of the movie sets, I met Natalie Wood just before she died. She was so tiny I thought she was a child when she first got there. Dolly Parton is a tiny women too except for the chest area. I always wore heels and no one ever looked down at my feet so they always thought I was taller.

The boys and I started hanging out with Erik Estrada before Chris was born. I knew he liked me, but he had a girlfriend so I stayed just friends. The first day I met him he tried to kiss me. He got his badge caught in the lace trim of my dress.

I started to back away to keep him from kissing me. I just calmly smiled and told him that I would kick his ass if he ripped my dress. We were friends for many years after that. The last time I saw Erik he had a bad motorcycle accident on the set.

Not long after Chris was born I quit going to the sets very often. I concentrated on my relationship with Chris' father. I kind of regretted that later because he wasn't nearly as nice to me as everyone on the sets were. But as a bartender he drank a lot.

We lived right between Knott's Berry Farm and Disneyland. We went to both places all the time. If you go in after six p.m., it is cheaper and the lines are shorter. Since we were there so much we would just go on our favorite rides. My mom was right when she said that I spoiled my sons and I loved every minute of it.

I want to tell you before you get the wrong idea about my next statements. This is so you will see the contrast of how my life was then and where it goes later in my story. I had an amazing life. This is not just me bragging. I am stating facts so you can see the difference.

My two young babysitters that were also my neighbors liked to go to the mall with me. They said they loved to watch how everyone's jaw would drop as I walked by. I was told by so many men and women all the time that I was their fantasy.

They told me that I was the most perfect human being that they had ever met. I didn't let any of this go to my head. I had better upbringing. I would say, "Thank you but most things are better left as fantasies."

One of my best friends used to say, "You really know how to wrap it." When I asked him what he meant, he said that I always dressed very feminine and very sexy. He said that the way I carry myself, like a lady at all times, made me very intriguing. People would say that I reminded them of Ann-Margaret or Elke Summers.

Another friend told me I had very striking features. What I remember the most though is that every time I hugged someone, either before they backed away or shortly after, they would always say, "You give good hug." I realized years later that they meant that it was a sincere hug. I genuinely loved people.

Chris was about three when we were all in a 6.5 earthquake. My king size water bed was bouncing so hard and so fast off the ground from the earthquake it took me a while to get out of my bed. I felt like I was trying to surf a huge wave.

When I got out of the house the huge pillars that held the street lights on the 91 freeway just above our house were still swaying, hard. I realized then that there is no warning and nothing you can do.

We had been in a lot of small tremors over the years but nothing like this. I didn't feel California was safe for my sons anymore. This happened about 4 AM. I threw my sons in the car, grabbed a few clothes and headed for my mom's in Alabama. I was still shaking when we got there three days later.

Adam was now about fifteen. He had just came home a few days before with a bunch of girl's phone numbers written in his hands. He said he had won the championship foot ball game for his high school and these girls were all over him as soon as he walked off the field.

He looked at me and said, "What should I do mom?" I said, "Go wash your hands and play your video games." He shook his head, kind of laughed and said, "That's cold, mom." I said, "You are still too young for girls."

I raised my three sons by myself so I was a very strict mom. He washed his hands and went to play video games.

Adam was a very hyper child pretty much from birth. I took him to a pediatrician that specialized in these kinds of kids while we lived in California.

He said that Adam had a chemical imbalance in his brain. Probably due to the things his father had to take to keep his truck driving job. He said that Adam was so active when he was awake that when he fell asleep he was literally dead to the world.

When the earthquake hit, Adam jumped up and grabbed his brothers to get them out of the house. Adam first said, "Stand here in the door way." I was still trying to get out of my bed so I screamed, "F_ _ _ the doorway, get out of the house."

I explained to him later that a lot of the guys that did construction around there always talked about how they got drunk and high at work all the time and rarely ever put as many nails in these houses as the building code asked for. They knew that if a big quake hit, all those buildings were coming down.

Adam was walking around but he was still asleep. I told Adam and Brian to go to sleep in the back seat of the car, and I put Chris in the front seat.

Early the next day as I topped the hill going into Albuquerque, New Mexico, Adam woke up. He said, "You did it, didn't you? You said you wanted to leave California and you just did it." To this day he still gets mad at me for taking him out of California.

As we topped that hill, we watched over five hundred hot air balloons just lifting off. They have this event there every year. It was such a beautiful sight that for a few moments Adam forgot we had left California.

I left Adam and Brian with my mom for a few weeks to go back to California with Chris to finish working my last contracts and to get my car. Chris was too young for my mom to try to keep up with.

I made good money so I rented huge houses in California. Party houses I called them. One place had a huge fire place and bar in a sunken living room. I had a house once that had an Olympic sized swimming pool, plush carpet in every room, silk brocade drapes, crystal chandeliers and stained glass windows all through the house. The kids had their own big sand box to play in.

You could park twenty or thirty cars in that driveway. I had so much furniture when I left California that I packed the largest moving van I could rent, top to bottom, end to end and still had to leave my garage full of furniture and clothes. I mean you couldn't have squeezed anything else in there. I left my car in storage and came back for it later.

I loved that old 69 Chevy Belair. I had bought it from a little old lady from Pasadena, California. She bought it new and had taken excellent care of it. She looked so much like my mother that when she came to the house to show me the car Chris ran to the door yelling that granny was there. I just stared at her. Then I had to tell her why I was staring. She was like mom's twin.

I drove that car for over twenty years. It broke my heart to scrap it. It was like part of my family. I got a lot of compliments from people of all ages on how good this antique car looked. I drove that car all over California and Mexico.

The boys learned very quickly that you can live cheaply in Mexico. It is so pretty down there that I would actually have to bribe them to get them back to California every time we went. I had to take them to SeaWorld.

I had friends with houses on the bluff right over the ocean in Mexico. They had all the rooms arranged so that when you sit up in bed in the morning you have a gorgeous view of the ocean.

The beaches sparkled every day from the mix of black sand, white sand and flakes of gold. My sons and I would get up early to collect sand dollar shells on the beach. We would go down on the rocks before the water rose to see what kind of sea life got trapped in little tide pools.

I could see how massive the Milky Way was there. Every night you could sit and watch the moon over the ocean as you drift off to sleep. I partied with college students for spring break and college professors the rest of the year, down there from San Diego.

I even tried to drive my car onto the beach in Mexico once. I saw trucks out there so I tried it. When a four wheeler suddenly cut in front of me I hit the brakes and my car sank to the frame. I had to have one of those trucks pull me out. I hadn't thought about the fact that the trucks were four wheel drive.

My sons hated my old Chevy. I would have to drop them off a block before their school.

Every time the boys and I left that area to go exploring I would say, "See ya later." My friends would be really upset because we wouldn't come back for several days.

I would say that was what "exploring" meant to us, to see it all while we were there. Years later I realized that our lives impacted people much deeper than I realized at the time. We were just enjoying life. In just a short span of time people get very attached to me and my sons.

I stopped at a truck stop to eat one time as I was going to Mardi Gras in New Orleans. I talked to three truck drivers for a while before I left to party. I stopped at that truck stop four days later on my way back home.

The same three truck drivers had sat there all this time to make sure I was okay. They told me I had more Moxy than any woman they had ever met before. I just saw it as my love of adventure. If someone mentioned a place, I wanted to go see it. I still think their concern was sweet.

There was one professor in Mexico that everyone just called shit head because that is what his girlfriend called him. He said you can live there cheap and even build a house cheap, but they will never let you buy land there, even if you owned the house that was sitting on the land.

One night after drinking a lot, a bunch of us talked about going in the caves under shit head's house to look around. By the time we decided to actually go it was high tide and everything was under water. We could have all gotten trapped down there and drowned. I miss those idiots.

I grew up in Chicago and saw a lot of tornadoes in my time. Personally I like the storms. I will go sit on a front porch swing to watch a storm while everyone else runs for cover. There was one storm in Mexico though that had me running for cover. Even then I didn't feel safe. The next day I couldn't believe the damage. Huge ships had holes the size of cars in the sides of them.

The houses on the beach had been under water over night and there was water and sand still in all of them where the furniture used to be. I still like to watch storms though. Brian hates storms. He still paces the floor and looks out the windows and doors just like my mother always did.

I got stopped by the police a lot in California. Mostly because they wanted my phone number. After a while this got really aggravating so I started cussing them when they stopped me. I only cussed them if they stop me for no reason.

One young rookie cop stopped me once because Chris' father was mad at me and called them. I knew when he said he had a warrant for me that it was a mistake but there was nothing I could do about it out there on the street, so I turned around and put my hands behind my back.

A while after we got to the station, he came to release me and apologized for my having to go through that. I told him I was fine with it.

There was a big black woman that sat next to me and kept everyone else from bothering me. Some of the women in that cell were a little too happy to see me walk in. They were on their way to Chino women's prison out in the desert. They weren't going to see a woman in a dress for a long time.

She just laid her head in my lap while she talked to me. Here again this would have scared the hell out of most women I know. To me it was just another one of life's experiences I chose to embrace.

Then the cop got mad and started looking through a law book. He said he was going to see what charges he could put on Mick for doing that to me.

The cop told me when he first walked up and saw it was a woman he got nervous. Then he said, "When I saw you were a redheaded woman, I thought oh damn, I'm in for a fight. I was so relieved when you just turned around and gave up."

We were driving down the freeway one day and this guy was waving for me to pull over. Adam and Brian were in the backseat. I ignored the guy. After a while Adam said, "What is it with these guys? It's not like you are Christy Brinkley or anything." I just said, "Gee thanks." He said he was tired of guys always trying to get my attention. He said, "I wish you looked like everyone else's moms."

Guys constantly stopped me and said they would fill up my car with gas if I would just stop to have coffee with them. I was offered condos and houses and Cadillac's. One guy even offered me a million dollars to marry him.

He said the money was mine even if I wanted to divorce him two weeks later. I always knew there were too many strings attached. I politely said, "Thanks but no thanks." I was always proud of the fact that my parents hadn't raised a gold digger.

Adam came running in from school one day and gave me a big hug. While he was hugging me he said, "I love you so much mommy. We had a discussion about parents at school today. Do you know that some parents aren't very nice to their kids? I love you because you are my mom but I like you because you are a good person." He patted me on the head and said, "You're a good kid mom."

Just a couple days before this, I was really upset with him and Brian. I had spent the day and the whole night painting my living room. When I got up the next day there were grape juice stains running down every wall. Adam and Brian had decided to have a grape fight in the house. I had to wash down the walls and re-paint. I just told them they were lucky they were so darn cute.

Adam was hyper and into everything all the time. He was a rough and tumble kind of kid. I had to remind him to not play so rough with his brothers and his friends. He even wrestled the little girls that came to play.

Brian was the shy quiet one. He was very meticulous about everything he did. He stopped to think about everything before he did it. This drives his wife crazy. She says he has to research everything on the computer for months before he will buy it.

Chris was at the park with us one day and a little girl walked by. Without saying a word he dropped my hand, did an about face and started following her. When I went to try on clothes at the store I would come out to find Chris helping the sales girl do her job.

Even when I would take him with me to get my body wraps done I would come out to find my attendant sitting on the floor just totally engrossed in conversation with him and he was only two.

Every woman that baby sat Chris said they hated to charge me because he was so much help that they loved having him there. They said he totally entertained himself all the time.

Because of these so very different traits in my sons I always said Adam is the brawn, Brian is the brain's, and Chris is the lover. As a tomboy I gave my parents so much more trouble than my boys ever did me. I was truly blessed.

All three of my sons were into video games. When I got home from work everyday, half the neighborhood was in my living room playing games.

Adam kept everyone in line. I only went in there if they got out of hand or used bad language. I would give their friends one warning.

If they misbehaved a second time I would call their parents and send them home. I heard Adam a few times telling someone to settle down. He would say, "If you keep this up, my mom will be pissed and trust me you don't want to piss my mom off." I wrote Nintendo once and told them they were the best babysitter I ever had.

Chapter 2

Before my father died, he had left me a piece of land in Crossburg, Tennessee. After a year or two in Alabama, I decided to move there to start a home for us.

Driving through Crossburg the first time my two oldest sons said from the back seat of my old Chevy, "We need to get out of here before rush hour, don't we?" I said, "This is rush hour here baby." My sons looked very puzzled for a minute at each other then said, "I thought you said we were moving here to slow down mom, not stop!"

A week later driving thru town, Paul Harvey comes on the radio and says," If you want to get away with murder, move to Crossburg, Tennessee." This kind of threw me for a second, so I asked around and I was told that was only drug related murders. Since I was never into drugs, I figured we had nothing to worry about. That really will teach me to think.

Driving through town a few weeks later I noticed someone hanging out the window of a car waving and yelling my name saying hello. I had just moved here, I thought to myself, how do these people know me? Then I said, "Oh yeah, it's a small town word travels real fast."

The land my father had left me was an acre in a resort area. I thought, no problem I have worked the last twenty six years and raised my three sons by myself. I will get a job and build a house. I had built up excellent credit in California for the last fifteen years. Being a single woman with three small children building up credit back then was no small feat.

Moving to the south I found out voided all credit I had spent all those years building up. I was told that the United States was split into four sections. If you move from one section to the other you have to start all over on credit.

Jobs in this small town was explained to me as, either you are related to someone here and they get you a job or you wait for someone to die and leave you a job.

When I first moved here, I had written to the White House and asked how I would go about opening a business there. I had wanted to open an arcade. That way the boys could help and they would have something of interest to keep them busy.

They had just started talking about virtual reality games. That sounded like it would be worth checking into. I got a letter back from Al Gore saying they would pay ninety percent of a small business loan for me to start a business here. I started looking into getting a building.

Soon after I moved here I became violently ill. I couldn't even get out of bed. For the next five years I went from doctor to doctor. They told me either it is old age or all in your mind. You don't go from being as active as I always was to being too old to get around over night.

All these years I took care of three very active boys and a huge house. Cooking, cleaning, working and helping friends with their businesses and hanging out at the studios. I finally found out I had allergy problems.

I was then told that since I moved to a much higher elevation here on the plateau, just before the Smoky Mountains, that the thinner air made my allergies much more severe. I took a lot of allergy shots and medicine to get thru it.

I still have to take the meds. every morning just to be able to breathe. I had to give up the business idea because I was too sick to get out of bed for five years. It took them that long to figure out it was allergies.

I don't even remember exactly how many different doctors I had to see before they figured it out.

Getting through all that, I set out to find a driving job. I drove semis with my ex-husband when I was nineteen. I drove them here and there different times over the years. Even when I had to hitch hike with truck drivers over the years, they would have me drive for them so they could take a break.

When Adam was little he woke up one morning to find me driving a brand new hand built Mormon truck. As a boy he really liked seeing his mom do this.

I started out racing motorcycles with my brothers and uncles when I was fifteen on old gravel back roads in Indiana. I drove car haulers out of Chicago, Arena Auto Auction when I was nineteen and drove package carriers for UPS one holiday season. I have driven everything from bikes to semis.

My mom's best friend was a preacher's wife. She kept saying I was having a girl when I was pregnant with Adam. My mom asked her one day why she was so sure it was a girl. She said, "Because she shook it's balls off in them trucks." I drove car haulers with my husband until I was about seven months pregnant. Then it just got too rough to take. Back then we didn't have sleepers or air ride seats.

Well, I found out that many places here will not hire female drivers at all. They claim the insurance won't cover female drivers and I was told I was too old to be hired at UPS. They won't hire anyone over thirty. It made no difference that I had already been trained by UPS.

This pissed me off, but I didn't have the time nor the money to fight it. I thought back to when I first started driving. I was a teenager. I was barely five feet tall back then and weighed about ninety pounds soaking wet.

The steering wheel was so big I could barely reach the width of it and there were times I had to stand up just to hold the clutch in. There weren't any female drivers back then. It would freak these truckers out when I would back this forty foot trailer between trucks so close the mirrors would almost touch. A female, a good driver and one that tiny?

Then I fell on a concrete floor that had flooded with water and slipped a disc in my neck. Outside of being very painful I found out that when the disc slipped out, it hit a nerve that made my arms go numb.

You can't drive semi's when your arms are numb. So I had to file for disability. It took me another eight and a half years to get disability. They only paid me for one year back pay. I couldn't afford an attorney to fight that either.

For the next ten years, the people of this town would go out of their way to stop me and just rave over how much they all really liked me and my sons and how well mannered my sons always are.

Teachers would tell me they loved to call me so they could brag about a child for once instead of complaining. Here and in California. We were even friends with several police officers here.

The female officer went to school with Brian. People told me my sons were welcome at their home anytime. They said even if their kids weren't at home they were welcome because they were so well mannered and down to earth that they liked talking to them.

It's nice to get a pat on the back for your efforts once in a while.

People everywhere I lived told me that they would have never guessed my sons came from a single parent home because they were so polite and so grounded.

I constantly told my sons how much I love them and when they asked about their father's, I always told them that it was their father's fault they chose not to be with them, not theirs. I told them that it was definitely their loss because I still love every minute I get to spend with them.

When I first moved here, we lived in a nice house in one of the other resort areas. This was about thirty miles from the land my dad gave me.

It was late when I got there, so I parked in the carport and decided to unpack the truck the next day. I woke up to freezing cold and two inches or more of snow. When I couldn't find a job we had to move to a much smaller place in town.

I had to drop off a truck load of my things one night at the Good Samaritans building. They were closed, so I just left them on the curb. They simply wouldn't fit into this much smaller place.

Times were hard, but I always try to keep a good sense of humor about what ever life threw at me. We had tough times before and I always told myself things would get better and it usually did.

Several years later, when Chris was the only one at home at that time, I had to go to Good Samaritans to ask for Christmas gifts because I didn't have my disability yet.

This wasn't easy for me to do. I had taken care of my family on my own. Now I had to ask for help. I convinced myself that it was okay since I had given them a couple thousand dollars worth of furniture, clothes and silk goose down comforter's years before.

I wrote down his name, told them he was a boy and wrote BOY, in big letters on the paper. I told them he had outgrown his bike and asked if they could get him a bigger one. I knew the man that donated hundreds of new bikes to them to give to kids every year.

I stood in line and watched all these people walk out with brand new bikes with nice ribbons tied all over them and bags of nice toys and clothes. I thought even though we have gone through so much at least he will have a nice Christmas.

They handed me a bag and rolled out a bike the same size as the one I told them I needed a bigger one for. Not only did it not have ribbons; it didn't have even one speck of paint on it.

Even all the spokes were rusted out on it. I wouldn't take it. They got mad and told me that I still had to drop off Chris' good bike to them so they could give it to someone. I refused. They said they had promised it to someone already. I said for them to give that one to them. Without thinking he said, "I'm not giving that piece of crap to anyone."

When I got home I found that the toys were all broken and had missing parts and it was girls' clothes. The clothes weren't only girls' clothes, the jeans were all ripped and the shirts were ripped and had missing buttons. I had to throw it all away and go to the dollar store and get him a few cheap plastic toys. Chris was still happy because I never mentioned what they had done to us.

Adam had a harder time than the rest of us adjusting to a small town. Tommy Lasorda lived in our neighborhood in California. Adam would stop on his way home from school everyday to talk sports with him. He asked Adam to come to work with the Angels Baseball team with him once.

Adam had to tell him he was only twelve at the time. You have to be sixteen to join the team. At twelve Adam had one of those Tom Selleck looking mustaches so he always looked much older than he really was. He was tall and had those wide shoulders too.

I was asked by a company that was writing a book about the "Women of the Eighties" one time if I would have a stripper party for my friends. They said they would pay for it if I let them get the women's reactions for their book. They said they would put me in the dedication.

When Adam walked in to get Chris his bottle, the women went nuts. He was a very good looking kid. I had to tell them he wasn't the stripper. They were all very disappointed. I had a huge house then. The boys were in their room at the back of the house. I had to carry a big stick to run off all the older women that hit on Adam over the next few years.

Adam was popular at school too. Adam is Russian and Cherokee Indian on his father's side. Dark curly hair and olive complexion. I don't tan. I just freckle. To look at us both together no one ever thought he was my son.

As he got older, most people would assume he was my boyfriend. They always said we got along to well to be mother and child. I was twenty when Adam was born. I always say, "We grew up together."

As I said, we lived right by Knott's Berry Farm in California. Adam went there a lot with friends from school. At curfew the police would run all the kids out of the park. Adam looked so much older so he would stand there waving bye to his friends. He would talk to the police a while then go back into the park. He really hated moving away from all that.

Adam had met a girl in Alabama just before we moved to Tennessee and wanted to move back there to be with her. Adam thought I would be mad. He was a little shocked when I said, "I will help you pack." and drove him to the bus station. He was eighteen by then so I really couldn't have stopped him.

Most of my family was there to help him. He got a live in job helping to care for a woman's mother while she worked.

He lived there several years and stayed this woman's friend long after her mother died. He moved back and forth the next few years from Alabama to Tennessee. He is much older now and still moves home from time to time. I really love taking care of my babies no matter how old they are.

They all get upset when I call them my baby, but as every mother knows, they will always be my babies. My birth sign is Cancer so I end up being called mom or sis by most people because I end up babysitting everyone, young and old. This really upset Adam when he was little.

One time a truck driver patted my hand at the lunch counter when he was talking to me. Instantly, Adam was between us and looked up and said, "That's my mom and you don't need to be touching her." The guy just laughed about it and said, "This must be your kid."

Adam hated anyone calling me mom. When one of his friends called me mom, Adam would put his hand on his hip and say, "Hey, that's MY mom, not yours!" My sons take this baby sitting trait from me. All their friends tell me how my sons only drink one beer to their case then safely drive everyone home. That's why people like them so much. I got it from my father. I love people but no one comes before my sons, ever. Never have, never will.

Adam even fussed at Erik Estrada once for running up and giving me a hug and kiss at a restaurant. Erik always called me Imogene Coca first, to remember my name.

Adam knew him from us being on the set a lot, but Adam felt the kiss was inappropriate for a public restaurant. Like I said I considered dating Erik at one time but because he had a girlfriend I decided to just stay friends. This was quite frustrating to Erik. His crew teased him about it.

Larry Wilcox was going through a divorce. He wasn't very nice to anyone back then.

At my dad's funeral years before, a woman much older than my dad came up to me to tell me that my dad was always like a father to her and many other people. She said he took care of everyone and had done this his whole life.

As I had said before, we were poor. My father working at the steel mills brought us up to middle class status. I remember going to his funeral and looking back at the cars behind us.

I was almost shocked at seeing that the line stretched for miles. I was amazed as I watched them coming over hill after hill. I love that this sweet, calm natured man touched so many lives.

A group of bikers pulled to the side of the road and stood in a row and took off their hats and bowed their heads as we went by. Even with all the people that came to the funeral, my mom said she received money and food and cards and phone calls for months afterwards. He always reminded me of John Wayne. He looked a little like him too.

My mother told me she was so mad at him one time because someone at work had a bad week so my dad signed his paycheck and handed it to him. She yelled at him and asked how they were going to feed thirteen kids. She said my dad calmly said, "We always make it honey." She said what pissed her off the most was he was right.

A man was talking to my dad once and saw a man coming up the road. The man asked, "Well, who is this stranger walking up here?" My dad said, "I don't know. I never met a stranger before. It always ends up a friend I hadn't met yet." That's how I chose to live my life. He always said to treat everyone like family. He said we had such a large family that they just might be related.

So many friends would get mad at me over the years because total strangers would come up and sit down and start telling me their life's story instantly. It never bothered me. This had happened to me my whole life.

I remember one of my older aunt's boyfriends that always talked to me while my aunt was getting ready for their dates. He told me once that he was breaking up with her because I was so easy to talk to that he was falling in love with me. I was much to young to date so he kissed me on the cheek and never came back.

All my life, after talking to me for even a short period of time, people would tell me I was an angel or a God send. They would say that when they needed someone to talk to the most, God made sure I was there.

Shortly after Chris' father and I split up I found out that he had gotten both hands cut off in a work accident. I had left him when I caught him with his ex-wife's sister. She talked him into going to Vegas to live. She told me she was doing this to keep him from paying me or her sister child support. She said she had three kids that she felt needed his money more than his own child did.

When he couldn't find bartending work, he started working with metal bending machines.

He was trying to un-jam a piece of metal, and the safety broke and cut off both hands at the wrist. I saw him a few years later and they had fused one of his thumbs by his wrist so he could still somewhat use one arm to do things.

When I couldn't cover our bills, I filed for disability for Chris against his father's account. For the next several years I got one to three dollars a month from them for Chris. At the end of every year they sent me paperwork and told me that I had to pay taxes on a thousand dollars that we never received. I asked them why. They said this was Workers Compensation Offset. This is their term for, you just got legally robbed.

I found out years later that California was collecting child support from him in Chris' name for over twenty years. When I asked where Chris' money was, they said that his dad had so many children that they were keeping it for them.

I still get a letter every month telling me how much they collect from him and that we still get nothing. How nice of them to decide that Chris had to pay for his father's other children, don't you think? Robbed again.

When I first moved to Crossburg, the police were a little pissed that I drove everyone home from the bars when I moved here. They knew that was safer but they had no one to give tickets to and make money.

I talked to the women that owned the local cab company once. She told me I was part of the reason she was put out of business. I apologized because I had no Idea. She said she never blamed me because she knew I didn't do it on purpose. I felt bad about it anyway.

After Chris' father and I separated, I had decided I didn't want to ever be in any type of relationship again. I just took care of my sons and never even dated for the next eleven years.

Some of the men in this town asked if I was a lesbian because their feelings got hurt when I turned them down.

Just as many women has hit on me as men over the years, so no, I never went with a woman either. My old roommate Maureen told me once that I should write a book about the most original pick up lines all these guys used. She said that she could remember quite a few of them.

One day my doctor did some kind of test and told me I had a hormone deficiency and started giving me hormones. I started getting kind of horny. This was a feeling I hadn't had in years. I tried to ignore it and did a pretty good job.

I went to the bars sometimes just to find people to talk to but never slept with anyone. I love spending my time with my sons, but there are only so many conversations you can have after awhile. Everyone needs an adult to talk to once in a while.

Chapter 3

Ike approached me one night in a bar and talked for quite a while. Then he asked if I wanted to smoke a joint.

I had quit drinking when I got pregnant with Chris and stopped smoking, except on occasion, not long after that. I will also add the fact that in California smoking pot and drinking lots of alcohol were legal when I lived there.

Then Ike said it was at his house and we could stop by there on my way home. I ended up having sex with Ike, then sat and talked for awhile with him and his room mate Rink.

I never sleep with strangers, not even all those years I drank a lot. I loved to dance a lot so I usually danced off my buzz instead of letting it get me into trouble. Most of the men I did sleep with I knew sometimes for years first.

Guys would always challenge me to drinking contests because I was so small. They thought I would get drunk really fast. I would usually end up having to drive the guys home in their cars after they passed out. If they passed out before I found out where they lived, I would drive them to my house and let them sleep it off in their car out in the driveway.

They were too big for me to carry in the house. My brother would look out the door and laugh and say, "So you drank another one under the table last night, huh!" I got to drive a lot of really nice, really fast cars that way. The freeways are just about empty early in the morning after the bars close in California, so I had my own little speedway.

I was walking to my car once in California and a bunch of guys came out of a house and asked if I was the entertainment. It turned out they were having a bachelor party and the girl didn't show up, and they said it was a real flop. I felt sorry for them and said I could play bartender for a while and wait to see if she showed up.

I made a lot of really strong Kamikazes. They never once gave me a hard time. They all gave me a hug and a kiss when I left and thanked me for making their party fun. All I did was talk to them. Sometimes people forget that a pleasant conversation can make a man's day.

I told myself that sleeping with Ike seemed logical at the time. I hadn't been with a man in so, so many years. And the fact that he was a stranger here from Ohio, I thought I may never have to run into him again.

Sometime later that morning five little girls came bursting out of their room, naked. They ran to the fridge and started shoving and hitting and scratching each other with one hand and grabbing food and shoving it into their mouths with the other hand. They were calling each other names and their hair was matted to their heads.

Before I could stop myself my jaw dropped to the floor and I said, "Oh my God, they are like a pack of wild animals." I apologized to him and said I didn't mean to say that out loud. He got a little angry and said that was his daughters and their mom had just abandoned them for a younger man, His former boss.

After talking a while he asked me if I wanted to baby-sit for $600 a month. He said he lost his job when Brandy took off with his boss, and if he had a sitter, he could look for work. I told him I would think about it and went home.

My disability hadn't gone through yet and I was about to lose my house back to the government agency that was "supposed" to be helping me buy it. So I said yes. I thought God had me meet these people for a reason and they very obviously needed my help.

I told the agency that owned my house, Compassionate Creation, that my disability back pay would be in soon and I could then buy the house I had rented from them for the last five years. They decided they wanted another five years rent instead.

Without any warning they suddenly threw me and my sons out on the street. I mean they sent the police to take us out of our home and they put all my things in storage. They wouldn't let me move anything or even go back in to get the phone number to where Chris was spending the weekend so I could call him to tell him what happened.

They lied to the courts to get me moved out. Chris came home to an empty house and sat down and cried until my neighbor came over and told him what happened and where we were.

When I got mad at my sons once I jokingly said I would move while they were in school one day and leave no forwarding address. Chris thought I had done just that. He was only twelve then.

These people destroyed most of my things. They didn't even get boxes or cover anything with furniture pads. They just threw it all in the storage space. They kept my fridge and all of the ceiling fans I had put up all through the house. I paid three hundred dollars a piece for every one of those fans before I left California.

When I walked out of the courtroom, Ike Mathers from Compassionate Creation walked out right behind me and said, "We know you don't actually owe us money, so we will never try to collect it. Nothing personal, it's just business."

It is probably still on record that I owe them money. I don't owe them anything and they always knew that. I think destroying my furniture and my credit and lying in court about me is extremely personal, don't you?

A local millionaire started a newspaper called The Watchdog. It talked all about how crooked the police and sheriff's department in that town had become. I still didn't think we were in any danger. I had never had a problem and neither had my sons. Eventually the police shut down the newspaper. I would have thought that with the money he had that they couldn't touch him.

I heard they even beat up the guy's wife when she was stopped for driving drunk. At one point I remember hearing that the sheriff had to pay the hospital more money than the people that lived there did because his men were beating everyone up.

When I lost my house, Ike said to move in with him so I could be there to watch his girls while he looked for work. I thought I would stay there for a while, save some money and get me another place.

Brian had just started college at Tennessee Tech in Cookeville. He stayed in the dorm at first. He majored in computer science. Brian started working with computers in the second grade in California.

He told me that they were offering computer classes and asked what I thought he should do. I told him and all my sons that if someone was willing to take the time to teach them anything, to go for it. You never know when you can use it later in life. I also told them that I thought computers would be the wave of the future.

I am so proud that all my sons cared enough about me that they actually listened to me. Adam had just started at Roane State Community College while he was home recuperating from a car wreck.

Chris was at that age that he spent most of his time out with his friends. So I thought, okay, I can deal with taking care of this new family. I was even more convinced that this was all happening for a reason.

Ike called the girls his little tornados. They were definitely a handful. But as I found out in time, they were nothing compared to having to deal with him. I took on six infants that day, not just five.

Let me say one thing to you ladies out there, a nice smile can hide a truly evil heart. My sons laughingly called the girls the spawn of satin. I had no idea the true terror I was leading my family into.

A day or two after I first met Ike I needed to go to the store. Ike asked if he could go with me and Chris. I saw no problem with that. While we were shopping, several people stopped us to talk. They talked about how nice they think I always am and they told me that my sons were so nice and down to earth and that I had done such a great job raising them.

Chris' music teacher stopped me to tell me how Chris played several different instruments extremely well and asked if I would mind if he taught him more than one instrument at a time.

He said he never does that but that Chris mastered every instrument he gave him in just a few weeks time. I told him he could teach him as many instruments as he could handle, if that is what Chris wanted to do.

Ike suddenly gave me a dirty look and said, "So you and your kids are little Miss Popular, huh. Well, I will put a stop to that." It was years before I understood what he meant by that and what he had done against us. You will find out later in the book. My nightmare was just beginning.

I spent the next week, day and night with three pair of reading glasses on picking lice and their eggs (nits) out of his five girl's hair so the oldest could go back to school. Lice are tiny little things.

When their family members took them for a day or two, they came back with lice or ring worms. Luckily she didn't come to take them very often. One time they got lice so bad I had to have the girls' heads shaved.

I felt so bad but it was during the summer and it grew back quickly. They were beautiful little blonde haired, blue eyed girls. Their ages were one, two, three, four and six.

I am going to pass on a tip the doctors won't tell you. They want you to buy the shampoo. The girls got lice so often I started worrying about using this toxic shampoo so much.

A doctor told me to mix together half Vaseline and half Mayonnaise. Put it on their hair as thick as you can and wrap their hair in saran wrap. All the way to the hairline for four hours. I washed their hair with Dawn dish detergent about five times to get it all out. I washed their sheets and pillow cases too.

When I checked not only were the lice gone, so were all the eggs. No more picking nits.

Ike spent the next year getting drunk with his buddies everyday instead of looking for work.

He started getting very verbally abusive, but I was still determined to protect those girls. I found out that some of these guys were convicted child molesters. He still let the girls run around naked in front of these men. I quickly put a stop to that. Feather was the hardest to break from it.

One day Tiffany came in to show him a picture she drew for him. She was smiling and skipping down the hall. He was very drunk and slapped her so hard her head smacked the wall, and then she landed back in the middle of the floor.

I have never in my life stood by and watched someone be hit. I have never felt that anyone had the right to hit anyone. Without even thinking I shoved him and said, "Swing at me, I know how to swing back." He said it was his child and that I needed to stay out of it. I said, "If a child misbehaves, you pick them up and swat them on their ass, but you don't hit them."

I learned raising my kids that if you put them in time out and take their favorite toy away for a while, it is a much worse punishment. He was mad, but he said he was sorry and calmed back down. Later he kind of laughed and said, "You were really going to fight me weren't you?"

I decided to let him know that one of my former jobs was as a professional kick boxer. I went to Taiwan before Chris was born and was trained by the championship kick boxer of Taipei. They are into self defense, not to go beat people up. I was taught that you may have to walk around your opponent and take a few punches but everyone guards their weak spot. Even if they don't know it's their weak spot.

When you see it you can bring anyone down in one to two punches, no matter how big they are. This is very similar to how Mike Tyson fights. One thing they told us was to never fight angry. They said if you fight angry you have already lost.

I made the mistake of taking everything I could with me to Taiwan. I had to move all these suitcases every week from one hotel to another. Now when I travel even with all three of my sons, I take one bag. If we need anything else, I buy it.

The first night we had a boxing match in Taiwan a few doctors asked us to have drinks with them. There are so many people there that they all drive scooters. There are no red lights or stop signs in towns.

We were all on these bikes going about seventy mph through town in heavy traffic. When I looked up, I saw a bus coming straight for us. After that we all agreed to share a cab everywhere we had to go.

The people there loved us. We were treated like celebrities. Crowds would gather in the street and wave up at us in our rooms. When we walked into a store, they would switch over to an English speaking radio station. All the teens there wore saddle shoes and poodle skirts.

I am a short person but even in a huge crowd of people, I could see over every bodies heads. I saw schools of small children going through rigorous exercise routines that would stop most adults.

They are so proud of boy babies that when they are babies they don't make them wear diapers.

In the big cities there would be deep open sewers with boards over them so you could cross to the other side of the street. You can't drink the water there either.

There is no middle class there. There is either high rise buildings for the rich or slums for everyone else. Everywhere we went they played old sixties music. This was in the eighties.

They were a little behind the times in music, but they were so far ahead of us in electronics.

I saw things there then that are just now coming out here thirty years later. I lost a lot of weight because Chinese food there is nothing like any of our food here. They had Pepsi and a McDonald's. That was the only thing I recognized so I ate a lot of Rice.

After we started boxing, they told us we had to start boxing topless. We trained as professional boxers, but the shows ended up being more like exhibition shows at the theaters. All the other acts were from Australia. I now have many friends in Sydney, but I have never been there. They were the only people there that spoke English.

Our Chinese M.C. for the shows spoke a little English, so one of the girls asked how to ask for chicken. We were all a little tired of just pointing or trying to order our food by playing charades.

I knew by the way she laughed when she said, "Chi pie," that she was not being totally honest. One of the girls went to order at the restaurant and the waiter just looked at her in shock. A woman came out of the back and started talking to him. They talk so fast that it almost sounds like they are arguing but they aren't.

The girl repeated Chi pie, and tucked her hands under her armpits and started flapping like a chicken. The couple just laughed and brought her some kind of chicken. I think it was chicken anyway. We found out later that Chi pie, means p _ _ _ _, and I don't mean the cat.

In Taiwan they ate live monkey brains and live prawns soaked in wine. They bought something they called a beetle from the street vendors. They chew it and spit a snuff like substance out of their mouths wherever they happen to be standing. They say this is the same effect as cocaine. I guess this is why they are always smiling. It ruins their teeth though.

The vendors would smack a hanging piece of meat that was black with all the flies hanging on it and cut off a piece and sell it. That is why I ate a lot of rice and lost so much weight.

One time my friend left her glasses in her room so since she couldn't see very well and I didn't want her to fall into one of the open sewers, I ran back to the room to get her glasses. I was running so fast because we were about to go on stage that when I fell I slid like a baseball player trying to make home plate.

I wasn't hurt but when I got to my feet I saw that people were filming me. It was embarrassing but I just smiled and waved. I was always afraid it would show up on a blooper show. Maybe it did, over there.

I started watching the promoters that had hired us when we were out in the evening. I told the other girls that there was something I didn't trust about them. Even though I don't speak Chinese you can learn a lot by watching someone's body language.

Just before they said we had to box topless, my sister called me to tell me my father had a heart attack, but that he was back home and doing fine. I told them I wanted to go home when they said we had to go topless. I told them that was ridiculous. The one girl was so big busted that she would beat her eyes black all by herself every night.

When we first got to Taiwan, they took our passports. They said it was to get our work visas. We also found out at the airport that they don't have toilets.

They have a footprint hollowed out on either side of a hole in the concrete you squat over. It was kind of funny every night watching the other girls squirm while we were out drinking waiting to get back to our rooms to use the bathroom.

I would just hold my nose and run in and squat. Living in the south gave me practice for this. I have had to go in more than my share of outhouses, fighting spiders and snakes to do it. The hotel rooms had toilets, but they also had huge rats that liked to play in the toilets.

There was one girl that couldn't get a work visa for some reason. They tried to make her work in prostitution. I knew I didn't trust these guys. It was all over the news when I got home about how they would trick girls into coming there, and they would sell them into white slavery.

We were out one night and this guy from London threw a huge plastic roach on the table as a joke. I looked up and pointed to one on the wall too. The one on the wall was bigger than my hand. After a few minutes the one on the wall started walking away. It was a real one, not plastic.

The promoters told me they couldn't afford to send me home yet. I ended up having to go to the Military police to get my passport back. They told me that they had me a ticket to Hawaii and when I got to the airport in Hawaii a ticket to California would be waiting.

I didn't sleep that night. I half expected them to come and shoot me in the middle of the night rather than pay for my ticket. Later the girls told me I was right. After I left, they never got paid and barely got food money.

Guess what? No ticket in Hawaii. I was stranded there for two weeks. It was the best vacation I ever had. I met a taxi driver the first night. He liked me so he gave me his card and said to call anytime. He took me everywhere I wanted to go every day the whole time I was there. Thank you very much, Steve.

At the bar my first night I met this guy Eddie that was going to go to the main land to try out for a pro football team. I told him he was welcomed to visit if he made it to California. He said that he had a couple of roommates, but that if I didn't mind sleeping on a couch I could stay with them until I got a ticket home.

I got to spend the next week with three gorgeous, buff, Hawaiian guys. They walked around the house in bathing suits all day because the weather there was great. They cooked my meals, did my laundry and took me out dancing every night. The taxi driver spent everyday taking me to see the sites. I got to see all the local hangouts and the tourist hot spots. I saw a few celebrities while I was there too.

At TGI Fridays I met these guys that said they had a fifty foot catamaran that they took people on tours around Maui with. They were on Oahu where I was at, for repairs on the catamaran.

They asked me to go to Maui with them. We left early the next day. It took all day to sail to the other island. I was a little sea sick so I took a nap. When I woke up the captain, the one called Preacher, was steering this huge boat drunk on his ass. It was a trip just watching him. He had a great time.

I spent another week there. These guys lived in a commune type of place with all the waiters, waitresses and bartenders on the island. I was invited to a different place every night. I ate and drank everywhere for free. And for the record, Maui Wowie was the best pot ever.

I got the drunkest I had ever been there. I ended up calling my sister who was at my house in California and asking her where I was at. A few days later Chris' father called me to tell me he had bought me a ticket home. I didn't want to leave yet. I stayed a few more days, and then I flew back to Oahu and then back to California.

On the way back, half way across the ocean, one of the engines went out. The pilot asked if we wanted to turn around or go on. We all said to go on. A week later they said on the news that the same flight I had taken from Maui to Oahu had just lost a big section of the plane in flight and sucked a bunch of the passengers out of the plane. I don't think I have flown anywhere since then. Oh yeah, Chris was born a year after this trip.

When I was still in Hawaii, I met about five other people with the same birthdays as mine. I went back five years later to meet up with them and spent a week on Kauai. I took a helicopter tour of the volcanoes. I highly recommend it if you go there.

I did however hate the geckos. They get between your sheets and crap all over. I had to check for this every night before I could lay down. That isn't easy to remember when you are out drinking all night.

While I am talking about vacations, a friend of mine that was building the Pyramid Hotel in Cairo, Egypt asked me if I would go to Cairo to talk one of his men out of quitting in the middle of the job.

He said if I did this he would pay for me to go to Germany to see my brother who was in the army and he would take me to the playboy club in Zurich, Switzerland on the way back. I agreed. It turned out that I didn't have enough time to get a visa to get into Egypt. He still said he would pay for my trip to Germany since I was at least going to try and help him.

On the flight back from Germany I had a lay over in London. I went site seeing and met Efrem Zimbalist Jr.'s Brother-in-law on the bus. He was a shrink for the UN. He traveled all over the world sorting out all the world leaders' problems. I get to meet a lot of interesting people. I had a lot of fun.

When my brother and I were traveling around Germany, we were out with his friends one night and an Italian jeweler bought all our drinks all night. He begged me to stay another week. He said it was almost time for Fasching. He said the whole country closes down to celebrate for a week. They all put on costumes and party hard all week. I really wanted to stay, but I had to get home.

I mentioned before growing up on a farm with my brothers, sister, aunts and uncles. Also at thirteen I was suddenly bigger busted than Dolly Parton. I was also the only virgin still around my neighborhood, so I grew up having to defend myself from all the local boys. These guys would jump out of trees to try to get me.

Over the years I grew to appreciate the tomboy side of my life. When I was twelve I was so flat and so skinny. I decided to go buy a product called Super Weight On. I woke up after taking only one spoonful and looked like someone had smacked me hard, in the chest with a baseball bat. I never took anymore.

It took years to lose those inches. I lost two inches of bust line with each of my sons. I produced a lot of milk but chose not to breast feed. I had to bind my breasts to stop the milk production which resulted in losing inches. I was happy with this. Men had stopped looking me in the eyes.

Back to the story. One time I took Ike to get some more beer. He instantly gets belligerent when he drinks. He started in on me on the way home. I asked him to stop, three times. He just kept bitching at me, and then he leaned over and said, "I will kill your kids, too."

I swear this was a knee jerk reaction, I punched him, hard. He grabbed his beer and said, "Let me out." I said, "Jump." He once again said, "Let me out." So I said again, "Jump." As he opened the door, I started to pull over to let him out, but he jumped first.

I looked in my rear view mirror and saw Rink just rolling in the back seat laughing. I had forgotten he was there. He said he had waited for years for someone to have enough balls to do that to Ike. He said that Ike had deserved it a lot but no one had ever done it. I felt bad about hitting him. This wasn't my nature.

After a lot of constant verbal abuse, I had enough and told Ike I was moving. I had sat and watched him get drunk every day and pass out and wet himself, day after day. Ike shoved me out the door and said, "You aren't taking anything." At that point most of my things were still in storage.

I had only brought a few personal things for me and Chris and an older portable dishwasher I had just had rebuilt. I bought the top of the line motor for this dishwasher. It cost me over $500 to repair. I sat on the curb to think about what I was going to do. Adam saw me and stopped to see what was wrong. I told him.

Adam was always very protective of me even as a child. Now he was a very big man with big broad shoulders. Since he was a football player in high school, he was a little intimidating. He went to the house and walked in and asked where Ike was. He was told that he had just left, so I got a few things and we started to leave. The very drunk woman that was there came running out behind me to grab me.

Adam put his arm out to block her and she ran into his arm and fell back. Then she grabbed Adam by the shirt collar to try and drag him back in the house. She weighed at least 300 lbs. My son picked her up off her feet like a feather and sat her back in the house and said, "I wouldn't try that again." We left with her cursing us and threatening us.

In the meantime, Ike found me and begged me to come back to take care of his girls. I had nowhere to go and my disability still hadn't started yet so I went back. Ike said that he was just angry over his wife leaving and not having a job and that he would never talk down to me again.

My sons are calm people like my father was. Totally non-violent. I always told my sons if they ever hit a woman or got one pregnant that after I beat their ass, I would take them to the girl's father to do the same. Thank God they listened to me.

A drunk is not supposed to be able to take a warrant out on anyone until they sober up but as you will understand later this ends up being a very crooked town.

The drunk woman had Adam arrested on assault. When it went to court, she was so high and so drunk she just kept walking in and out in the middle of the hearing. They finally decided to drop it, but only if Adam paid a big fine to dismiss it.

While all this was going on Ike had taken Rink's car on a beer run and wiped out going to fast around the corner and ran from the scene. Both passengers were hurt but not seriously. When they went to court Ike pointed at Rink and said, "It's his car and he was driving." Rink lost his car and his license and went to jail for a year.

The first thing I found out was that Ike sold my dishwasher while I was gone, for more booze.

This pissed me off, but I didn't say anything. I wouldn't have minded if he had used it to feed the girls.

Adam wouldn't come back, but since he had just dropped out of college and was working and staying with friends, I told him it was probably time for him to be on his own anyway. I always told my sons that as long as they were in school I would support them. He was twenty six now. I was also a little afraid of what he may do over what Ike had done and what Ike may do.

I had bought Brian an old car for college. It was sitting out front until I could get it up to him.

I had just had a new motor put in it. When Ike got mad, he had it towed. By the time I found out where the car had been taken, the tow and storage fees were so high I had to just let them keep it. Ike just thought all of this was so funny.

When Ike heard what the drunk had done to Adam he said, "So it doesn't matter to the cops here if you are right or not they just listen to whoever calls first huh. That is really good to know."

Shortly after that Ike got a letter from his landlord telling him he needed to move because he had called the police on his neighbors ninety nine times in one month. It turned out he was stealing everything he could pawn from the neighborhood to buy booze. Then he would call the police to say they were all starting trouble with him for no reason.

Ike then told everyone that the landlord didn't like me and that it was my fault we had to move. All my life I tried to find good in everyone I have ever met but I have no tolerance for a liar, a thief or a bully. As I quickly found out Ike was the worst of all three.

Not long after that, Ike drug me out of bed from a sound sleep and screamed, "Lets see what you got bitch." I kept saying, "Leave me alone. I don't want to hurt you." He just backed me into a corner in the bathroom and started to swing at me.

I punched him several times then grabbed his shirt as he fell back. He backed away and ripped his shirt off his back getting away. I went back to sleep. The next day I asked him if I was just dreaming or did he attack me in my sleep? He said, "I just wanted to know how well you could handle yourself."

He laughed and said, "Man you hit me five times so fast and so hard, my knees buckled. Then before I could think you grabbed my shirt to bring me back for more so I took off. I will never do that again." I truly wish he had meant that, but then my story would have a very short ending. That was probably the last time I slept soundly for the next thirteen years.

Chapter 4

Ike was supposed to be looking for a place to live. Instead Chris and I slept in the car while Ike slept on different friends' couches. He wouldn't let me out of his sight. We ran into some people Ike said he knew from Ohio. They had five little boys. They asked us to stay with them.

One day when Chris was gone Ike got mad and dragged me out of my car through the window by my throat. He threw me on the ground and grabbed my feet. He started dragging me up and down the gravel driveway on my ass. Chris came home and said he was tired and was going to bed so he could get up for school. I didn't want to upset him, so I told him to go to bed. I didn't let him know what Ike had done.

Someone heard us arguing and called the police. I was standing there with the rear of my pants all ripped up, my ass bleeding and out of nowhere three cops tackled me. They twisted my arms up behind me and drug me to the car. I didn't even argue with them about arresting me because I was getting away from this lunatic. I asked them to get my son first.

They said no. I said, "You don't understand. The last thing Ike said to me was that when Chris feel asleep that he was going to slit his throat if I left him."

I begged this officer over and over to go get him out of that house. He refused. Ike had told the police when they got there that I attacked him and that I was a kick boxer and that they had better be careful arresting me.

One of the officers recognized the woman that was there and came back to arrest her on an old warrant. Ike told this couple that I snitched on them to get out of trouble and that was why she was arrested.

When I bonded out the next day and came to get my things, Chris wasn't there. The man was screaming at me, wanting to beat me for getting his wife arrested. Ike just stood there laughing because they asked me to move and let him stay. I was moving anyway. I was getting away from Ike so I gladly packed my things to move.

I had made the mistake the night before of telling Ike that the woman said she couldn't take these horrible kids anymore and was going to tell Ike he had to go. His girls had came back from their grandparents. This is why he got mad and attacked me. She said Chris and I were welcome to stay if we wanted. So Ike got his revenge on me, not her.

I called the school the next day to see if Chris was okay. They wouldn't tell me anything. They said it was against their policy, so I had to wait till school was out to know if he was alright. One of the longest days of my life.

I got away from Ike for a short time, but he found me as soon as that couple kicked him out. He sent the girls to Ohio again with Brandy's parents.

Then we moved to the State Park in a tent. This wasn't too bad. When you rent a site at the campground, you get a stone bench, a big grill, a water faucet and an electrical plug in, right there at your site. They have nice shower rooms. I brought my TV and VCR to watch movies with.

I almost felt human again. I have never liked having to live off someone else. In most cases unless I have to, I don't even like to spend the night away from home. I have had my own place since I was fifteen. This is how Ike had lived most of his life. He was quite comfortable with using people.

When we went to the park to stay, Chris asked if he could spend the summer with his friends so I let him. But every day I had this nagging feeling something was wrong, so I would go find him and ask him to stay at the park with me.

He would assure me he was fine and just wanted to hang out with his friends. Mothers, don't ever ignore those motherly instincts, no matter what your children tell you. I will tell you later what I found out was happening.

When Ike stole my antique white gold and diamond ring off my finger in my sleep, I once again tried to leave. It had been appraised at a thousand dollars years before this. I am sure it was much higher by this time. It wasn't the value that pissed me off as much as the fact that it was a keep sake from a friend. I was starting to see that I had become this man's prisoner.

Ike said he got a job in the rock quarry and that the job came with a trailer and he needed a sitter. I was happy to be in a home even though I am claustrophobic and have a hard time with small enclosures.

I just wanted my son home with me so I agreed to watch his girls a little longer. I liked helping with the rock. He would dynamite large sections then peel them up layer by layer. They were such beautiful colors all swirled together like a piece of marble.

The constant verbal abuse really got worse then. Ike would start as soon as Chris left for school or would go to his friends on the weekends.

Even Ike's friends jumped on him for how he talked to me. They would get mad and say, "This poor woman was sitting there watching TV and minding her own business until you kept on and on. Now she wants to kill all of us. You are really screwed up man." He didn't listen. He just thought it was funny.

I would take anything he had to say about me, but when he would threaten to hurt my sons, I got in his face. It didn't take long to realize that this is just what he wanted.

I brought all my things to this place from storage and bought the girls bunk beds and gave them my console color TV for their room. I had the phones, cable, and utilities put in my name, since I had lived there for so long and paid all my bills on time.

With all I could see that those girls had already been through, I didn't force them to talk to me in any way. I let them come to me in their own time. One thing I had learned in being the baby girl of a very large family is that children do what they see, not what they are told to do.

I talked to my sons about everything that happened to me when they were little so they could learn by other peoples mistakes and by trying my best to set a good example. I am not perfect and I have never in all my travels met any one that was.

Having one side of the family being heavy drinkers, the Irish side, I learned patience and acceptance. My parents didn't drink, but you knew my mother was Irish when she got mad. My father would just go out and have a seat in the shade until she was over it.

So I learned tolerance. My parents didn't argue in front of us much. They would usually go for a drive, argue it out and my dad would come home and sleep on the couch.

Chris' father was a bartender. I went to see him one afternoon where he worked when we still lived in California. This was a horseshoe shaped bar. Sitting across from me was a couple.

I noticed that they looked straight ahead while they drank. They didn't speak to each other or even look at each other.

All of a sudden I heard a big BAM. The man had backhanded the woman off the bar stool. I slide off my stool to walk around and ask him what he was doing. Two men very gently grabbed my wrists and said, "You really don't want to be in this. Just sit and watch a minute first." The woman brushed herself off and calmly sat back down next to her husband. Ten minutes later we hear BAM. She had knocked him off the barstool.

The one guy leaned over to me and said, "They do that the whole time they are here every time they are here. The problem is if you say something to him she will jump you and if you say something to her he will jump you." From this I learned that sometimes it is best to pick your battles instead of jumping into all of them.

When Brandy did finally come to visit, she looked at me in shock and said, "What did you do to him? I have never seen this man so calm in my life." This man was verbally abusing me every day, all day long. I thought this woman must be nuts. Little did I know he was just getting started.

I am so calm that most dogs don't even bark at me, not even police dogs. They come up smiling with their tails wagging to be petted. If I sit anywhere for any length of time people will come up to me, sit down and start talking to me. Even at the park all the animals would gather around me at the table if I sat there very long. Wild deer would walk right next to me to drink from the lake.

The girls, as I said, were quite a hand full at first too. Every time I would spend a day doing laundry and folding it and putting it away I would walk out of the room for a minute and walk back in to find all the clothes out of the drawers and closet, lying all over the floor.

They were throwing them around playing with them. I didn't say anything. We played this game a few times, then I brought them all in the living room and sat them down and started explaining to them that they could have just as much constructive fun as they were having destructive fun.

After that if they misbehaved or hurt each other, I would put them in time out. When I had to put them in time out, I would sit down to ask them if they understood why they were in time out. It didn't take long at all for them to calm down too.

After a short time I noticed that if I wore leggings, they all put on leggings. If I wore a dress, they would put on dresses. They slowly started coming in to talk to me or just sit down and watch cartoons with me. One thing that was a problem was the fact that for breakfast he would throw a box of Little Debbie cakes on the table.

He came in one day and was angry at me because he said ten minutes ago they were all sitting there quietly watching TV with me, and now they were bouncing off the walls, and he was demanding to know what I did to them. I told him it was all the sugar he had just given them.

The specialist that I had taken Adam to when he was younger told me that children's bodies can't break sugar down properly so giving sugar to a child is like giving them poison. They can't handle it.

Ike thought a good dinner for them was to open a bag of potato chips and set a bottle of hot sauce and one big glass of Kool-Aid in the middle of the table for them to share.

I started cutting up fruits and vegetables and leaving them in the fridge.

I got different colored squeeze bottles and filled them with water and put them in the fridge and told them to pick out a color they liked.

I never told them they had to eat or drink anything I put in there. Everyday I had to refill the bottles and cut up more fruits and vegetables. Not long after that people would come up to me and tell me what beautiful little ladies they all were.

When I went to Wal-Mart I took one or all five girls with me. Ike would demand I take them but I really didn't mind. One day at the counter a woman looked at me and said, "I have watched you coming here for years. All of us here think you are a saint. We want to just hug you sometimes."

She said, "We see people with just one kid here just screaming at them and slapping them around. You come in with all five of these girls and calmly answer all their questions. You never seem to get upset."

One of the girls called my name to ask me something. The girl looked so surprised and said, "They aren't even your children and you are this patient? You really are a saint."

One day during an argument I told Ike I wasn't going to take him threatening me anymore.

He had already escalated from threatening to kill me to threatening to kill my sons. He grabbed me and started to choke me. I got his hands off me and called the police.

They came out and told me that since I willingly moved in there with him that this was domestic and they couldn't do a thing to help me. Ike only saw that they were not going to stop him. He swore he would never do that to me again so I had to let it go.

A few days later I was in the shower. I had just soaped up my body and my hair. All of a sudden the water stopped and the lights went out. My eyes were now burning from the shampoo and I heard the door open.

Suddenly all I saw was bright pops of light and heard Ike screaming, "You aren't going to use my shower to clean up to go see some man. Brandy did that to me for years and I won't stand for it anymore." I then realized the pops of light was him beating me in the face. I think he broke my nose.

I said that I wasn't planning on going anywhere. I was just taking a shower. I heard him leave. The lights and water came back on so I finished my shower. I got dressed and went out to confront him. He was sitting there shaking and crying and once again swore he would never do that again.

I knew already there was no point in going to the police, so I went to see a lawyer in town, Tommy Turner. I told him that I wanted to get my son out of there. The only way I could do that was to sue John Alex, the head of section eight housing, for illegally stopping payment to Compassionate Creation, which got me illegally put out of my house.

I handed him a big bag of paperwork to prove that this had all been done illegally. I am a pack rat, so I keep everything. He told me to come back in a few days and that he would check my story out.

When this first happened about my house, I went to Knoxville section eight and told them what had happened and showed them my paperwork. They told me that if I won in court that they could fire John Alex and undo what he had done to me and everyone else. Before he was hired for housing, John managed K-Mart. He was fired for embezzling lots of money.

I met a man that said John paid his cousin under the table for working there. His only job was to follow John around the store and everything John pointed to the guy had to put out by the dumpster where there were no cameras. John would pick it all up on his way home from work.

I said I couldn't afford an attorney. The man at Knoxville section eight smiled and said, "You just explained your case so well to me that I believe you. Get an attorney to get you a court date and you state your case to the judge yourself and give him this paperwork and I guarantee you will win. It won't cost you much that way."

When I went back to see Tommy. He said he would get me a court date for six hundred dollars. I was now supporting six more people on my small paycheck, so it took me a while to save up.

I told him that I thought that the attorney Douglas Stevens was a part of this too and he should have to answer to the courts also. I think he knew all along they did this illegally.

Tommy took my money and said he knew Stevens and he wanted to talk to him first before he set a court date. Stevens was now a judge and Tommy said he had to let him know he was going to be named and charged in my lawsuit. I said to hurry, we couldn't take this anymore.

For Chris' birthday that year Ike said as a surprise he was going to get a tent and give him a nice party with his friends. A few days before his birthday, I asked him if he had done anything yet. Ike looked at me and yelled, "Surprise! The surprise is I'm not doing anything because he ain't my kid."

At the last minute I got a two room tent to set up behind the trailer. I put Chris' stereo, TV and games out there. I went out and bought all the drinks and food to last the whole weekend and filled two big coolers with ice.

Chris was so happy. He said he loved hanging out there those few days with his friends, girls and boys. Chris also told me that he had stopped eating at home because every time he came into the kitchen for anything Ike and the girls would give him dirty looks and glare at him like he was eating their food.

I told him to get anything he wanted any time he wanted. I paid for everything there except the rent. And technically I was covering half of that. The rent came out of the rock Ike turned in. I helped him in the quarry when the older girls started to school. That is on the days my back held out. So I was paying for everything.

I noticed after that Chris still wasn't coming out to eat, so I put that big cooler in his room and started putting food in his room just for him and his friends when they came over to play video games.

This really set Ike off. He said that it made his girls feel that I thought Chris was more special. It didn't bother him when they were starving my son, but it pissed him off when I made sure he was eating.

For every one of the girl's birthdays I had gone out and got cake and ice cream. I rented games and movies and cartoons and bought pizza, and they had their friends over. This wasn't enough for Ike though. He had to feel like he took everything away from me and Chris and handed it over to them. I'm a truly stubborn Irish woman. I wasn't about to let him break me.

With my allergies being so severe, once a year my immune system just shuts down. When this happens, I can't even lift my head off the pillow for about three days.

I was in bed during one of these times and left my door open so I could see and hear the girls. The girls' names starting with the oldest are Feather, Tiffany, Linda, Angie and Louise. Feather and Louise were sitting right out side my door on the floor.

Feather leans over and says, "Go along with whatever I say." Then she said very loudly, "Do you remember when Imogene hit us and called us names the other day?" Louise said, "No that never happened." Feather grabbed her and said, "I will break your arm."

Before I could even roll over to ask Feather what she was doing, Ike ran in the room and dragged me into the living room and started beating me. I couldn't even lift my arms. All I could do is roll over so he wasn't beating me in the face. Louise tried to stop him and said it wasn't true but Feather dragged her into the back bedroom.

Feather was grinning like the Cheshire cat the whole time. Feather constantly bullied her sisters. She lied to get them in trouble all the time. If she was caught doing anything, she would blame it on her sisters and just grin while their dad was yelling at them.

After that as soon as Chris left with his friends for the weekend, Feather would make up another lie about me to get Ike to attack me. I would run out the back door through the briar patch just to keep from being beaten. Later I would get my car and sit on the corner all weekend in my car. I not only watched for Chris to come in, but I was there to keep an eye on the girls too.

I had no food, no water and no bathroom to tend to these sometimes deep briar cuts. The girls would sometimes sneak me out something to eat. Ike would have all his buddies over to get drunk and laugh about how he ran me off again. When he passed out, I would watch all his drunken buddies walking out with bags full of my food.

Ike would come out on Sunday night and say he was sorry. He would say he needed me to come back and watch the girls all week. I didn't have a court date yet, so I had to go back. I didn't tell Chris this was happening. I thought I was protecting him from it.

As soon as I got back in the house, Ike would yell at me and tell me I had obviously not bought enough food because there was nothing there to eat. He said that I had better get out and find some way to have food in the house before he got off work.

I had to start going to the churches and start begging for food. I stopped helping him in the rock quarry. I didn't even want to be around him anymore.

This wasn't a once in a while occurrence this went on every weekend for years.

My disability finally went through. I got a ten thousand dollar back pay check. They only paid me for one year not the eight and a half years I had to see all their doctors to prove my case.

I didn't mention it to Ike because the verbal, mental, emotional, physical, and financial abuse had really gotten bad by this time and I really wanted to get away from this man.

I had also after many years gotten good credit again and had a lot of credit cards in my purse. I was going to keep them for emergencies only. Ike found them and ran them all up to the limit. When I got the bills, he just said they weren't in his name, so they weren't his bills. He ruined in a few months what it took me years to build back up.

I paid them off again and I charged a ten by sixteen vinyl storage building. I charged it because I didn't want Ike to know I had gotten my back pay already.

He put the building together for me behind the trailer and hooked the phone, electric and cable to the building for me. I moved into it.

I was hoping I would have a little privacy to start looking for a house for me and Chris. I wanted to put Chris a bed out there too, but Ike wouldn't let me. I had to buy a new closet for the shed. I filled it with food and drinks for me and Chris.

Tommy said with this paper work I had a real good case and as soon as Judge Stevens cleared it, he would have me a court date.

A friend of Ike's came over to tell Ike one day that he had a problem with a guy at work. Ike told him to call the police and say the guy had done something to him, even if he hadn't done anything. He said the police would tie the guy up in court so long that it didn't matter if he was guilty or not. He would be ruined in that town.

Then Ike said, "If you are really pissed at the guy just say he did something to your kids, That will really ruin him." His friend said he didn't believe him, so Ike looked at me and said, "Who has pissed me off lately? I am going to prove I know what I am talking about."

After the guy left Ike started threatening once again that he was going to kill me and my whole family so I said, "If you aren't happy with me why don't you just move back to Ohio?" He got mad and left and was gone all night.

The next day Chris went to his friend's house early. I told him to be back soon because I wanted to go to see Brian at college and take him out to eat. It was a day or two before his birthday. I wanted to celebrate over the weekend so I wouldn't bother his classes during the week.

Ike came home and came to my building to talk. I said there was nothing to talk about. Next thing I know a cop is at my door. I said, "I didn't call you." I looked out the door and Ike was sitting on the back steps of the trailer and he said, "I called him because we are going to fight and I don't want it to get out of hand." I said, "There won't be a fight because as soon as my son calls I'm leaving."

I found out later Ike took an axe and cut all the lines to my building so I couldn't call for help or get a call from my son.

Before the cop got out of the drive Ike was in my building. I could still hear the cops tires on the gravel drive. I heard Ike ranting but I pulled my covers over my head and ignored it until I felt a sharp pain in my leg.

I sat up to see that he had taken all of my things that he could pick up and threw them at me. I had a very large very heavy case of video tapes sitting on my leg. When I got up to defend myself, he ran to the trailer.

Since he knew I could defend myself he would run up and grab me from behind and get me off my feet. I grabbed an old axe handle thinking I could use it to pry his hands off me if he did it again.

I wasn't angry enough to even think of using it to hurt him. The trailer door was locked, so I walked to the front. It was locked too. So I knocked and said for him to come out and talk to me.

I heard the girls say they were going out back to play on the swings. I started to walk away saying, "What is wrong with you?" At which point when I turned the axe handle accidentally hit the window and broke it.

Ike opened the door so I went in to talk to him. He came up behind me and picked me up. I tried to use the handle to pry open his arms, but it didn't work. He walked to the back door and threw me way up in the air and out the back door.

My feet landed on the bottom step, and I wrapped my arm around the banister in barely enough time to keep my face from smashing on the quarry rock at the bottom of the steps. I found out later that this tore the ligaments out of my arm for the third time in fights trying to defend myself or the girls from him.

To this day I have to take two pills a day just to be able to use my arm without intense pain. I have arthritis, bursitis and tendonitis all in the same arm.

He also ripped the muscle off the bone in that arm at the shoulder. I was told that the muscle could be reattached, but that the nerve damage would be worse from the surgery than the muscle gap is. I still have a big dent where the muscle used to be.

I tried to phone the police, but the line was cut so I went to my car to leave. I was just going to wait until Chris came home and we could leave.

57

I thought I would just go see my attorney on Monday, go to court and get my house back. Then I thought, well I will drive around to my building and get a change of cloths first.

Ike started throwing my planters at my car, so I turned around. Then I realized I had $5,000. in cash in my safe left after paying a few bills. I started back to my building. He continued throwing plants at my car, so I realized that he would never let me in my building so I turned around again.

I decided I would come back later to get it when he was gone. It had rained all week so my turning around so many times really tore up the lawn.

I was up the street when the police flew past me so I thought I need to talk to them now before he can make up lies. By the time I turned around he had told the police that he was minding his own business when I broke the window in his girls' faces and came in and started beating him with the axe handle. Let me say again I was not even angry yet. I thought I was just going to move away and be done with all this.

People that have known me my whole life say I am so easy going like my dad that they could never even picture me angry. As soon as I pulled up, they arrested me and put me in the car. The cop that had been there earlier came up to the car. I tried to get him to open the door so I could find out what was going on. He just gave me a dirty look, shock his head and walked away.

Until I met Ike I had been arrested twice in my life. Once for drinking with my sister when I was fifteen and a DUI in Ca. I don't count the one where they had to let me go when they realized there weren't any actual charges. I still thought, "No problem." I will go to court and tell the judge what happened and get this all behind me."

The arresting officer came to my holding cell the second time to read me a list of additional charges. He snickered all through the list like he was just so proud of himself for thinking up all these things to charge me with.

One of the Judicial Commissioners came running into the room cussing me and tried to grab me so the officer stepped between us. She was calling me a child beater. I didn't say anything. I knew there was no point. I also knew that if I thought someone had hurt a child I would feel the same way. I decided to just take it and wait for court.

Ike used to laugh when he told people how we could be arguing like crazy and I would be so mad I wanted to tear into him, and if one of his daughters walked in to ask something, I would stop and very calmly ask them what they needed.

I would answer them then ask them to go play, so he and I could finish talking. In the five years I raised those girls I never even spanked one of them. I threatened to spank Feather a few times but never did. This was only the first year.

When I bonded out of jail, I went to Knoxville to two local news stations and told them what happened and asked them to be in court with me. When I got to court the judge was Douglas Stevens. He should have stepped down, but I still didn't think much about it. I told the judge what happened and that I had hired an attorney for another case and he could represent me.

Tommy stood up and said, "I have no idea what she is talking about. I already finished the other case, and I am not her attorney." He hadn't even gotten me the first court date.

They gave me a public defender Wendy Liars and set a court date. This all turned out to be front page news for quite sometime. My name was on the local radio for a long time too.

I went to Tommy as soon as I bailed out and told him to give me back my money and my bag of letters I had for proof of my case and he said, "What letters? And you can sue my fat ass for the money."

As he was walking out, I asked what I could do about my and Chris's things, and he said that since Ike was still at the courthouse I needed to go get some clothes. He said that the court couldn't keep my personal belongings from me.

His secretary asked me to come back in a few days. She saw me give him the letters and heard everything he said about taking my case. She said to give her time to find them.

When I went back a few days later she said, "He must have destroyed them because they aren't here. But if you do sue him, subpoena me to court and I will tell them everything I heard him say to you. I will tell them I saw that big bag of letters and heard him say you had a good case. And that he had to talk to Judge Stevens first."

I went to grab me and Chris some clothes, and Ike came home. He called the police, and I was arrested again. The judge said he told me not to go there. He never said that to my knowledge.

When I went to court Wendy Liars wouldn't say one word to me. She just folded her arms and glared at me so I had to speak up for myself.

I had gone to get my things on the advise of Tommy who then denied saying it. I got two weeks in jail for contempt of court. I spent my birthday and the Fourth of July in there. What upset me the most was that I had planned to take my mother to see George Jones when he did his come back show with Loretta Lynn on the fourth.

They were both my mom's favorite singers. My friend's brother was part of Loretta's band for years. I could have taken her back stage to meet them.

I heard from a friend that Ike had moved a young lesbian crank whore in the day after I was first arrested. Her name was Debney Tramsey. She slept with men for drugs. I was told they were selling my things, buying drugs and staying in my room day and night while the girls ran the roads begging for food.

Many people offered to go to court with me to testify against Ike over the next few weeks, but I thought all I have to do is tell the truth and I can go home and get my things to move. I guess I really was still very naive.

I called Judge Stevens at home and told him what was going on. He told me not to worry that he would take care of all of it when we went to court. When we went to court the judge said to Ike, "Did you pay for any of these things?"

Ike, who thinks quickly said, "Yes, it's all mine." So I was told without this man even showing one receipt for anything to forget it, that it was his. I had all my receipts with me. The judge wouldn't even look at them.

I was told that I couldn't even go to get my clothes, but they would send someone with Chris to get his school clothes and books and nothing else. The judge even gave him all of Chris's furniture and belongings. I came back one night while Ike was passed out and found out Ike had broken a key off in my shed door to try and keep me out.

I figured out that with a screwdriver the door opened easily. I got a change of clothes, my paperwork for court and my money out of my safe. Good thing too. He beat the hell out of that safe trying to get it opened.

All he would have found now was my passport, my sons' identification papers, their pictures, shot records and fingerprint papers. I'm slow, not stupid.

I was told that people from both news shows I had went to see were there every time I went to court. They asked me later what the judge had against me. They said the judge seemed to make it personal.

I still wasn't thinking about my case that I was going to take out against him. They said they heard me very loudly tell the truth and the judge just ignored everything I said. He seemed to only listen to Ike.

They said they couldn't say anything at the time because they couldn't get involved in domestic cases, but if I decided to sue the judge, they were willing to go to court with me and testify that everyone sitting there could tell I was telling the truth and was purposely ignored by this judge.

I knew then the only way I was getting out of this was to prove my case myself so I went to the DA and asked him to wire me so I could get a confession out of Ike. He said he couldn't because he was prosecuting me but he said the police might. Of course they refused.

While I was in jail, I asked Brian to go to my building and get the land deed my mother had given me when I first moved here so they could hold it on my bond.

He said when he pulled up Ike came out swinging a metal bat. Brian said this didn't scare him because he trained in Hokkaido in college. He said he thought it was kind of funny when he realized it was in fact his bat that Ike was swinging at him. He said Ike's eyes looked all weird and crazy.

Either way he couldn't get to my building to get to my safe for the paper work. Brian had asked me a few weeks earlier if Chris could spend the summer with him. I told him that sounded like a good thing for them both. Chris went to Brian's house.

Adam went to my mother and talked her into sending a copy of the paper work on the land with him to give the bondsman. Adam wanted to stay and help me in court but I said, "I got myself into this and I will get myself out of it." I wasn't fully aware I was dealing with a crooked court.

I knew my sons didn't need the stress and I knew if they had helped, Ike would see them as even more of a threat and try his best to harm them. Away from me was safer for them. I just didn't think it would take so long to be rid of Ike.

When Ike had asked me to baby sit for pay I wasn't aware that the state was the ones he was expecting to pay me. The state said that since it was on record that I owed a government agency money, Compassionate Creation, that they couldn't pay me. All of this was what I had wanted to prove, or should I say disprove if I had gotten the court date I had paid for.

Also Ike was supposed to pay me first, and then they would pay the difference. So I ended up supporting those girls at my expense for the next five years. Most of the time I didn't mind because I loved those girls like my own. I did how ever hate that I was forced to support him all those years, only to get constantly beaten down for my trouble.

Compassionate Creation was supposed to be a non-profit government agency started for the sole purpose of helping low income families buy houses. My land lord came to me before he sold his house, very cheaply I might add, to them. He said they told him they were going to help me buy it, so my family would always have a home. That is the only reason he sold it to them and sold it so cheap.

I saw Ike Mathers in a store a little over five years later and asked him if he sold my home to the next people. His answer was, "No, the company decided that they need another five years rent." Non-profit my ass.

Knowing what I paid for rent and that they probably raised the rent on the next people, they had already made over three times what I know they bought it for. They bought up a lot of homes on that pretense. I wonder if they ever sold any of them to these families. Probably not.

When I walked into the jail that first day, the girls ran up to me and kept saying I couldn't have done anything to be there. When I told them what happened, they told me that they all belonged there for the things they had done but still agreed that I shouldn't be there.

When you are in jail, the guards leave the speakers on, so they can hear everything you say. I was eating one day and a female guard stood next to me for a few minutes. I finally looked up to see what she wanted. She said very quietly that she had heard what I said and that I should have just shot the man. She said that I would have gotten less time for it.

She then offered to put a gun she had that the numbers had been filed off out in the lobby bathroom for me. She said it would be there when I got bail. I said, thanks but no thanks. I couldn't even make myself just hit the man after all he had done. I knew I couldn't shoot anyone. Knowing now all the people's lives this man purposely destroyed I sometimes wish I had considered it.

I knew I had to get a confession from Ike to end this. I bought a recorder and went to find Ike. I found out that when he was gone all night that first night he had met Debney.

He did all this to me on purpose to prove what he had said to his friend about setting someone up and so he could move this girl into my home with him and the girls.

I wanted to get away from him. He didn't have to do this. If he had came in and said he found someone to watch the girls, I would have gladly put everything in my storage building and found a way to move it to the land my dad had given me.

I got him to admit he lied under oath to keep me away while they partied. He said he lied the first time because he was high on meth when the police showed up and he was afraid they would figure out he was on drugs and take his kids. He couldn't lose his paycheck.

When they ran out of things of mine to sell, they sold Debney's fourteen year old girlfriend to Ike's friends for meth. I mean Debney's lover, just in case you didn't catch that. I took this tape to my attorney along with the names of the people that wanted to testify against him.

She never even looked at it. After this drew out for months in court, she gave me back the tape and the list of names, still sealed in the original envelope. She never once spoke to me or tried to defend me. She got paid for this by the state. How can they justify that? If she didn't want to defend me, she should have asked them to get someone that would.

Ike called my friends and begged them to tell me to come get my mail while this was still going on. When I showed up, he had me arrested again for violation of order of protection. He even had me arrested once saying I came and started screaming at him from the road.

I hadn't gone anywhere near him. I had no car. I was driving down the street and suddenly my transmission stopped working and before I got completely off the road, my engine died. I sat there a couple days wondering what I was going to do. A man Ike has known for years from Ohio, came up and started screaming at me.

He said the police came and told him that I said he had bought my stolen tools from Ike. This was kind of funny to me since I told the police that I heard he had them and that I wasn't pressing charges. I said that I only wanted them back.

The police told me they didn't find anyone that had any of my things. They said they couldn't find even one person that knew anything. I still feel that if these guys knew it was my stuff and that Ike stole it, then them buying it was the same as stealing it from me. I would have never done that to them.

For years Ike swore he didn't know what happened to my car. Then one day when he was telling me what an idiot he thinks I am, he said that I was so stupid that I hadn't realized that while I was in jail for the fourth he came to the Justice Center parking lot and punched holes in my radiator and oil pan. He said he then tore the wires out, so the idiot light wouldn't warn me they were over heating on me. He just laughed about how slick he is.

I went to the Justice Center once to ask the Judicial Commissioner if she would please let me take care of the girls because he wasn't. When I pulled up, Ike was just going into his anger management class.

It turned out he had a history of beating women. He ran in screaming that I was there to kill him. Two officers came out to arrest me, but when I told them I didn't even know he was there and what I was there for, they let me go. They reminded me he had a order of protection.

I never raised a hand to this man after the first two times I had told you about the year before and HE, had a order of protection. I let Chris go to Brian's house to stay. Brian had rented a house just off campus. I picked up Chris one day and let him come to Crossburg with me so he could see his friends.

I called Ike to tell him that for the girls' sake I was going to leave the cable, utilities and phone on until this was done. I was still hoping the judge would come to his senses and do the right thing.

I had missed a court date. As soon as I remembered, I called the bonds man and told him I would be there first thing next week to tell the courts what happened. He said no problem. In the mean time, Ike had called and said I called him to cuss and threaten him and his girlfriend and that she was his witness to this. This is how Ike repays everyone for kindness.

The bondsman told me that if I came to his office he would rent a room for me and Chris. When I got there, I was arrested for failure to appear and violation of order of protection. Since Chris was with me, they put him in state custody. Chris said it was basically a prison for kids, the other side of the state.

When I bonded out, I had to go to court for a custody hearing. Judge Stevens said that he wanted to wait and see if I got into any more trouble before he gave me custody of Chris. He did however agree to let Chris go back to stay with Brian. I didn't fight it because that was where he was to begin with but I already knew what the judge had just done was illegal.

I had heard him many times in court jump all over attorney's for trying to pull that. He told them that they knew full well that they couldn't hold against anyone, what they may or may not do in the future. And yet he just did it to me.

First of all when I told the judge what Ike did to me the first day of court, he asked me if I had ever had sex with Ike.

I asked what that had to do with anything and he said to answer the question. I said, "Yes." He replied, "Then that is domestic and I can't hear it." If that were true then as soon as Ike said the girls weren't in the house but that I hit him, which I didn't, Then it should have been immediately dismissed.

Even though he was selling my things and running up my bills, all I could think of was what those girls were going through. I begged the court again to let me take care of them until this was done, but they didn't seem to care what happened to those girls.

I ran into that couple with the five boys one day. They said they were sorry for getting mad at me before and they finally figured out it was Ike, not me, causing the problem. They said the boys were with their dad's mom.

They said that I could have a private room and bathroom all to myself if I came to stay with them while I was looking for a house. She said she would take me house hunting. She was very pregnant, I think they said with twins this time. Since I had no car and nowhere to live, this sounded great.

When I found out Ike had gotten evicted for not paying rent, I went to hopefully get my things back and found everything gone, including my brand new building. I found a few things hanging on the wall and some garbage bags with what I had hoped were some of my things. I took the bags back to this couple's house to sort through them. Every bag turned out to be garbage that had sat in the sun for days.

I had to go through every bag because in each bag was a some small item of mine and Chris's. Also in each bag was a bra or panty or nightie with cum stains, to make sure I knew what they did. These were not old clothes they left behind. They were left on purpose for me to find.

In each bag I found a cut up piece of my clothing with a chunk of human crap globed on it. You could tell that they took a knife and cut pieces of crap to put on each piece of my clothing they had cut up. I can picture them enjoying doing all this to me on purpose. How sick is this?

Even all my photos of my sons were stuffed in this garbage. Most of the pictures were unsalvageable. All of mine and my sons' things were sold or destroyed just to buy them drugs. I cried a lot and threw up a lot, but I got through it.

It turned out that this couple that said they would take me house hunting were just borrowing that car from a relative. So now I was stuck thirty miles from town and had to walk to town to look for a house. On top of that my name was in the paper so much that no one would even consider renting to me. And yet, my troubles had just begun.

The pregnant woman woke me early one morning and told me that she was starting to go into labor and begged me to go to the store and write her a check so that she could go to the hospital to stop her labor. She said she would go first thing Monday and pay it off. Monday she came home and said she paid it off and said she ripped up the check.

I got a call from my bank that checks were bouncing. I keep very meticulous count on my checks because I can't afford all the bank fees to bounce one. I found a piece of paper on the kitchen table with my name written all over it. I asked her what it was for. She said their friend Steve must have written it because he had a crush on me.

I went to the bank and found out that about a hundred of my checks had been stolen. I filed the paperwork for stolen checks. The bank assured me that since I did that, nothing else would happen.

I told that couple I had filed with the bank and the police for stolen checks. She started freaking out. She said, "Oh my God, one of those stores made me put my finger print on a check." She then told me that while I was asleep Steve went through my things, stole my checks and took some of my paperwork to practice my signature.

They had spent the last few weeks doing coke at my expense while I was walking to find a place to live. I told her the bank said it was all covered.

Rink was out of jail, so I moved to his friend's house next door to Rink's, so Rink and this man could fix my car. The next thing I know I am being arrested again.

She didn't pick up that check and the courts let three other places illegally file against me, ignoring the fact the bank and the police said they couldn't do this. I went to court and was set a court date.

As soon as court was done, they came up to arrest me on one of the same checks I had just had court about. I reminded Wendy that check was covered in court just seconds before. She crossed her arms and just glared at me as usual and I was arrested again.

This big ole farm boy sheriff was sent to get me. He looked down at me on the way to the van and said, "You don't look so mean to me." I said, "What are you talking about?"

He laughed and said. "They told me to come over here to help the other officer because you are the meanest woman in Crossburg." We both got a laugh out of that. I asked for another attorney, since Wendy was obviously not going to help as usual.

They gave me another attorney on the check cases but wouldn't consider it for the trial I really needed a good attorney on. They purposely didn't want to give me a fighting chance.

I went to court and admitted to the one check and explained that she told me she paid it off. I told them I would pay it off. To begin with, this store didn't wait the required thirty days to file. And I had gone to that store as soon as I figured out what these people had done to me and told them I would pay them. They refused to let me pay it. So all of this was illegal.

I also told them that in all the years I lived there I had never even set foot even once in any of the other three stores. Judge Stevens said, "Thirty days, a year probation, court costs and restitution." My attorney grabbed my sleeve and pulled me out of the court and said, "No sir, I am filing an appeal and taking this to another court."

Even after we told the other court the whole story they said that since it was my checks I was still responsible. They said I had to pay court costs, restitution and pay and serve a year probation. But I only had to do four hours in jail. I was forced to take a guilty plea for something I had nothing to do with.

As soon as we got out in the parking lot my attorney said to me, "I am so sorry but you just got screwed by the courts. This system is for the rich and you ain't rich. If it makes you feel any better they screw over a thousand other people every day." No this didn't make me feel better.

It made me sad that everyone knows this and no one is doing anything about it. I ended up getting one of the owners at the probation office as my worker. He said he knew I wasn't guilty because he was in the court room.

He didn't make me pay probation costs and I only had to call him once a month for a year instead of coming in. But it is still on record that I was guilty, when I wasn't. I could see this is starting to be a habit with this court.

I found out later that all of Steve's uncles were attorneys for that court. Steve did this to a lot of people, including his own father. I was told by one of those store owners that they knew none of these were Steve's checks but they cash them all the time anyway. They said they just sue the check owner to get their money back.

I finally told Wendy in front of the DA once that Ike knew he had a court subpoena because they told him when he went to his anger management classes every week. I also mentioned the fact that he had lied under oath and was afraid he might not be able to get away with it a second time.

When Ike didn't show up for court a dozen different times, they finally threw it out and said to expunge it. I had told the DA when I asked him to wire me that time, that he was welcome to check my record, that I was clean. He said in court that he had in fact checked and found that I had no criminal record, of any kind, anywhere, ever.

This was now sent to a different court. I stood up and asked the judge if I could say something first before he dismissed it. The DA jumped up and covered the microphone and said, "Just let sleeping dogs lay. I am letting you go." They had destroyed my name in that town for things I never did, but I had to let it go.

Ike said to me later that he was so high when he went to court that he kept having to go throw up and he didn't remember anything he had said.

The guy from the newspaper said if I proved I wasn't guilty they would print a retraction. I went there straight from court and I asked the women up front if I could also have them put an ad in the paper to find other people that had lost their homes illegally to the people I wanted to sue when this first happened.

The women told me she knew who I was and that she owned the paper. She said she wasn't printing anything for me. She said that I had two seconds to get the hell out of her building and she reached for the phone to call the police.

Ike's mom told me after this was all over that he has done this his whole life. She called it his spring fling. She said at least once a year he would find the sleaziest thing he could and hole up for weeks doing drugs. He did this all through his marriage.

Until all this happened I thought he was just a drunk. I didn't know about the drugs. She told me he had spent a year and a half in an Ohio prison on three drug felonies.

She told me that she knew Ike was in his room doing hard drugs since he was ten. She said she was an alcoholic so she didn't care what he was doing as long as he was out of her hair. She said he had spent his whole life in and out of detention homes, jail and prison.

This information would have helped a lot a year earlier, but as I soon found out it was much too late for me and my family. Ike denied for years doing anything to my car, selling all my furniture and my building or lying to keep me in trouble. He didn't remember I taped him. I even showed him the tape once.

I really should have seen this. For months when I first moved in, his mother would call every couple of days, drunk. She would cuss him like a dog and tell him how much she hated him. She would tell him to never visit and never call her again. A day or two later he would get drunk and do the same thing to her.

Chapter 5

After that the police constantly stopped me to search and harass me. I asked once if they had nothing better to do than bother me. The cop replied, "No. As a matter of fact I live for it. I miss the good old days when we could hang the niggers and bust down doors just to beat up people."

Even when I just walked down the street, they stopped me. Male cops would frisk me, which is illegal, they would search my purse and put me in the car. Then they would call to see if I had any warrants.

I'm sorry people but I personally hate the N word. It really offends me to even hear it said. I was born in the south but raised in the north. People are people no matter what color their skin.

I walked thirty miles to town every day to look for a place to live. After being front page news no one would rent to me. Some of them even cussed me. I finally found a women that said she would rent to me because she knew it would piss her husband off. She said she wanted a divorce anyway.

Even though they all knew my case had been expunged because it never happened. When someone called the court house to check on my record, they would tell them about all my arrests and tell them what they thought I had done. Again illegal but they didn't care. They were still out to ruin my name.

This house was in a subdivision I had lived in before, but this house was at the end of one of the streets and didn't belong to the owner of the subdivision. The landlord said her husband had taken care of the couple that had lived there, and when they died, they left him the house.

When I got Chris back, Brian gave him his old bed because he had gotten a new one. So we moved into an empty house with one bed. We were just so relieved to be there alone. I didn't even mind sleeping on the floor.

While Chris was in school, I was sitting on the floor wondering how a person could be this twisted to do this to the only person that was honestly trying to help him and his family. I got this strange feeling I wasn't alone. I suddenly got sucker punched from behind and heard Ike yell, "I told you the cops can't protect you twenty four-seven, bitch."

When I got to my feet, he was nowhere in sight. All the windows and the door were locked. I have no idea how he got in or out. It was pointless to call the police, so I never said anything to anyone not even Chris. I didn't want him to worry.

Not long after that Ike called crying, telling me he was in the hospital and had almost been beaten to death and asked if I would please help him. Debney's father and several relatives saw him on the street and beat him with bats. They left him in the ditch for dead. He already knew where I lived, so I told him he could stay in the living room until he got on his feet.

Instead of being thankful, he made everyday for the next twelve years a living hell for me and Chris. Every time I helped him it was for those girls, not him. He had spent his whole life using, abusing and conning everyone. I hoped I could break those habits so he would be a better father. I failed.

My new landlord came over to meet his new tenant, me. To his wife's surprise he liked me.

He said he liked the way I kept my house clean and the large lawn mowed. I had to go buy a new fridge, stove, washer, dryer and lawnmower.

The landlord and his wife brought me over a dining room table and chairs, a couch and chair and told me I could use them. Then they gave me a mattress set to have. They weren't so happy when my new house guests moved in. I assured them it was only temporary.

Since my car wasn't running yet a friend that owed me some money gave me an old truck. A truck I never even got to drive.

Ike said he would fix my car if I would give him the truck. My nephew brought me an old engine my brother had left in Alabama, so Ike put it in my car and I gave him the truck.

Two weeks later I am being towed home. Ike laughed and said that if he had only put a cheap set of bearings in that it would have kept running. Then he said, "I only promised to get it running, not keep it running." He left them out on purpose so I would be stranded again.

Since everything in this place was in my name I paid for everything including his girls' food. I had them twenty four-seven while he spent their state check and food stamps to run the roads. He spent all his time chasing drugs and women. I had made him promise to give up the booze or he wasn't moving in even temporarily.

As I said, I didn't know about the drugs at the time. I have been around people doing drugs and none of them became so increasingly violent on them as this man did. He walked around mad at the world all the time and took it all out on me.

With no warning and for no reason, he would suddenly burst into the room screaming, trap me in the corner and I would have to fight for my life. He would always scream that it was because his dad beat him as a child, his mother hated him, his ex sucked black guys for dope or one of his drug buddies just screwed him on a deal.

In all the years this went on I never raised my hand in anger to hit him or one of his children, ever. He tried to beat me every day many times a day and constantly threatened to kill me and my sons.

When he jumped in my face, I jumped back in his face. I wasn't about to just take it. I did try to ignore it as long as I could but he wouldn't quit. All I ever did was block any punches I saw coming, pry his hands off my throat and face and get my legs between us to kick him off of me.

By the time I would get to my feet to defend myself he would start shaking and crying and tell me it wasn't him it was the drugs. He would always say that he would never do that again. An hour later, I would have to fight him all over again.

He would wait until everyone was a sleep or until everyone went to school. He made sure there were never any witnesses. If one of the neighbors heard us and called the police, he would drag his girls out of bed, even in the winter and make them lie to the police.

He would make them say that he was minding his own business and I just went off and started beating him for no reason. He would say, "She is a professional kick boxer." They always assumed I was the aggressor because I knew how to protect myself.

I got beaten for no reason, then went to jail over and over and over for things I didn't do.

I kept telling them the truth and kept begging them to help me get him out of my house and get him help, they ignored it. Ike started hanging out with a meth crowd.

I went to visit a friend one day that had just gotten out of the hospital and I went by the store to get a few things on my way home. When I got home, Ike came out the door smiling. I thought how nice, finally he is going to help bring things in for once.

He walked up and punched me right in the face. Bags of food flew everywhere. He screamed that it took me too long. This broke out two teeth and several filings. A neighbor saw this and called the police.

Ike went in and dragged his girls out and told them what to say as soon as he heard the sirens. He said to say they saw me pull these teeth out with my hands just to frame him. One of these teeth was bolted into my jaw on a wire with a cap on it. I couldn't have yanked it out with pliers.

Louise said no that she wasn't lying for him anymore, that lying was wrong. He picked her up by one arm and said, "If daddy goes to jail, when I get out I will break your arms, your legs and every little toe you have. You will never walk again." Then he threw her on the ground, hard.

He was shaking and crying as the police got out of their cars. All ready to put on his show. Then we heard the door of the house open and Chris stepped out. Ike didn't know he was home. Ike suddenly stopped the tears and said, "Kiss daddy goodbye girls, daddy is going to jail."

Even after they figured out that the problem really was him, every time they arrested him they would arrest me too and say, "You are still with him, you must be guilty too. Birds of a feather flock together." I truly grew to hate that saying.

Since he only worked briefly, twice over the next few years, I was stuck paying all the bail, court costs and probation money for us both. After a while I realized that was why they kept arresting me too. Even they saw me as a paycheck.

I had to sit through parties I didn't even want to be at and listen to him brag that he kept getting away with attempted murder over and over because the cops were too stupid to do their job. He would say that as a matter of fact the other guy went to jail every time. He didn't tell anyone he was talking about me.

I had to walk to the stores and bring food home in the girls little red wagon and go to churches to beg for food for his children while he was running the roads in my truck.

After we were front page news for so long the churches literally cussed me and told me to get out of their buildings and slammed doors in my face. So now those girls were the ones paying for their father's lies. This still didn't stop him.

Ike used to make me lay down with him to watch TV. After a few minutes he would shove me out in the floor really hard. He would laugh. Then he would get mad and ask me what happened to my sense of humor. Several times I could barely use my arm afterwards, but I don't think I broke it. He would shove me harder the next time.

When Ike got out of jail after busting out my teeth, he screamed and threatened as usual. He could see that wasn't getting the results he was expecting so he told me if I dropped the assault charge he would pay for my dentist.

When I went to court and said I wanted to just drop it. The very pregnant DA said, "Fine with me."

"I wouldn't believe anything this child beating bitch has to say anyway." When we got out the door Ike was laughing really hard and said, "I told you I would ruin you in this town. No one will help you now. All you got is me."

Once when Ike and I fought, Chris and I went to a battered women's shelter to stay. The women liked us so much they said they tried to vote me in as house mother. One night while we were at the shelter, a man broke into the basement.

I got all the women calmed down, then I went to the basement to confront the guy. He had already left, but the women started depending on me a lot after that. After everything Ike did to me, no one would help me, not even the shelter. They said they couldn't get involved. We were now all on our own in this town.

For the next five years, I watched my teeth rot out of my face. I found a dentist that was willing to take payments. I even found free dentists at church clinics and he wouldn't let me go. He said they were male dentists and I might sleep with one of them because Brandy always did.

He told me once that she collapsed a lung doing so many drugs and he still caught her in the bathroom at the hospital doing a black guy for more drugs. Ike said it was his fault that Brandy was on drugs and that all their girls were crack babies.

Ike rented a trailer for a few months when this all first happened. Brandy and her fiancé moved a couple doors down from him. I thought I was done with all this, so I was fine with it.

Brian got engaged on my birthday one year. The next year he graduated from college and shortly afterwards was going to marry the girl he dated and worked with and went to college with. Brian had gone to college for three extra years just so he could graduate the same time as Sara.

I was looking forward to the wedding, but I still hadn't gotten my teeth fixed from when Ike knocked them out. I was too embarrassed to smile or talk a lot to anyone. It was a beautiful wedding on the lake.

I ended up a little late because I had trouble with the directions. Adam and Chris were the best men so they were already there. As Brian and Sara walked away from the preacher, she told Brian she wanted lots of kids. That made me very happy.

They waited almost eight years though to start a family. They both worked and put their money in the bank. Brian ran the software department for the credit section of a big bank. Sara taught third grade at one of the wealthiest schools in Georgia.

They had a huge house with state of the art security. That is why Ike never threatened to go after Brian. He knew he couldn't get to him. Also since Brian didn't come to visit a lot, Ike never felt he was a threat to him. I didn't like not seeing my son very often but as long as he didn't have to deal with Ike, I felt he was safe and that was important to me.

I had kept my same cell phone. Brandy called me in a panic. She said Ike was geeked out on drugs all the time and that she was afraid for the girls. That sounded funny to me since she was an addict herself. She said that I was the only one he would listen to and asked if I would please come to take him to see a doctor.

I went by there after the wedding to see the girls running all over the trailer park in the middle of the night unsupervised, so I stopped to see Ike.

He came out throwing rocks at me and asking everyone that passed by if they wanted to rent me from him for five bucks. He then came out swinging my son's metal bat, the same one that he swore he didn't take because he was still saying he had left everything of mine sitting there at the rock quarry for me to come and get.

He tried to break out the car window. He was swinging at my head. The window didn't break, but he left several big dents in the car. My car had been hit several years before with seventy mile per hour golf ball sized hail in a tornado. The little dimples it left were almost invisible. The only way you could even see them was if a car was behind me with lights on.

Ike left huge dents with the bat. He was swinging that hard to kill me. I left. I thought about the girls all night so I went back the next day to take him to see my doctor.

Soon after that my car quit again. Remember this is how Ike repays everyone for their kindness. He always makes you regret helping him. Like a snake he bites you in the ass every time. He told me to find a car and he would buy it for me. I found a car and took it by to show him.

I told him it was someone we both knew so the guy sold it cheap and said he would take payments. Ike was drunk this time, and his roommate told him I probably screwed someone for the car.

Ike went out and poured brake fluid all over it and put a knife in one of the tires. He came at me so I took off. He chased me down on this winding old road at night in the rain with a flat tire.

Every curve he would rear end me trying to make me spin out. I had already told him the brakes were really bad on this car. The last time he hit me, I spun out and barely whipped into a drive way and asked the people to call the police.

When the police went to Ike's house, both he and his roommate swore he never left the house. Even as drunk as they both were, they believed him and nothing happened to him.

Ike said later that he really was trying to kill me when he hit me with his car and was swinging the bat.

Ike bought a van and said it was for me. I didn't take it. I walked to his place to check on the girls one morning. He came out screaming he was going to kill me, so I jumped in the van and went down the street. I didn't want the van, I just wanted to not be hurt. I called and told him where he could find the van, just a block from his place.

When I got home, the police came and pushed Chris out of their way and came into my home to arrest me for theft. I was changing clothes when I heard them coming up the hall, so I stepped into the closet to pull my pants on. They said I was trying to hide, so they added evading to the charge.

My clothes were all on hangers and my shoes were on the floor. Where did they think I was trying to hide?

I told Wendy Liars I was going to sue for them shoving my underage son out of their way and that I could prove they were false charges to begin with. They dropped it because Ike hadn't even signed the warrant.

Ike was only trying to get me out of there because Brandy had gotten drunk and spent the night with him and he didn't want me to find out. I called the radio station to tell them to not put this on the radio like they had done everything else.

The woman that writes the news said she had been in court every time I went and that she knew I told the judge the truth. She said she knew the judge ignored everything I said. She said that after that if anything came in on me, she reported the story but left my name out of it.

She then told me if I ever sued Judge Stevens to please call her as a witness. I really wish I had enough money back then to take this to court. With all these great witnesses, I might have been able to stop these people from ruining this town.

Ike lost the trailer so of course he came crying in the middle of the night that his girls had no where to go and promising he would be different this time.

Every time I left the house he would make me take one or all of his girls. I really didn't mind but he forced me to not ever take my son with me so I would wait until Chris went to a friend's before I went to shop. I made sure to never leave Chris alone with him. Ike threatened to kill him just to spite me too many times for me to be that stupid.

I always knew that for Ike that was just a matter of time before he would try to prove that he meant what he said. It is so hard to explain because the first time I saw his blue eyes turn white and ice cold, I knew he meant it when he talked about killing me and my family. This was not just an idol threat like everyone else has always tried to convince me.

Even though I knew I was fighting for my very life every time I HAD to fight him, I refused to let him scare me or intimidate me. I did however shower and sleep with one eye open for the next thirteen years. When I saw that look, I said to myself, "Ikeee isn't home anymore."

He shipped the girls off to Ohio again. I was glad his girls didn't have to see him like he had become. I tried to get his family to stop sending money. When they did send money he just did more drugs and tried to kill me more often. It wasn't fun for me having to fight this man for my life many, many times every day.

When the truck he basically stole from me broke down, he got a job long enough to buy a car. Then he told me to go to a check cashing place to get money to feed his girls. He said not to worry that he would pay it back since he was working now. He didn't go to just one place he went to eight places.

He would tell them he was working and showed them a check stub and said he didn't have a checking account yet. He asked if they would just let me give them a check until he opened up an account.

After two places I told him we needed to get to a grocery store. He stuck a knife to my throat and started screaming that after he cut my throat he was going home to cut my sons throat if I didn't do what I was told.

He borrowed $1,600. and dropped me off at home with mine and his hungry children and stayed gone for a week. When the checks came due, he said they weren't in his name and he didn't owe me a thing.

That $1,600 cost me over $16,000. to pay back with interest over the next five years. I told the police what happened and they said that it was domestic, and that they couldn't get involved.

I told the state that he never once spent the girls money on them for anything. That he was spending it all on drugs. They called him in and asked him about it. He said it was just a jealous ex starting trouble. They never even came out to check on the girls. I told him I told them.

He not only spent their state money and food stamps, he returned all their Christmas and birthday gifts for drugs for the next five years. His grandmother sent the girls gift cards. They all went for drugs too.

He would tell the girls to leave all their presents in the package so they would stay pretty for them. The next day him and the presents were always gone.

Ike would get out on the porch when the owner of the subdivision would drive through. Ike would cuss him, flip him off and moon him. Ike knew he didn't own that house and couldn't stop him. The guy did however tell my landlord. I was then told that I had to move because he was getting a divorce and had to move in there.

The landlord's wife picked up the rent the next time it was due, and then I was suddenly in court for not paying rent. When he saw the receipt with her signature, he dropped it, but I was still going to have to move.

Ike asked if he could take the money out to the landlord once because he had pulled up and I was busy. I didn't think anything of it. He only had to walk ten steps out the door.

Ike kept seventy five dollars, that I had to pay back later. Of course he denied it. Ike even pulled a knife on the landlord when he asked about it. The guy's wife called and asked if Ike would provoke him into a fight again. She said she wanted her husband arrested.

Adam called me once and said he and his long time black friend was coming to visit. Ike had a fit and said, "No nigger is ever setting foot in my house. I will beat the f_ _ _ out of all of you."

It was too late to ask them not to come. They were on their way already.

Adam's friend had bad cataracts and was almost blind. He had been a wrestler though and was a real big man. He could have busted Ike up easily. When Adam called back, I asked if we could go out to eat. He said that was what he planned anyway.

We were on our way back from diner when I realized that Adam had come to see me because it was his birthday. Ike had me so stressed out I forgot my own son's special day.

I usually made this Philippine dish my ex mother-in-law taught me called manoak. It was a teriyaki chicken dish. Adam loved it. I was so upset with myself for forgetting it was his birthday, then I was very angry at Ike for making me forget.

My ex had asked me when we were married if I wanted to meet his family in the Philippines. He said they owned a huge restaurant in Manila. He said his father was in a wheelchair but that he was still the right hand man to the First Lady of the Philippines. He said we would be royalty there. I should have went when I was in Taiwan.

Not long after that Louise was sitting on my lap. She was about two or three at the time. She took her little hands and held my face and started crying. She told me that she was so sad when her dad and Debney were selling and destroying my things at the trailer.

She said, "That wasn't right of them to do that." I told Ike what she said later and said that it was really sad that his girls were going to grow up long before he did. He insisted she was lying.

One afternoon a woman from across the street came over. She got really angry when she saw me playing games while I was bathing the two youngest girls. She said, "I heard him screaming at you all night. Now you are in here bathing and playing games with his kids."

I smiled and said, "They didn't do anything. It isn't their fault he is an ass." Ike constantly hit on this woman in front of me. I asked him once if he thought I couldn't see this. He said that he didn't care. He said that I didn't need any friends and if he hit on everyone, that eventually I wouldn't invite any of them over.

I got really sick, like I do every year and was in bed for three days. When I felt better, I got up and went out to get my new lawnmower from under the house to mow the lawn.

The lock was on the ground, and the lawnmower was gone. I called the police and filed a report. I was told several weeks later, by a neighbor, that they saw Ike put it in his trunk and leave with it. All of a sudden Ike started calling me a retard. With all the horrible names he called me over the years why was he now calling me a retard all the time?

I found out later that Ike was trying to sleep with our other neighbor's retarded sister and had taken my mower to her house to mow her lawn. Something he never offered to do for me.

When she refused to sleep with him, he got mad and left my brand new lawnmower sitting there. I never got it back. I was still making payments on it.

That girl came to me crying. She could barely walk or talk. She had this scrunched up, deformed face. I felt so sorry for her. She told me Ike left flowers on her doorstep for weeks and wouldn't leave her alone.

I don't remember getting flowers either. I guess he knew that I knew he wasn't sincere. He scared her, but there was nothing I could do. I tried all the time to talk him out of the things he was doing. He never listens.

Ike constantly screamed and tried to beat me for doing laundry. He said clean, wrinkle free clothes weren't that important to him or his girls. I had all their clothes laying on the couch every morning for them for school. This made him really angry for some reason. That didn't stop me from doing it for them. I could tell they really liked that everything matched for them.

One day Ike told me he would kill me if I made any more payments on the furniture that I had to charge when I moved there. He was holding a knife to my throat and his eyes were all weird. He meant it.

I called and asked the store if they wanted the things back. I hadn't had them very long. They said, no thanks. I tried to tell them I couldn't pay them anymore. They didn't care. Ike said that him and his girls needed my money more than the store did. Of course the store sued me.

Just before we moved from this place, Ike started going into Chris's room with him and his friends. He said he was only playing video games and that it was harmless. He wouldn't let his girls go in with him.

I kept telling him to stop locking the door while he was in there because it was teen age boys and girls. I don't close my doors. Part because I am claustrophobic and part because I always wanted to see what my children were doing.

One day Ike came in and started screaming at these kids. Everyone left. I asked what was going on. I got no answer. I found out by listening to conversations later that Ike had started smoking pot with my son and his friends.

When Ike found out that two of Chris's friends started buying pot from someone he knew, Ike went in the room and threatened to kill those boys and their families if they ever bought from anyone but him.

Chris got suspended from school for a year and had to go to what they called alternative school because they smelled pot smoke on him one day at school. At alternative school they put everyone in a cubical facing the wall and they are told to just study.

Chris lost a whole year of school for this. Ike said it wasn't his fault of course. Chris took the punishment but said he didn't deserve it. He said the thing that pissed him off most was that the teacher that reported him was the teacher that everyone knew was selling pot to all the high school students. Chris wouldn't snitch not even to help himself.

I told Ike if he didn't move I was leaving. He said as long as I was getting free rent, he wasn't going anywhere. The landlord had stopped charging rent while I was looking for a new place so I could save some money to move on.

When Ike would trap me in a room, Louise would kick and scream and cry and beat on the door and beg him to let me out. He would go spank her or just throw her somewhere and tell her to shut up. One time it gave me enough time to dive out the window.

I didn't even take the time to check to see if the window was closed or not. Luckily all I hit was the screen. While I was walking to the police station, he drove past me saying, "I will beat you there, bitch."

When I walked in the police station, the officer came out and started yelling at me. He was saying to leave this poor man and his girls alone or he would personally take care of me, himself.

Every time Ike attacked me he would take the phone off the hook so I couldn't call for help. Isn't this premeditated? Feather started bragging to everyone that she was mean to everyone and hated everyone just like her dad.

Feather went to one of the neighbors and told them I called her names and locked her out of the house. That never happened. I always left the door open to see the girls and so I could see when Ike was coming back.

Those neighbors came to my house to fight me over it. She just stood there grinning because she got away with it. Even her mother's aunt stopped picking the girls up. She said Feather was causing too many problems when she kept them. So she stopped picking any of them up.

Just before Feather did this a female officer that had gone to school with Brian came to ask me if I was alright. She said Ike had ran out in front of her car earlier, flagging her down and ranting that he knew I had called her to check on him but that he wasn't doing a thing.

She said she could tell he was really high at the time and wanted to check on me. Ike drove by and saw her there so he was really convinced I had called her then.

She was the one that came out when the neighbors came to jump me later. Feather started shaking and crying just like she had seen her dad do so many times.

I couldn't believe that this officer that I thought was my friend believed her. I had just about had it with this whole town.

Ike didn't say anything that night, but as soon as everyone left for school the next morning, he trapped me in the bathroom. Most of the time, up until then when he trapped me in a corner and tried to beat me, I blocked the punches. It made me angry that he kept trying to hurt me but I was never really scared of him.

This time I sat down on the toilet and calmly listened to him scream that he knew I had called the cops on him the day before. I explained to him that I hadn't. That she came by to check on me because he stopped her. The more I tried to explain the fact that him flagging her down was why she came to see me, the angrier he got.

I then explained to him that even though he started this nothing happened to him anyway. So he had no reason to be angry. She didn't arrest him, she didn't go in the house where he was at, she didn't question him in any way. I found out later they were cooking meth, right across the street from a grade school.

Ike took my head and shoved me over into a back bend. My ears twisted forward and jammed my head between the wall and the toilet. I couldn't move. I tried every way I could to pull my head up. I even grabbed my own hair and kept pulling. It seemed like he beat me for an hour. All over my face and body.

As I gave one last hard jerk on my hair and finally pulled my head out of the hole, I saw a knife in his hand swinging to cut my very exposed throat. As I sat up I turned my head and the knife stuck in the back of my head, right about the crown area. Ike heard kids talking and knew the kids were getting home from school. He told me he was going to finish off my son for what he thought I had done.

As I came out of the bathroom going to stop him, I saw him waiting behind the door as it opened. He jumped out and swung the knife.

Usually Chris walked in several minutes before his girls every day. On this day Chris had stopped on the corner to talk to a friend. Ike's girls jumped and screamed. He put the knife away and said he was only playing with them.

Then he came and told me if I went out of the house and let anyone see my face he would kill me and then slaughter my whole family. I had so many bumps on me I couldn't lean my head or body on anything without screaming for over a week. I slept sitting up and leaning forward in a chair.

I avoided seeing Chris that week thinking that I was keeping all this from him so he wouldn't worry or be scared.

It was several weeks before I had my regular doctor's visit. My face was still every color of the rainbow. I have never seen these colors of bruises before.

I had asked my doctor a few months earlier to see Ike and the girls. I asked him to see if Ike's outbursts were a chemical imbalance. My primary care doctor was Don, but I had seen his physicians assistant Barry for years.

When Barry walked in and saw my face, he quietly motioned for me to follow him. We walked to the back of the building. He said, "I know you wanted it to be an imbalance but it isn't. I just informed Ike that I am not able to see him or Feather anymore."

"I told him that he and Feather need very serious professional psychiatric help." He said, "I wake up every morning scared to death that I will read in the paper that he has beaten you to death. Please get away from this man as soon as possible." I said, "I can't, I have tried." Barry walked out in tears.

I started looking for a place and told Ike he wasn't moving with me. My landlady called to tell me that she was in a car wreck and she was moving in with her sister and couldn't afford to keep her house. She asked me to please rent her place so she wouldn't end up losing it.

Ike disappeared with my money and was suddenly gone for a week, so I rented her house. He had taken the girls with him this time.

I told her what happened and that he wasn't moving with me. Since my car was still not running, I moved everything I could in the girls little red wagon. I walked up and down hills everyday that whole week, day and night moving mine and Chris's things.

After about three exhausting days of this, the police stopped me. They said the neighbors were complaining that some strange woman had been walking the streets for days. This kind of ticked me off. Not one person ask to help me, but they jumped right on trying to get me arrested. This officer apologized for the general public and told me that there really were good men still out there. I think he was new to town.

The last day I found a friend with a truck to move the bed, washer and dryer, fridge and stove. I was pretty sure they weren't going to fit in the little red wagon.

Ike told me later that he kept driving past me moving my things in that little wagon and laughed and said to the women with him that I was an idiot for moving our things while he was out doing drugs and getting laid. What kind of woman would be impressed by this?

I couldn't believe the mess this new place was. I have cleaned up some really nasty houses before but nothing like this place. To look at her, you would think she was a clean person. It took me one straight week just to clean this place and take out her garbage.

Something in the back of my mind kept telling me that I should take pictures or have someone come in to witness this mess. I always try so hard to believe in people and take them at their word, even though I know better. Once again I ignored those instincts and you will find out later how badly it bit me in the ass.

Ike was pretty pissed when he came back and found his and his girls things still sitting there. I cleaned everything up and made the mistake of leaving the garbage bags sitting there. Ike said for weeks that he was going to leave eggs out to rot and throw them around places where they wouldn't be found to ruin this house just to piss off the landlord.

I told him this man was being more than generous for giving us several months free rent and plenty of time to find a place. It wasn't his fault he was getting a divorce and having to move in. Ike sees any action as being against him. I did talk him out of tearing up the place or so I thought.

When I came back to tow my car, Ike came in swinging a metal bat at me. If I didn't have fast reflexes, I would be dead. He was swinging right at my head. My friend heard the noise and called the police. I told them he wasn't moving with me. I left with my car being towed to my new place. Just as my friend was leaving my new place Ike came pulling in and started throwing his things on the lawn screaming that he was going to kill me if I didn't start putting his things inside.

My friend called the police again and they came out and finally arrested him, only because there was a witness this time.

It started raining while he was in jail and I didn't want the girls' things to get ruined, so I put them in the smaller house out back. When Ike got out of jail he called the landlady, and she told him he could live in the small house if he would do some repairs.

The police said that even though I paid the rent the owner said he could stay and there was nothing I could do about it. I let the girls move into the big house with me and Chris.

Since I had my own appliances I had the landlady's very old fridge and stove moved to the little house. They were so nasty that even if I didn't have new stuff, I would have gone out to buy new things instead of trying to clean those. I thought since she told him he could live there he could use her things.

Pretty soon he started having parties. These parties were very loud and lasted until all hours. I usually had to go bang on the door and tell everyone they had to leave because it was keeping my son and Ike's daughters up on school nights. Standing on my back porch I could hear everything that was said by Ike and his friends.

The conversations quickly turned to meth. and cooking meth. I told him I wouldn't tolerate this because I wasn't going to lose my son or my home or his girls because he wanted to be an ass.

He said he loved me and would never consider doing anything to put me in any jeopardy. He said that he kept everything from me all those years because that way the police couldn't bother me and that was his way of protecting me. B.S. He knew I would fight him and try to talk him out of being so stupid.

I transferred all the electric, cable and phones without a problem. The water refused to transfer. When I went in there I was told that the landlady owed a very large bill. She told them to bill the new tenant. While I was trying to pay off her bill Ike goes out and connects the water himself at the meter without telling me. The next thing I know we are both being arrested on theft of services.

I had to pay both our bonds, both court costs and a very large connection fee just to get water. Jail, court and having the police in my face constantly was already starting to wear on my nerves but as I said, this man was just getting started.

Ike then started going to this couple's house about a block away. Right across from a grade school and the same place where he had flagged the female officer down that one day. I could tell by the attitude he was now on hard drugs.

The verbal abuse started to be more and more. The mental, emotional, physical and financial abuse started getting much worse too. He accused me of sleeping with every man, woman and child we ever met.

Brandy and her fiancé pulled up one afternoon. We lived on a busy street by two schools. I was still pissed over the water stunt he had pulled and said that one way or another I was going to get away from him. He pulled out a 357 loaded with hollow tip bullets and pointed it at my head.

I have never understood exactly why but someone pulling a knife or a gun on me doesn't scare me it just really pisses me off. I started walking towards him. He then looked around and noticed all the traffic waiting for the light and all the people looking at him so he put the gun away.

As I said before, he always makes sure there are no witnesses. This time he had been too high to notice. I found out years later Chris had seen all this too. He was in the house.

One weekend Ike said Brandy was taking the girls and he invited this other couple over. I started noticing he always hung out with guys that were dating or married to women he knew were sleazy enough to eventually sleep with him. But by this point I hated him so much I didn't care what he did. I just wanted him out of our lives.

I fell asleep on the couch. When I woke up, there was a huge four foot flame in the middle of the kitchen. Ike put it out and told me everyone had gotten hungry and he fixed burgers. He said the grease caught on fire and when he pulled it off the stove the floor caught on fire.

I found out later that when I fell asleep he had decided he was going to cook meth for this couple, right under my nose. We really got into it that night. He didn't try this in my home again. He started going to the other two couples houses when I went to sleep. They were all cooking meth.

I started staying in my room more and more doing picture puzzles, just doing my best to block out everything he said and did. One day Chris came to my room and said, "I love you so much mom, but I am moving with one of my friends." He stood there quietly for a minute then he said, "Do you realize that since Ike moved in we have become prisoners in our own home?"

I gave him a hug and said, "I am so sorry honey, I have tried to stop this but the police just won't help." Chris said, "I know but I don't have to take it anymore." This broke my heart.

He was almost eighteen so I let him move. I was thinking that if he were somewhere safe where Ike couldn't get to him then I could some how get away.

The couple that was trying to help him cook meth when they caught my kitchen on fire came back. I told them to leave. They refused so I had to call the police. It turned out the guy had a warrant against him so he was arrested but they didn't make her leave.

Ike instantly started flirting with her and picked a fight with me. He was trying to get me to leave the two of them in my home. He was trying to do what he did before with Debney.

He was going to move this woman into my home and take everything I had bought to replace what he stole the last time. It was that time of year again. I didn't let it happen this time. I refused to leave so he moved to her place for the week while her boyfriend was in jail.

When he left once before Louise looked at me and said, "I hope he didn't move back to Susy's house. She was mean." She then told me that the week he was gone and left me to move every thing by myself he had moved into this woman's house that had drug parties day and night. She said the woman's twenty year old daughter ran around naked for all the men. Nice place for a man to move his girls to huh.

She said she was mean to the girls and picked a fight with Ike and told him to get out. Another woman told me that during this time Ike had gotten mad at Louise for messing with one of his shirts and threw her at the couch so hard that she bounced into the middle of the floor. They were afraid she was seriously hurt. I think she was like four or five now.

When Ike took the girls back to Brandy this time I told Ike that wasn't a good idea but he did it anyway. I just had one of those gut feelings that by now I should know better than to ignore.

The landlady called and said that she wasn't supposed to move out of that house during her divorce and now that it was being finalized she was moving back in. She asked me to lie for her in court and say she had lived there with me the whole time. I told her no. After I cleaned everything and paid her bills off she was putting me out AND wanted me to lie to the court.

Chris was moving and I thought this is perfect. I will put everything in storage and find me and Chris a place. I had always told the girls that if anyone, even their parents, ever did anything they didn't feel comfortable with, for them to tell a teacher, a councilor or a cop.

I told Louise because she was the last one home with me that family means everything and that she needed to always protect her sisters.

I had also told myself from the beginning that I would protect them until they were at least school age. Then they would be old enough and could tell someone if there was a problem. It was now summer. I think it was the last day of school and Louise would start school the next year. I figured Brandy would ship them off to her parents in a few days like she always did. I was finally done with this.

My car was still not running because Ike purposely left those bearings out. This was over a year now and he wouldn't even consider fixing it. I was still walking everywhere I had to go but at least we were in town now.

Out of the blue a woman from child services called me. She just kept apologizing to me. She said she was sent there to review cases and she was appalled when she read what the courts had done to me and Chris.

She said she read my case cover to cover several times to make sure of what she had read. She said that the judge and child services was so wrong. She said that they never had any reason or any right to do this to us. She said that they never should have been involved in the first place.

She asked if she could do anything to make it up to us because a thousand apologies was simply not enough. I told her she could pay to fix the motor in my car.

I had it towed to a garage a week later and she paid the bill. Chris would soon be safe from Ike and the girls were away from him. I was about to put my things in storage and find a place he didn't know about and I had a promise of my car being fixed. I was on top of the world, for a moment.

I started moving Chris's things to the car before they towed it so it would be easier for him to pick his things up after school that day. After I moved Chris's things to my car Ike came in after being gone all week.

I told him that I had to move again and I told him to get out that he was no longer welcomed. I told him I was going to get the police and that I was really done with all this. When I left he hurried up and grabbed all of his things and Chris's TV that was in my car.

He was gone when I got back. So I started checking on storage places. This was all starting to look like it was all falling into place. Since the girls were with their mother I thought it may turn out ok. I really should stop thinking, huh!

Chris came to get his things. I told him not to worry that I would get him a new TV or get his back. As soon as Chris left for his new home with his friends I suddenly get this frantic call from Ike that the police are at that first couples house a block away by the school.

They were all being busted for cooking meth. He said the police were going to force him to come back to my place.

I didn't mind because I clean my house all the time. I knew nothing was there. I had just spent all morning cleaning and moving Chris's things out to the car.

I walked outside to see Ike's car pulling in with Chris's TV in it and all of his things in it and tied all around it. The first thing I told the police is that I wanted my sons TV put back in my car. They said only if I let them search. They said that they knew it was just him doing this and that I would never be charged with anything even if they found anything.

I knew nothing was there so I agreed. This was my first introduction to three dirty cops. Mark Verdick, Tom Sternman and Stan Johns.

They tore my place apart, his little house too and found nothing. Sternman walked in and said that he heard my name a lot lately in the drug world. I knew he was full of crap because every one that has ever met me knows I don't do drugs and never have. Most people are shocked when they hear that I used to smoke pot.

I didn't even drink all those years I went to the bars there. That is why I ended up driving every one home for years. I even drove home the lawyers I knew there. One night a friend said I could use his van if I drove him and his mother home too. I ended up with about ten to fifteen drunk people jammed in the van driving everyone home.

All of a sudden Sternman asks me to come out on my back porch and he pointed to a bag and asked me what that was. He was pointing to a clear plastic bag full of garbage. I said I had no idea.

Since I had spent the morning going in and out of the back door taking my sons things to the car I knew it wasn't there before they all showed up. He had them bring Ike up and he asked him the same thing.

I was standing right in side the door and heard Ike say, "I moved out a week ago, whatever it is, it's hers." Remember, his things were sitting out there still tied to his car where he had just moved out and I know for a fact this clear bag full of garbage was not there ten minutes earlier. The garbage ran earlier that day. If it had been there I would have put the bag in the garbage for pick up.

The police walked in and told me that since the lease was in my name it was now my stuff and I was arrested. I bonded out and moved my things to storage and moved to the mission so I could look for a place to live. They didn't let Ike bond out.

I was then arrested on theft charges. My landlady said that she had left all her husband's furniture when she moved and that I had stolen it, including a riding lawnmower that I had never even seen. Yeah, you can say it, I really should have taken pictures when I moved in.

My bond was five times higher than what they said I stole. When I bonded out I went to see the guy that had tackled me that time and refused to get Chris out of that house to safety. I told him they could go with me to my storage and that I had receipts for everything in there.

I told him he owed me that much for risking Chris's life. They were now starting to see that I was telling the truth all along and Ike was the problem.

They dropped the case. My landlady said it was nothing personal. That since she had the wreck and lost her paycheck, that she had done all this to take my paycheck. Don't you love it when someone screws you over for no reason and says, "Nothing personal."

When she went for her divorce hearing later, her husband asked me to come to make sure she didn't lie about any of this. When we were in court, three cops pointed at her and said that she had five trucks full of furniture sitting in front of her house the day she moved out and that I didn't steal a thing.

I found out that no one would rent to me once again because I was front page news again. No one cared that I kept proving that I wasn't guilty.

I also found out that I had a $2,000 judgment against me. When Ike moved his things out of the other house, when I didn't move his things, he tore open my garbage bags and threw it all around. He broke the dining room set into pieces and pissed all over the living room set. Then he turned on all the water faucets inside and out and left. $2,000 worth of damages.

He knew that since it was in my name I would be blamed. The landlord said he knew it wasn't me so he would never try to collect. It is probably still on the court records that I owe this.

My doctor Barry volunteered to go to court with me. He told me that in all the years he had been my doctor drugs never showed up in my tests and I had never asked him for any drugs. He also said that since he could tell Ike was on drugs that he had started paying more attention to my eyes and skin to make sure Ike wasn't exposing me to anything. He assured me that he knew exactly what signs to look for.

When I told the court this they said it made no difference, that the stuff was found on my porch and I had to plead guilty for meth garbage. They said they would just let me go after I plead guilty because it was my first time.

Ike sat behind me in court threatening to kill me if I didn't plead guilty because they wouldn't let him out until I was found guilty. I had to take the charges. I then found out that in the mean time Brandy was caught cooking meth, with the girls there with her so the state took the girls.

This broke my heart. I was so afraid they would split the girls up. With all they had been through they needed each other more now than ever. I fought so hard for five years to keep this from happening, now it was done and there was nothing I could do.

Chapter 6

Ike moved into the mission as soon as he got out. Ike knew I wanted to get away from him so from then on he wouldn't let me get out of his sight. He started pulling guns and knives on me more and more. His steady paycheck was gone now. He had nothing to lose.

No matter how early I got up and tried to leave, Ike would come running out and jump in the car. We went out in the woods every day looking for ginseng because the preacher told Ike he was making all kinds of money selling it. All we ever found were big patches that had already been dug up.

It turned out that the couple Ike got busted with was the mission owner's daughter. The preacher and his wife told me and a lot of other people that were sitting there, that they knew for a fact I had been set up.

He said he was there when they busted his daughter. He said that Sternman and Verdick held the clear plastic bag open for him while he took all the meth garbage out of his daughter's garbage can. Then they told him to take his grandchildren out of there. The bag ended up on my porch ten minutes later.

All bags at the stores are white, brown or black. I can't even buy clear bags anywhere. The police have clear bags. I went to the courthouse and I told Judge Stevens I wanted to change my plea and go back to court. He said I was one day too late to do that. I doubt that was true, but what can you do? I don't have the money to fight them.

The girl Ike spent the week with while her boyfriend was in jail ended up getting a year in jail when they found Ike's meth lab under her trailer.

She lost her kids too. She wasn't the last person to have to take charges for his labs.

This man has never once cared about the lives he destroyed, least of all mine or my sons or his daughters. I could see now this court definitely didn't care about the truth either, only their conviction rate.

When I was arrested the year before for the charges with the girls, I begged these people to please go talk to the girls. I told them that if Ike wasn't there to threaten them, they would tell the truth. No one did. They don't care about the truth only about who they can railroad into pleading guilty and paying their ridiculous fees. They hide behind the law and destroy lives.

When the judge took the kids later I asked him to please get the girls help because of all I could see that they had gone through with two drug addicted parents. He told me it wasn't his problem, that it was up to the foster mom to get them help.

I had no way of reaching her so I have prayed for years for them to find the help they needed. It was obvious to me that the courts couldn't have cared less what happened to them.

After a few weeks we were told we had to leave the mission because someone said we were out in the woods making meth because we were taking water with us every day. It was summer, we out in the heat walking everyday. We weren't supposed to take water to drink?

I'm not sure but I would imagine that it would take a lot more than the two, two liter bottles of tap water we were taking with us to cook meth. Also I have heard Ike tell people he used distilled water to cook with.

The preacher's daughter said Ike was sneaking out to see her after curfew and that Ike was cooking meth in the church basement every night when everyone went to sleep. I told them I wasn't doing anything. They said it didn't make any difference because I was still with him. No one ever cared that I was there against my will.

Just a few days before this. Ike had gotten into a fight with one of the alcoholics that was staying at the mission. I was told that it was because Ike was playing with his fourteen year old daughter's butt right in front of the guy. Ike thought he was too drunk to notice I guess. Ike denied it of course.

For the next year I slept in my car and tried to find a place to rent. I got away from him for a short time here and there. I got to spend some time with Chris, and I went to my storage unit and watched some movies a few times.

Ike found me again. Ike dragged me from one of his drug parties to another. I knew if I left he would find me or look for Chris. I always just went out to my car to sit. I was at one party and was watching him put out lines of meth for this girl he was hitting on. I told him she looked under age.

I reminded him that he was the oldest man there and this would bring some really serious charges for him. He just screamed and threatened me and told me to stop trying to ruin his fun.

Then the girl started yelling at me because she was getting very wasted so I went to my car.

The next day a guy came in and told him that girl was his neighbor and that she had just turned thirteen. Ike almost fell out of his chair. He had obviously been with her and the reality of what I said to him was setting in.

Of course he denied all of this for years. Ike told me later that was what he called panty blower Meth. He said they purposely ground up Magnesium in it to make women horny. One day he got really high and started bragging about all of it.

People started coming up to me to tell me things Ike had said about me and my sons. He told people that he busted his ass to pay for everything and me and my sons just lived off of him and treated him like dirt. He was playing the victim.

They said that Ike said the only reason I didn't date all those years was because I was sleeping with my sons. I was horrified. This is what he was saying about us to anyone that would listen?

I have known people that were molested by their parents. Every one of them said that if they ever saw that parent ever again that they would kill them for what they did to them. Everyone of them said they hated them for what they did. This traumatized these people for life. What kind of sick mind would even think to say this?

Every time I told him what someone had said, he would try to beat me and tell me they just lied to break us up. He would say he was angry that I had the nerve to believe them, over him. When I said some of them were church people he would get even madder.

At one of the parties that Ike made me go to I suddenly smelled a really bad odor coming from the kitchen. I started to go out and get some air. Ike grabbed me from behind just as I reached for the door handle. Ike picked me up and threw me on the couch and said that he would kill anyone that even tried to open that door again.

I was finally getting angry when I realized they were cooking meth with me and all these people sitting there.

We weren't only forced to breathe these toxic fumes but our lives were at risk from not only going to jail if the police had shown up, but also of us being blown up if something had gone wrong.

I have seen on the news where entire houses were blown to pieces from it or blown off their foundation. I knew that if I told the police Ike would just lie and find a way to have me arrested for it. Since I didn't actually see it, it was hearsay.

The next week we were at a different apartment. Ike was gone and the people there were going somewhere too. I asked them if I could shower while Ike was gone because I was leaving and not coming back. They said for me to lock the door when I left. When I finished my shower, Ike was back, but I was going to try to get away anyway. Once again my son wasn't where Ike could find him.

Ike came over to the couch and handed me a can of Vienna sausage and sat something on the floor by my feet. I had assumed it was a drink for me. While he was busy unpacking what he had just bought, I saw my chance to run. Before I got off the couch there was a knock at the door. I told him to not answer it since it wasn't our place. He did any way and it was the police. They had a warrant for him.

The cops pointed next to my feet and said, "What is that?" He had set a big stack of pills by my feet, not a drink. One of the ingredients of meth. I'm in a police car again for something I had no idea was going on.

The two cops were the ones I told you I had been friends with. The male cop told me not to worry, that they all knew I didn't do drugs. He said that they were only looking at Ike and the people that lived in the apartment.

Ike must have snitched on these people like he always does to get himself out of trouble. But of course he convinced that couple that I snitched on them. I had no reason to tell the police any thing and actually didn't know anything to tell.

For some reason people believe what he says. When the couple got home the woman was cussing me and screaming that I snitched.

She and Ike told the cops they needed to go search my storage. I told them I would gladly take them over there. It was right across the street. I took them over there and they didn't find anything. That was only because Ike didn't have a key to it.

Ike said he had something bad in his trunk but managed to drop his keys before he was searched. I was just glad he hadn't put anything in my car this time. I was just let go, which even further convinced her that I snitched.

The next time Ike got arrested for drugs for some reason I ended up doing his community service and paying all his fines because he claimed he had heart problems. While I was picking up garbage in his place, he took my car to chase more women and drugs.

It turned out that the last time he tried to beat me he injured my back. When I bent over to pick up paper, pain shot up my back and I instantly fell to my knees. I couldn't move.

Luckily I had just finished all my time for community service. Or should I say all of his time. I went to the hospital. While I was in the hospital for that week for tests, he stayed there with me. He screamed at me every day to get up and get him something to drink or get him some ice cream.

It took me ten minutes to just get out of bed. I had to take baby steps all the way down the hall. I was in so much pain. When I got back, he was always mad because it wasn't what he wanted or it took me too long.

Ike would steal my car and go to another girls house to do drugs all night. She lived an hour or two away from the hospital I was in. The same car I might add, that he purposely tore up twice and refused to work on for me for over a year. Once I got it fixed, it was suddenly his car again.

The only reason I even found out he was gone was because I woke up one night in pain. When I asked if anyone knew where he was, I was told he left every night as soon as I went to sleep. He would spend the night doing meth then scream at me the entire next day over every little thing he could think of.

The doctor couldn't find anything wrong with my back, so I had to leave the hospital. I always had the feeling they thought that since I was homeless, that I was faking it. I am sure they were all tired of listening to Ike constantly screaming at me all day too.

They didn't even bother to take any x rays or scans. It was years before they did and found out the problem. It was there all that time. They just didn't bother to look for it. They wanted Ike and his constant screaming out of there. It made no difference that I was in so much pain or that I begged the police to get him out of my life.

I started hearing more and more that Ike was bragging about sleeping with all these women he had heard had AIDS. They said he would brag that it was all good to him. When I asked him, he would look me in the eye and swear that he loved me far too much to ever risk my life that way.

Ike would tell me he wanted to marry me and grow old together sitting on a back porch swing. That he would never risk my life that way. He already knew I was never going to marry him. I was always up front about the fact that I was only there to protect those girls.

I started noticing that he had needle marks on his arms too, so I stopped sleeping with him at all.

At a party once I saw him take drugs out of the same spoon a lot of other people had just used.

One day his wife's aunt told me that the woman that lived with Ike just before me, she knew for a fact had AIDS. And that when she told Ike that this girls last two exes died of AIDS he went in the bedroom and slept with her right then. He then came out bragging how good it was.

When I met Ike, he had told me that Brandy had just run off right before I met him. I definitely didn't want to be with him for any reason now. He had risked killing me from the very beginning and never bothered to tell me. Then he flat out lied to me every time I asked him about it.

I always tell my sons that no matter what the girls say, you use a condom. I really should have listened to my own advice. You truly cannot trust anyone these days. So many women trust untrustworthy men. They may not even know they have it. Ike knew and never bothered to mention it. I get my blood checked once every year as a precaution. I've been doing this for twenty years now.

If I went to the bathroom at a gas station, Ike would be standing out side the door when I came out. I asked him where he thought I was going to run to since it was my car sitting out front. Ike started disappearing again a lot. He would strand me somewhere and take off with my car.

He had met this stripper, barely eighteen, and it turned out she was a meth cook too. She and her lesbian room mate for some reason decided they were going to be my friends.

She started telling me she liked me much more than Ike and told me about all the women she knew he was with.

I don't think anyone ever realized we were no longer a couple. I didn't care nor was I surprised or hurt by any of this, but people insisted on telling me everything about what he was doing for many years. She said this time that he was with a woman everyone knew had herpes. She had even given them to her kids and her kids were taken away.

More and more women would come to cry on my shoulder and tell me they were so sorry for sleeping with what they thought was my man but he convinced them he was in love with them. When he got what he wanted, he would then chase their friends and relatives right in front of them. I always tried to tell them that he wasn't worth crying over.

I never tried to fight or hurt any of these women in any way. I patiently listened to their problems just like I had everyone else's all my life. Ike told everyone I was a psychotic monster that would beat them, like he told everyone I was beating him. But they came to me for comfort anyway. They all told me I was nothing like he said I was.

Ike would say and do anything to humiliate me in front of people all the time. Ike met one guy that he said was a big time cook and dealer. Ike decided he would start getting pills to sell this guy and make money to rent a room with. I refused to stay with anymore of these people.

He went from one end of the state to the other and started stealing a lot of pills. He tried to force me to start stealing with him. I told him he would have to fight me first. Since it wasn't yet illegal to buy these pills

I did say I would buy a few but not steal anything. Ike would turn right towards the cameras in the stores and stuff boxes of pills in his pants. I kept hoping he would get caught. No such luck.

We went to a lot of different counties to rent rooms. Within a week the police would show up with a dog to search the room. Ike would freak out and run and leave me to go back and move everything to the next place. I kept trying to tell them this was a waste of their time and a lot of harassment for me because as usual he knew if I found drugs I would either flush them or call the police myself.

I found out later though that he rented two rooms a couple of times, and when I went to sleep he would go over there with his friends and cook meth. I didn't find this out until much later.

I heard him say once that he had stripped so many matches and flushed them down the toilet at one place that they stopped up a toilet and did a lot of water damage to the room down stairs, which made the police come to our room one of those times.

One guy that had befriended Ike for the drugs he was making told Ike he would put his truck, trailer and bobcat shovel in both their names. Ike had cards printed up and made signs for them to get work to do. Ike told me that as soon as he put it in his name, he was going to sell it out from under the guy.

After the guy did a lot of Ike's drugs, he disappeared in the middle of the night. Of course Ike swore I told the guy his plan and tried to beat me for it.

Another guy was going to buy all new lawn service equipment for him and Ike to do lawns with and once again all Ike talked about was stealing all of it to sell. This guy suddenly disappeared too. I probably would have told these guys if I had had a chance. I hated that all this man ever thought to do was screw over everyone that tried to help him.

One time at one of the nicest places we stayed at, one of Ike's friends came to visit. The next day we found out that on his way out, he decided to steal a big color TV from the dining room.

The guy got busted. A day or two later a couple of his friends showed up and accused Ike of snitching on him.

They approached Ike in the parking lot. When I saw a knife in the one guy's hand I told Ike to run. The guy started to come after me, but he saw that I had a cell phone and had already dialed 911. The guy dropped the knife and both of them ran after Ike.

By the time I drove up the hill, they had beaten Ike and left. When Ike went to the hospital, I had to go move all our stuff. I kept waiting for those two guys to show back up while I was busy moving. The police tried to come in and search, but I told them the room wasn't in my name. They had to go get permission from Ike.

They did however wait in the parking lot and ask to search my car while I was carrying everything out. I was getting pissed, so I whipped all the doors open and told them to have at it. They had no concern with protecting me from drugged out armed felons there to harm me but couldn't wait to continue to harass me. So glad to know that this is what I am paying my taxes for.

The police were constantly in my face again now. A friend told me one day that he knew everytime I came to town because he had a scanner. He said the police would actually follow my car and talk about everywhere I stopped and argue over who was going to stop me and search me.

I proved over and over that I was not a drug addict and that I was doing nothing wrong, but it didn't stop the police from their harassing me. When I was walking back to the room, I almost stepped on the knife the guy threw down. I called the police. They said it wasn't their concern and they never came out to get it.

When I told Ike I wouldn't help him even buy the pills anymore, he started stealing my car at night. He would pick up a bunch of women and use my car to go party and steal material with.

I found this out from the stripper when they got pulled over one time by a state trooper. She said Ike went running back to the cop car with his hands up yelling that it wasn't his car and it wasn't his shit. He even told the cop where to go to find me. At that time I wasn't even aware any of this was happening.

She said she was pissed at me because Ike convinced them I had called the police on them. I didn't. I was busy walking to Crossburg trying to find my car. I thought he had just stolen it to go do drugs with his friend. A three hour walk I might add.

It turned out that since they only had one ingredient they couldn't be charged and were let go. But it pissed these women off so bad that Ike tried to blame it on me that they all refused to help him anymore. I guess at least one good thing came out of it. He stopped stealing my car for a while.

The same stripper told me once that she had been arrested many times on meth charges but she was let go every time because she was sleeping with Judge Stevens. A year later the judge lost his job and went back to being a lawyer when he was caught with what I heard was two kilos of cocaine. He didn't do any jail time either.

Ike stole a lot of different things to sell this one dealer over the years. These were big, expensive items at that same chain store. I prayed he would get caught, but of course never did. One night Ike said he had to go to the drug guy's house to pick up money this other guy owed him.

On the way up the hill I told him to stop and let me out because I didn't want to go there any more. He wouldn't do it. Then I said, "Turn around now, there are way too many cars at his house and his house is never that lit up." He kept going.

It turned out those three crooked cops that had protected the guy for years were there with the feds busting him. It was a case of they had no choice but to help so they wouldn't look guilty. We drove by and were chased by the police and forced to go back to the house.

They held us over night but didn't charge us. Everyone there told them they would tell the judge we weren't there until the police forced us to go there. Not all drug addicts are bad people.

When I got back to my car the next day, the windows were left down and it had snowed over night. My purse and everything else was dumped out and thrown everywhere.

We then noticed the crooked cops were there going through the guy's house while he was in jail. The guy said later a lot of cash, jewelry and other things were suddenly missing. The guy got busted so many times by the feds he is doing forty years in a Kentucky federal prison. I actually liked this guy. He was a honest decent man before the drugs took over his life.

Ike of course got away with all of it again. I heard later that Ike, the guy's girlfriend and another guy went there when he went to prison and left with about five truck loads of his things. Ike truly has no conscience and no morals.

One time I went to see Brian's new house for Easter. I came back by my doctor's. I started having a lot of pain and I knew it wasn't my period because I went through the change early in life. He told me I had Chlamydia, a very serious STD.

Ike had just thrown me down a few times and forced sex on me. He never lasted long so there wasn't much I could do. I called him the minute man. There was no point in asking the police for help and I knew it.

I got back to the room to find out some married woman had spent the week there because her husband was in jail. I knocked on the door and told Ike the doctor said he had to use this cream and I taped it to the door and told him what was wrong. I left.

I ended up having to take three of the strongest antibiotics made, all at the same time to get rid of it. The doctor said taking these three together could kill me but that it was the only way to get rid of it.

I wonder how this married woman ever explained to her husband how she got this infection while he was in jail. A week later, after the girl left, Ike tracked me down and said that it was all my fault he did this because I went to see my son. And of course he threatened to kill my whole family if I ever left again.

This is about the time he started trying to smother me every time he got mad. He had very large very strong hands. He would sit on me and put one hand on my throat and squeeze while he put the other hand over my nose and mouth to make sure I couldn't breathe. It really pissed him off when I got out of this hold.

My teeth were still all broken up. So to this day I can still feel the bumps on the inside of my mouth with my tongue. They are from the scar tissue where these cuts healed from when he would bear down so hard trying to smother me and it would cut up the inside of my mouth.

One day we were getting ready for Ike to go to court. Ike would force me to go with him. He said it had to look like I was supporting my man. Sternman and Verdick came to our room. They came in putting on their gloves and were obviously very pissed. They told me to go on to court and that they would bring Ike.

Ike asked me to wait close by. I heard Verdick scream at Ike that he screwed the wrong guy. He said that he had told Ike not to tell anyone that they knew each other. Ike was bragging to everyone about him protecting him. Somehow he talked these guys out of beating him.

Ike told me that these guys had been taking drugs off of the guy that went to prison for all those years and were now his buddies. Ike then started calling the cops right in front of me to tell them all the things everyone he knew was doing.

I heard him tell someone later that he did this every time he wanted to cook so they were busy busting his friends and wouldn't be looking at him. I also heard Ike tell someone that he accidentally spilled his soda in one batch. He said he didn't want to waste it so he poured it back in the soda can.

Ike told this one guy to take out his meth garbage. He said they usually just went out on a deserted road and tossed it out. Just before the guy took off he drank the soda. He hit a mail box and the police found him barely coherent and wandering the neighborhood. Ike just laughed because they charged that guy as having a meth lab in his trunk.

About a year later we heard that those three cops were busted cooking meth, using meth, selling meth and setting innocent people up to take the fall instead of their friends. They did no jail time.

They were told to quit their jobs and I heard they all went to work for other counties, still in law enforcement. They are cops walking around high on drugs, armed and on duty. This to me is a very scary thought. And it is still going on people.

With his protectors gone, Ike decided to go to a different county. All of a sudden his buddy that had stolen the TV from the other place showed up. He and his girlfriend rented a room next door. The walls were thin. I woke up later to hear Ike screwing her right next door. I just went back to sleep.

Early the next day while Ike was still gone, I went out to my car and saw the parking lot full of cops. Ike and that couple were cooking meth right next door. They had ran to the store to get more material and the maid came in and found their lab.

Ike came home and acted like he had no idea what was going on. This time it was the TBI in my room searching and asking a lot of questions.

Of course we had to move again as soon as they left. Ike showed me where he had somehow melted one of their bedspreads the night before. I was glad the room was in his name.

We started staying with this man we had both known for years. The guy was creeping me out so I left. Also the guy's brother told me the guy had Hepatitis C. When we were at his house one day visiting a girl came to tell me how she had just slept with ten to fifteen guys for drugs that one day and that Ike was one of them.

She said in the middle of all this Ike stopped to call me and threaten me into getting more phone minutes for him while I was out.

Ike would use other people's phones to call my cell phone and waste all my minutes, cussing me and threatening me. Then he would have his phone to use while I had to wait till the next month to renew mine. This way I couldn't call anyone, not even my family.

When I told Ike what she said, he started trying to beat me for it just like he always did. I drove away. He was hanging on to the car and I drug him a little way before he let go. I made sure he was ok. When I saw him get up, I kept going.

I had heard of a place that did land contracts with little money down and a small monthly payment. I had asked Ike to take me there many times, but he insisted that I was an idiot because no one did that kind of thing for anyone. I decided to stop and ask about it since Ike hadn't found me yet.

I drove for days looking at a lot of land. Everything they had came with a book of restrictions. I finally told them that I needed a place that had no restrictions so I could put a small trailer on it until I could afford to build. They said they had one place left. I told them that if I liked it that it was mine and I would be right back.

I picked up Chris, and we drove out to see this piece of land. I said that as soon as I could, I would get a house put there for us to live in. It was in the next county over, so Chris was worried about his friends and school. I told him he didn't have to move right then, that I would be there when he was ready.

At the last house we lived in Ike had ran the bills up so high and with all those check cashing fees I was still paying I couldn't even afford to eat let alone make the payments. I gave up the food so I could get the land.

Since Ike was no longer around, Brian said that I could either live with him and his wife in Georgia or he would help me pay off the bills. I knew I had to stay close enough to protect Chris from Ike, so I told him I wanted to start working on the land. I still hadn't told Brian or anyone else what Ike had done to us all those years.

For one reason I was still protecting my family and because Brian never asked me anything, not even when he knew I had gone to jail and the hospital. I figured he didn't want to know or he would have asked. Adam had told me he didn't come around because of Ike.

I told him I understood, but that I couldn't change that. I tried every way I knew how. I knew Brian was angry, but he never said why. This hurt me a lot, but I let it go on because he was still safer not being around Ike. As every parent knows, if your children are safe, you can endure almost anything.

I started worrying more about if Ike would try to find Chris like he always threatened to do. I checked on him as much as I could.

I was going back through town one day. There was a lot of traffic so I had to stop a lot. I had just dropped Chris off and forgot to lock his door back. Out of no where Ike jumped in my car, put a knife to my throat and started threatening to kill me and my family.

When he realized everyone around us was looking at him he dropped the knife, started shaking and crying and begged me to get him help.

He showed me his arms that were covered with bruises and needle marks. I mean a hundred needle marks or more. They were all up and down both arms. He asked me to please get him into rehab.

As soon as we got away from all the people he picked up the knife and started the threats again. I didn't tell him about the land. I had hoped that after sleeping in the car for a few more months he would have enough and just leave.

Early every morning for months a cop would bang on my window and tell me we couldn't sleep wherever we were and we had to move. They even did this to me when I went to the property my mother still owned and told me I could stay on. They were still into harassing me. We started going out to the interstate rest area to sleep.

I had to put stuff in the windows to block all the lights, but they did have a nice bathroom to clean up in so it wasn't too bad. I didn't have the gas to go to the rest area one night and got woke up again by the police.

I had enough and sat up and said, "This is why I bought that land so I would have a place to sleep peacefully." I didn't realized I had said it out loud until Ike said, "Land, what land?" Ike threatened and screamed and made me take him there.

My mother called Brian and told him Ike was back, so he was mad and stopped helping me. I didn't blame him, but here again, no one cared that it was once again not by my choice.

I had just told my mom that when I saw Brian during the holidays I was going to explain it all to him. She told him first so it looked like I was hiding it. I was only waiting so I could talk to him face to face. He didn't talk to me for a while, again.

As I said my sons and I are nonviolent. We don't even argue. We just don't talk for a while. I had to sneak away for a minute to call Chris to tell him why I wouldn't be able to stop by for a while. He said he understood. I told him to come out to the land to see me when he could.

Once again I was cut off from my sons. This heart ache was getting harder and harder to take. I had just got my family back; now they were gone again. I really started hating this man.

Many different times Ike would say to me and other people that he wasn't on drugs. He went to prison for drugs. He cooked drugs. He was dropped by his doctor when he found drugs in his system. When they took his girls they pulled his hair out to test it and surprise, he tested positive for drugs. Can you say, Major Denial?

He told people all the time that I didn't do drugs. He said it like I was the crazy one. When I quit smoking pot he thought it was funny to light a joint and put it in my mouth and hold my nose. I have to tell you, pot is a lot less fun when you are forced to do it, so is sex. I could see this man was losing it more and more.

Ike told me he would go up to drug dealers in Ohio and smack their hands so they would drop their drugs. Then he said he would drive over the dealers to get away. He laughed about how their bodies would bounce when he ran them over. When I got upset at hearing this, he would get mad and say it was just niggers.

A few times when Ike got high, he would start pacing the floor and ranting about how since his grandma had cut him out of her will that he was going to drive to Ohio and sneak into her house and cut her throat in her sleep.

He said he would be back before anyone knew he was gone and they would never suspect him. He said he would rob her of everything he could and they would think it was just a robbery. He would go on for hours about it even in front of the girls when they were still there.

He would also go on for hours about what he was going to do to the girl's mother too. I didn't have pleasant breakups with my son's fathers either but I would never cut them down to my sons. I told them they had to meet them someday and decide for themselves. I asked him to stop doing this in front of them but he kept doing it anyway. He would go on and on for days.

He had the worst road rage too. He cussed everyone on the road right in front of the girls. I told him that I wouldn't want him to talk like this in front of my grown sons let alone these little girls. He wouldn't stop. He said they were used to it. Used to it or not, it wasn't right.

One time I said, "How dare these people get on your road when you are trying to go somewhere, huh." He said, "Yeah, exactly." Then he realized I was being sarcastic.

Ike knew he wasn't supposed to have guns or knives even around him. Let alone try to use them on me. Since the police protected him he didn't worry about it.

He said while he was in prison he went to the law library everyday to study what he could and couldn't get away with when he got out. So he was well aware of how to bend the law on top of being an excellent liar. I thought that the police protected him because he was a snitch.

Even after Ike told me himself they took drugs from him, I didn't put that all together until much later. Even then someone had to actually tell me that was why they always looked the other way. I was told that everyone around knew he was giving the police drugs to look the other way for years. One by one everyone Ike knew went to jail on meth charges, everyone but Ike that is.

Ike went to that same big hardware chain store and stole a chain saw and started cutting down the trees on my land. He walked in and threw the chainsaw on his shoulder. He had a fake receipt in his hand and walked right out of the door. He did this more than once.

As soon as we moved in, he found a meth cook a block away. He would go up there and shoot up meth and come back and stay up all night cutting down trees.

He also dug us a driveway out of the side of the bluff. I told him he was cutting down too many trees, but he was too high to care. I hopped out of my car one morning and squatted to pee where I always went. I was half asleep. I turned around to see a family driving by waving at me. It was really embarrassing. There used to be trees there to hide me.

I met an older neighbor named Pete. He gave me water by the gallons to take back to my land to shower and do dishes and cook with. Since

I was still paying off my bills he gave me food out of his garden all the time too.

I said no at first but he would always insist that he had more food than he could eat and it would just go to waste.

I had found an old plastic fifty gallon drum and Ike put a spout on it. I filled it with the water I got from Pete. I had a bunch of shower curtains so Ike put a wood pallet on the ground and nailed the curtains to some trees. I bought one of those camp showers for the little stall he made from the curtains.

You fill the plastic bag with five gallons of water and lay it out in the sun to heat up during the day. So we had nice warm showers after clearing land all day. I got a five gallon bucket to sit in the shower stall for a toilet. We had to use the stall to check each other for ticks every night too.

Ike was a meat eater. He said his mother had been a butcher and fed him steak every night. He would go steal steaks at the local store and sometimes steal bags of ice. I didn't like it but there isn't much you can do to stop him. I preferred the vegetables I got from Pete.

I found a glass patio table and some chairs and a grill to cook on at the local dump. I bought a big cooler and we kept it full of ice for drinks and other food. Even though we still slept in the car it really wasn't half bad. My car windows started leaking a little bit so when it rained I always woke up wet and cold.

Ike started spending more and more time up at Pete's house and the meth cooks house. It didn't take long to figure out it was because young drug whores hung out at both places. You have heard the saying eight to eighty blind, crippled, or crazy? Well Ike chased them all. I wish I had pictures to show you. It was quite humiliating and at times just sickening.

The only time I ever said anything to him was if he hit on them right in front of me. I would call him on it right then and there. The women would get upset and instantly say they had nothing to do with it. I would just say, "Yes, I know that. That is why I didn't say anything to you."

For the next two years the courts gave Ike and Brandy time to get on their feet and get off drugs.

They did this so they could get the girls back. Neither one of them even tried. Ike was supposed to see the girls at a park every weekend near where they lived in a foster home. He wouldn't bother going and always made up an excuse. He was too busy still chasing women and drugs to go.

He was still too busy going from state line to state line getting pills for the new meth cook. Seeing his girls was too much of a bother to him. The case worker told me that Brandy walked up to her in court and said, "I told you bitch, I don't want them."

I can't comprehend this. How can you give birth to five beautiful little girls and walk away like they just don't exist?

The case worker started bringing the girls out to the land to see Ike. This pissed Ike off so he made up a bunch of stories about me so she wouldn't bring them out anymore. Ike's mom said she told her that I was too crazy for the girls to be around. She stopped me from going to see them at all. She said her insurance didn't cover me and she could only take him.

Ike started sleeping with her when she picked him up to visit the girls, and that is when she wouldn't let him give her anymore excuses. I was told she was fired when child services found out about it. She even offered to get him his own place if he left me. He told her no. I was his paycheck and punching bag now. He didn't need them.

When the case finally went to court, Ike and Brandy both were in police custody on drug charges so the girls were adopted by the foster mom and they were told they couldn't have contact until they were eighteen. I asked if I could take the girls if they got him away from me. They said I wasn't their parent, so I had no rights and that I was not involved.

I was told that since my case about the girls had been expunged that it couldn't be discussed by anyone because it never happened. My case and the fact that they both did drugs was all they talked about during the case against Ike and Brandy. Once again, illegal and they all knew it. I raised these girls for five years, risked my life to fight for them and I had no rights because of his lies.

At least the woman adopted all of them. They weren't split up. So I just busied myself with clearing my land and keeping the fires going to burn out the stumps that were too big to dig out.

We didn't have a lot of close neighbors out there. On one side it was a wild life preserve and a timbering company and a land company. There was nothing but trees, and there were no witnesses. The abuse got worse.

I asked the state for help with getting my back child support. This was something they were supposed to be helping me with for years. When the woman read about my case on her computer, the case that was supposed to be expunged from all records, she cussed me and told me to get out of her office before she called the police. Ike found that real funny too.

When I got to be friends with Pete I told him what Ike had just done to me in Crossburg. He told me he had a cousin Easel Bandstander that was a very prominent, very expensive attorney in Nashville.

He said to call him and ask him if he could help me. I called the guy and before I could even tell him my problem, he said he knew who I was and what I was calling about but that he couldn't help me for conflict of interest.

He said he had read my file and knew I was innocent of everything the Crossburg courts accused me of. He said the conflict was that he was on a committee board that was hired to investigate all Land County Courts.

He said that they had first been hired to figure out why people were getting less jail time for murder than for much lesser crimes. He said that they quickly figured out that the bigger problem was that they were forcing innocent people to plead guilty just to clear their docket and have a higher conviction rate. Of course nothing ever came of their investigation. It is still business as usual.

One time when Adam went to have a drink in Crossburg, a guy picked up his new pack of cigarettes. Adam told him those were his and the guy cussed him. Adam told him that he didn't need to be a little bitch about it, just sit them back down.

A girl came up behind Adam and pulled his shirt up over his head so he couldn't see. He said at least three guys started hitting him in the head. By the time he got up to fight back, the bouncer broke up the fight and everyone was told to leave. Adam had only had one beer and had just gotten his second one.

Adam didn't like it, but he went home. He said when he looked in the mirror he realized he was worse than he thought and started to the store for medical supplies. He needed a hospital but he didn't think he had insurance. On the way to the store he was pulled over and arrested.

Adam was driving Chris' car so when Officer Fendrick heard my last name come over the radio he ran out there with dogs and tore Chris' car apart looking for drugs. At that time Ike had never even been in this car. They had no reason to do this. Chris said they took screwdrivers and took everything they could get to apart and left it all laying there for him to try to put back.

Adam's breathalyzer test said .04 This is half of the legal limit. They had no reason to arrest him, other than not liking me. When I had to go to the court house to make a payment on Ike's many court costs they had stuck me with, I ended up in the elevator with the man that had just arrested Adam.

I told him that I knew for a fact that Adam repeatedly tried to tell him that he couldn't hear him because his ears were ringing from the beating he just had. I told him that I could sue for the fact that the ringing told me that my son had a concussion and should have been taken to the hospital, not to jail where he could have died when he went to sleep.

The guy apologized. He said that he was on his way home when Adam went thru the light, and it pissed him off because he had to stop him and would be late getting home because he now had all the paperwork to do for this. He said Adam did try telling him something, but he was too pissed to listen. He said Adam was very courteous and cooperative the whole time too.

Then he kind of laughed and said, "He was nothing like when I had to deal with you." I told him if I was pissed and cussing then I probably had good reason at the time. I don't just lose my temper for no reason.

When Adam went to court, the guy tried every way he could to let Adam out of it. He even said that the light may not have even been red yet, that he wasn't sure. Judge Stevens ignored it and bound him over to the next court.

Ike fought me everytime I went to town to go to court with Adam. I wouldn't let Adam plead guilty for something he wasn't guilty of, so they just kept dragging it out to more court dates.

They drug it out so long that he was fired from one job for losing so much time for court. He was about to be fired from his new job for the same reason. Adam called me just before the last court date to tell me that they called him in the day before court and told him if he pled guilty that they would drop it and just fine him. There wasn't even a Judge there.

Mostly they didn't want me there. Adam didn't want to lose his job so he pled guilty to their bogus, trumped up charges. I was pissed because now wherever he goes this will be on his record and he wasn't guilty to begin with.

They said they found a tiny roach of pot in the back seat ash tray. Chris said it wasn't pot. He said his friend had bought something at a head shop that they called cabbage leaves. He said he told the guy not to do it in his car even though the stuff was not illegal. I asked them to test it. They said it was too small of an amount. Again illegal for them to charge him with but they did.

Adam said he felt he had to plead guilty because Wendy Liars was his attorney and she wasn't even trying to defend him. He said that he could tell just by watching all her cases in court all those weeks that she would rather prosecute everyone, not defend them. Once again she got paid to not do her job. I wanted to take it to the State Bar Association, but Adam said he didn't have the time to fight it.

Every chance I got, I would stop when I was in town to give Chris a hug. Sometimes I would go in and give him a hug in his sleep if his friend's mother was home to let me in.

Chris told me he really liked seeing me. I made the mistake of saying this to Ike. When we were arguing, he told me that it wasn't him that ran my sons off.

I told him that Chris said he wanted to see me. All of a sudden, Ike wouldn't let me drive my own car anymore, so I couldn't go to see Chris. He started following me around the land to make sure I didn't even get a chance to call any of my sons.

He would scream at me that Chris was too old for his mama and he probably really hated to see me or hear from me. He said he would go beat him down if I tried to see him anymore. So I had to wait for Chris to visit me to see him. I now hated Ike the most for taking my family away again.

Soon after I showed Ike the land he started threatening me to put it in his name. When I went to make my next payment, he went to the office with me and told them I wanted it in his name. He was told that they wouldn't do that. That it was my land.

They did tell him that they could put his name on the paperwork. They said that once it was paid for, his name would only go on the deed if I asked them to leave it. She asked him if he understood that it was just my property before she let him sign the contract. He said he understood.

As soon as we walked out the door, he put his hand out and said, "$20,000 right now bitch or I sell the land and get my money." I told him I only had a couple hundred in the land at this point.

He drove away and left me standing there. He said he was going to get a sign to put it up for sale. He came back shortly saying he didn't have enough money to buy a sign with, but he was selling it out from under me as soon as he could.

After that every time I went to town to pay bills and buy food before I could even turn my car off when I got home, he would drag me out the car window by the throat. He would throw me on the ground and start pounding my head on the ground. He would choke me and scream that I took too long so I must have been out screwing somebody because that's what Brandy always did.

If I didn't mention it, I was about one hundred and twenty pounds. He was about two hundred and fifty pounds. He still didn't scare me though. He still just pissed me off that he thought he was going to get away with this. Even with all the names and all the sick things he constantly accused me of, I was determined he wasn't going to break me or bring me down to his level.

Chapter 7

Ike got one of his friends to bring him a bunch of wood pallets, the kind companies use to stack things on so they can move them with a fork lift. He built a small building out front on the bluff with the pallets. I thought this was for us to sleep in while we were clearing the land.

He put his lock on it and said it was for him and his friends when they came out to party. I still stayed in my car. He would even invite women over to party in the shed and lock me out.

Early one morning the new county's DEA, Shayne Kotter, showed up. He said they wanted to search the shed. Ike slammed the door and put his lock on it. They argued for him to open it. Ike told me to tell them to leave. He told them it was my land. Suddenly it is my land! I knew then he had something in there he didn't want them to see.

When they told him that if it was my land that they would arrest me if they found anything and not him, he opened the door. They found pills used to make meth breaking down in water. Since it was only one ingredient they said they would dump it out in the ditch and let it go.

Ike told someone later that he was going to go to the store and get heet to break them down in because it was faster but that he had been too lazy to go get it. That would be two ingredients. I would have gone to jail and lost my land for something I didn't even know was there, again.

I was really starting to have to fight the urge to beat this man. Counting to ten wasn't working as well as it used to.

I went to my mother's for a few days. Ike called me on my cell phone at three one morning asking who I was there screwing. I knew by the way he was whispering and what he was accusing me of that he was with someone. As soon as I got back home, a neighbor stopped to tell me he had some sleazy looking woman with him the whole time I was gone.

It pissed me off that he had brought her to my land but didn't bother me he was with her or surprise me that he did this. Everything he did from that point on disappointed me a lot but I was never surprised by anything he did. His cruelty to everyone saw no bounds.

It turned out to be the girl he convinced at that one apartment that I snitched on her when it was him that snitched. I went to her house and told her I knew what was going on. I told her to please keep him because I had enough.

When I went to the shed, I looked down to see a cum stained Kotex pad right in front of the door to the building. This woman was purposely trying to rub it in my face she was there. This is so sad to me that all these woman can find as an accomplishment in their lives is to take someone else's man. I didn't even want him.

The door was open and right inside the door was a cooler with meth chemicals in it. I knew he was going to try and cook on my land. I called him to tell him I was burning down the shed.

It took a while for me to pry open the little pen to let the baby chickens out. I poured gas on the place and lit a match. Someone called the fire department They jumped out to put out the fire. I stopped them and said, "No, I want it to burn to the ground. I checked first, there are no trees close by to burn, it will be fine."

They asked if they could stay around to make sure it didn't get out of hand. I said that was ok. I burned the table and chairs and the picnic table he had built too. Once it was all burned, I started to town.

I was going to get gas, pick up Chris, and go to Brian's until I thought Ike had given up and moved away.

I went in to pay for gas at the station. I came out to pump the gas and my car was gone. I called the police to report it stolen.

The police told me Ike had taken my car out to my land. Even though I said I had left him, the police said they still couldn't get involved. Every time I got mad at Ike for stealing my car while I was asleep he would always say, "It's just civil, so sue me." The police said it was civil and that I had to pay the courts to sue him.

I went out to my land to find that he had driven my car into a large section of downed trees and it was not only wedged in there, it was now out of gas, two tires were flat, and my purse was gone.

He did something to my car, so it wouldn't start even once I got gas. It took days to get gas, cut it out of the trees and get some tires for it. He still refused to give me my purse so I couldn't leave. He had hid it out in the trees but insisted that he didn't have it.

Then I found out that Ike went to the fire department and told them the shed burned down because I was trying to cook meth. He said that they needed to check the ruins for meth material and arrest me for cooking. Isn't he just the sweetest guy?

Ike told me later that while he was sitting there looking at the burned shed a woman stopped and handed him a hundred dollars. She told him to cheer up and rebuild. If she hadn't done that he said he was thinking about just leaving.

People came to tell us that one day while we were gone they watched the Land County sheriff search our land. This again is illegal because they didn't bring More County sheriff with them.

A couple had stopped by one day and said they would give us a trailer but we had to bring it from another city. I found out the moving permits would cost more than I could afford. Ike decided to go over to the place and take the water heater and light switches and electrical box. Someone saw us with all this and told Land County we stole all of it. That's what they were searching for.

For months I kept asking Ike to stop at this trailer place in our new town of Wartville to look at the used trailers they had sitting there. He would start cutting me down saying I was an idiot if I thought anyone was going to sell me a trailer with no money down.

As I said, I was in the mountains, and it gets very cold in the winter. I had already spent two winters in my car freezing. I wasn't going to do that again. Camping is fun for a while, but it was time to get a home, even if it was a temporary one.

One time that we went through town he had to stop a ways back from the light for traffic, so I got out and started walking to the trailer office. I told the man there what my situation was and that I could make small payments on something.

I showed him the trailer that was an older one that I was considering. About two days later I look up and the guy is sitting in the road with the trailer. I hadn't even put anything down yet. He pulled it in and strapped it down and told me when I got paid to come in and put what I could down and send the payments when I could.

I found about twenty cans of paint at the dump that someone had left. Most of them were white so I went and bought some dark brown paint. I mixed some cans until I came up with a nice beige for the trailer and used the rest of the dark brown for the trim.

I painted the inside and outside of the trailer. I bought orange oil and wiped down all the paneling and woodwork. Ike told people for years that he did it all himself. He didn't even try to help. He said heights bothered him too much. Ike had gotten insurance checks for him and his oldest two girls, so he put in new floors and redid the kitchen and bathroom.

We didn't have electricity yet, so he did it with a chain saw. He really did do a good job with what we had. He had the potential to be a good man, but the drugs and whores always won out with him.

One thing that bothered me about it was that he got those checks by lying to a chemical company in Ohio. He did it long before I met him but I still had a problem with it. This chemical plant blew up one time. His mom told him that she told them that he and his girls were living with her and they all got sick. He was nowhere near Ohio when it happened.

He had barely gotten the floor down when he showed up with this couple from Georgia and told me they were moving in. I said no, because we had no electric, no water, no food, or even drinks.

He sent me to get food and moved them in while I was gone. I can't remember their names but they were related to John Smelton that lived up above us on Island Ford Rd.

Two days later Ike just disappeared. Brian had bought me a little cast iron stove to heat with. He was still upset with me, but he was getting over it. That was all I had there, even for light. I told that couple that Pete would probably be able to help them. I asked them to go talk to him.

Brian had also bought a new radiator and front end parts for my car. He spent over eight hundred dollars on parts because Ike said he would fix my car. Ike was supposed to put this on, but he took off instead so this guy that was there tried to do it. He wasn't a mechanic, so it didn't get done.

Several days later Ike showed up. I went to bed because I have a hard time sleeping with strangers in my home. I was exhausted. I was also kind of pissed because in a few days' time these two had eaten a month's worth of my food and drinks and smoked all the cigarettes I had bought for Ike. They didn't even get off the couch to help me bring in firewood.

The next thing I know Ike has one hand on my throat choking me and one hand on my nose and mouth smothering me. When I put my feet up to try to get to my feet, I kicked him in the head. I still had my steel toed boots on. This action made his head bounce off the wall.

He started screaming that I kicked him in the head for no reason and that they were witnesses and he was calling the police to drag me out of there. He was once again trying to get me out of my home, so he could be with another woman.

That couple told him if he called the police they were leaving. It turned out they left Georgia to get away from the law. Great, now I am harboring felons. Ike just left.

The woman came into my room and said she wanted to come and help me but her boyfriend wouldn't let her. She said as soon as Ike came in he was whispering to her about the girl he spent the week with and all the drugs they did. She said she put her hand up and said she didn't want to hear it and this pissed Ike off.

Ike then went to the kitchen and started yelling at me. They said he argued with me for thirty minutes, then came and attacked me. Then they said, "But we both agreed that we didn't hear you saying anything." Then I told them that I didn't say anything because I was sound asleep.

He was arguing with himself just like he had done many times before. He wanted to make it look like he had a reason to attack me. He wanted everyone to think he was the victim. When Ike came back, I told him that they had to go. They took my advice and went to see if Pete would take them in. He did.

When they came to get their suitcase, Ike told them to go to the shed with him. He had built another one out of pallets behind the trailer.

I heard him tell them that I wanted them to go but for them to stay and he would get rid of me. I went out and told them that they all needed to leave including Ike. I told him that I heard what he said.

This man tried his best to stop me from buying land and buying the trailer. He has not helped me pay one dime for anything. He not only repeatedly refuses to help me do anything, but he tried to beat me over everything I tried to do here to improve the place.

Now he is trying to run me out of my home again for this women he doesn't even know. And acts like it is all my fault that I want nothing to do with him. The couple left.

I noticed the radiator wasn't there after they left, so I asked Ike if he had seen it. I told him I was going to look for it and if it wasn't there, I would have to call the police. Ike suddenly brought in the radiator. It was put back in the box and he said he found it out in the woods.

He said that guy was probably trying to steal it to sell it. It was in a locked shed when it went missing. That other guy didn't have a key. Ike was the one planning on stealing it. I knew by now that as high as Ike was there was no use in saying anything until he had sobered up. Pick your battles.

Ike suddenly burst into the house screaming he was going to kill me for running her off. I tried to get away until he cooled down. When he caught me right outside the back door, Ike threw me on the ground.

I could tell by the way he was putting his arms over my chest and head that he was going to try to break my neck like he had seen on TV. It was like I was watching this in slow motion and there was nothing I could do to stop it.

When he went to jerk my neck I turned my head as far to the left as I could. I heard something pop but knew my neck wasn't broke because I was still breathing. I couldn't stand up though.

He had popped two discs out in my lower back that hit the sciatic nerve. I was in a lot of pain. He had to help me up and he dusted me off, laughing, like he hadn't done a thing. He told me I was imagining things when I asked why he tried to kill me.

He was quiet for awhile but by the next morning he was pissed again. He ran in screaming again that he was going to kill me. I tried to run again.

This time when he grabbed me from behind in the exact same spot as he had before to do the same thing, hopping it would work this time.

He yelled, "You ran her off right when she was ready to put give up the p----."

I turned my head again and once again I heard a pop and I was in a lot more pain. My back went out off and on for the next few years. Especially when he would attack me.

Later that night he screwed the back door to the frame from the outside so I couldn't open it. He then took a big nail and put it in the front door frame next to the handle. He took copper wire and wrapped it around the knob and the nail so it couldn't be opened.

He threw me on the couch and held a sledge hammer over my head for hours screaming he could beat me to death before the cops broke in.

This was a heavy hammer he held over my head screaming at me for hours. If he had even dropped that hammer accidentally, I would be dead.

One of his friends came over, so he opened the door and started to brag to the guy that he almost beat me to death over this girl. He even admitted to the guy that he doesn't even know this woman. He was laughing about it.

His friend jumped up instantly, nose to nose with him. Without even flinching or looking away he tapped me on the knee and asked if I was ok. Then he told Ike that he already knew that I hadn't done anything and that he was going to drag him out in the yard and beat him to death.

The guy then told me to go lay down and get some sleep. He said he would stay there to protect me until I woke up. As soon as I woke up, he waved goodbye and left. He told Ike that I was his friend just as much as he was and that he had better not touch me again.

Ike settled down for a short time but the calm never lasted for long. Every time that guy came over after that Ike would try to beat me when he left saying that I probably slept with the guy.

Ike didn't let me see a doctor for a while. He was afraid I would tell him what he did. When Ike was mad at me he would scream and threaten me for days on end, day and night.

But when he did something and I even mention it, the beatings and threats would just start all over again. He would tell me to stop living in the past. I really had to carefully choose my battles. Most things I had to just let go. He never let anything go. If I didn't do anything, he would make something up in his head.

Have you ever seen an army movie where the guy would get up close and scream in everyone's ears? Ike would see that and comment on how that had to hurt, even if it was pretend. Ike did it to me all the time and never once said he was sorry.

I now have a ten percent hearing loss. I believe I have to wear glasses because of all the times he tried to push my eyeballs out with his thumbs.

He used to think it was funny to constantly flick his liter in my face, my crotch and at my feet. One time he lit my socks on fire. He never stopped doing any of these things to me. I had to tie my pants on to keep him from pulling them down, even in public. I don't wear panties. He would pull them down then scream at me and say I did it on purpose to get men's attention.

I mentioned earlier doing all the painting. When we were clearing the trees, he would cut them down, cut them into pieces and I would roll them or carry them to the stumps we were burning out. Every time he tells the story he did everything himself.

One time I was moving a tree and some woman gasped and said, "My God that tree is bigger than she is." Ike got mad and said it was a rotten tree and weighed a lot less than it looked. Then he started bragging that he had cleared all that land by himself.

Usually on my birthday he would steal any money my family would send and find someone to spend the day doing drugs with on my money. He spent a lot of time searching out some of the worst low life drug addicts I had ever met.

He would drag them into my home week after week and yet neither I nor Chris were ever allowed to bring anyone there. He would have a fit if anyone even called us. Chris briefly moved back in with me when he started college.

Chris had used a big part of his money to rent a place from what he thought was a friend. It turned out that they didn't tell their landlord about it, so when they were told to move, Chris lost his home and his money. He had to move in with me. Because of Ike he didn't willingly move back home.

Ike even cussed Chris when the people that picked him up for church called to tell him they were on their way to pick him up. Chris stopped going to church for a while. That upset me and Chris.

Ike has to control every second of every day for everyone around him. Even then he wasn't happy.

Almost every day Ike would get mad over absolutely nothing and squeeze my head like he was trying to pop it open. This would give me bad headaches.

He would put his thumbs in my eyes and try to push them out of the sockets. Then he would squeeze my head and shake it violently and turn me in all kinds of distorted positions to scream as loud as he could in my left ear.

He would twist my arms and legs up in front of me and do a belly flop on top of me. I hated this so bad but he knew I wouldn't just hit him. He always sees kindness as weakness and always turns it against you.

When we drove down the street he would start screaming that I had looked at someone. I needed glasses, everything was just a big blur to me all the time. I couldn't make out faces if I wanted to. He would speed up and scream that he was going to drive us off the mountainside or into a tree.

All these friends I mention of his; it was a new group every week. No one could take him for very long. He uses and abuses everyone.

I told him I could see that he just hung out with theses guys because he wanted their wives or girlfriends. He would say, "What do you think that I am trying to do, screw them in front of their old man?" Yes that was exactly it. He thought he was so slick that the guy would never figure it out. This was a challenge to him.

Most of them didn't figure it out until it was too late. Ike would romance the woman until he got what he wanted, and then he would break them up. Then everything would blow up and I would have to deal with the fallout.

I found out from a policeman that most of the time when Ike pissed these guys off, they would go to the police and tell them everything Ike had done. They keep telling me all this is on file to use against him. And still no one ever arrested him.

One day Shayne Kotter showed up to see Ike. As I went out to check the mail, I heard him say to Ike that he could bring a camper over and set it up at the end of my land and let Ike cook meth in it. He said he would put a camera in it to set up everyone that came to buy.

I told him it was my land and no one was ever going to cook meth there and that he was trespassing and needed to leave. I am purposely trying not to swear but in reality Ike had the worst language I have ever heard from anyone and being an ex-truck driver, that is saying a lot.

I always had to go to his mother's for the holidays because he would put those girls in the car, drunk and high and try to drive to Ohio. He would weave in and out of traffic, speeding and pulling right out in front of semis. I sat in the middle the whole way so I could grab the wheel. I know in my heart those girls would be dead if I hadn't been there.

It didn't take long for me to see that his abusive ways definitely came from his mother. She talked so badly to her husband that most of the time we went there he was in tears. She used to ask me how I kept from beating the hell out of her son. She said that even she couldn't stand how he constantly treated me and talked down to me. As I said before, he would do this in front of people to humiliate me on purpose.

So many times when he walked away, people would ask me if I wanted them to shoot him or break his legs. I would instantly say no thank you. I couldn't live with myself if I did.

One time a total stranger said to me that for $1500 his buddy could make him disappear, never to be found. It scared the hell out of me when I hesitated before I said no thank you. Then I was angry at Ike. He didn't have the right to press me so far that I couldn't answer instantly with a "no thank you."

So many times when he was too lazy to go to the store and he made me go, I would run into one of these couples that had been his friends. They would tell me that they really liked visiting me.

They said they could no longer put up with how he talked to me. So they stopped coming around before they said or did something they would regret. I would say thank you and tell them that I definitely understood.

The girl that Ike had stolen my car to party with when I was in the hospital showed up at my land. She said she was living in Kentucky now and asked me if I would move there with her and teach her to be a lady. She said she liked the way I carried myself. A lot of people has said that to me in the past, but I never knew exactly what they meant. That is just how I have always been. I said I had no idea how to teach someone how to act.

She then asked Ike to move with her to help her cook meth. This stunned me for a second.

I guess I still am a little slow because after she left, I realized that they had done more than just drugs together when I was in the hospital.

I kind of felt sorry for her. She was another one that had to feel like she took someone's man. I have never in my life felt like I had to have a man to make my life better. I always preferred it just being me and my sons. I didn't have to answer to anyone for anything. There wasn't much that I couldn't do for myself and yes that included sex.

A vibrator never lies, never cheats and never tries to beat you. As far as I can see they last longer than any man can. They are a woman's best friend. The battery companies should use that for advertisement and offer lifetime supplies of batteries.

I have been all over the world. I have never carried a weapon and never felt the need to. I greet everyone with a smile and open arms and I have always been treated the same.

One time when I was at a friend's house in California he had to excuse himself because him and his girlfriend were in the middle of an argument. When he came back in the room he said, "I always knew I trusted you but I didn't realize just how much until now."

He pointed to the desk. He had walked out and left his safe standing open, with stacks of cash sitting there. All his drugs were sitting there and all his guns. Then he looked at me and said, "I don't even trust my wife or girlfriend that much.

After I moved to Tennessee, I met this really nice couple in a bar once. Not long after that they were in a car wreck. She was killed and he was on crutches. I told him I would run the bar for him until he was off his crutches. There was a little trailer next door, so I brought the boys with me and brought their games to keep them busy. I had to be bouncer for the bar too.

One night two guys decided to fight in the parking lot. Shortly after walking out there, I realized that the problem was this woman I had known for a few years. I walked up to her and said I knew she was instigating this on purpose and getting off on the fact these guys were fighting over her. I told her either she stopped it, or I was going to stomp her ass. I hate to see people try to manipulate other people.

The guys fighting heard me. The one guy stumbled over to me, taped me on the shoulder and said, "I know you well enough to know that if you are mad, then I am doing something very wrong. If you find someone to drive me home, I will leave."

He hugged me, kissed me on the cheek and said, "Goodnight mama." From my life's experiences, I always knew that my and Ike's problems were always Ike's problems.

Chapter 8

Ike bought a truck from John Smelton. My nephew in Alabama said he had parts to fit it, and if we wanted to we could come get them. The truck broke down on our way back home, so we had it towed back to my nephew's for him to fix. They loaned us a car of theirs while he worked on the truck. When we got home, Ike was suddenly gone a lot again.

The police showed up one day saying they had a warrant for Ike, so I went to find him. Mostly, because I didn't want my niece's car mixed up in whatever he was doing. When I found him, he said he was going to the next county to a friend's place. I told him not in that car he wasn't.

He took off, and I had to jump into the car. When we got there and I saw who it was, I told her that if they had any kind of drugs there that I was leaving. She said they had just moved in and they were just there cleaning the place up, and Ike was going to fix her car.

I talked to her while she cleaned the carpets with a machine she had rented. She was using bleach to clean with. I was told that bleach and meth chemicals in the same place were definitely something you didn't want to do. So I believed them.

I told this woman that something in me just kept telling me to get in my niece's car and keep going. Ike and Tim said they were going to get car parts. I should have listened to that gut feeling. I found out later they were getting meth material instead of car parts and were seen by a state agent doing this.

When they got back Ike said we were going to go get something to eat. When we left, I said for him to take me home. He said he had to take them some food back first.

A block before their house we saw a few police cars at the gas station. I got that feeling that this wasn't going to go well, once again.

When we got to their house, Ike made me come in too because he was afraid I would drive off. He was right this time. I was thinking of doing exactly that.

Just as we reached for the door to leave, there was a knock. It was the police. They said they had a warrant for Tim. His girlfriend said he wasn't there and walked away. We had just gotten back with the food so I believed her.

Ike knew he had a warrant on himself too, so thinking it would get their attention off of him, he leaned over and said, "He is in the back room." They came busting in and in their search found him getting ready to cook in a locked back room. They took everyone out to search us.

They took everything out of my purse to search it. They even took all my makeup and lipsticks apart. I told them nothing was going on and if they smelled my clothes they could tell I wasn't near a meth cook. They agreed and said I wasn't under arrest but I had to be questioned.

When we got to the station they found the old charges in Crossburg that should have been dropped but weren't, so they charged me with everything they found in that house.

Pete came to bail me out. We had to jump start my niece's car. I got as far as Crossburg with it. When I stopped to have the battery checked it wouldn't start. I had to sleep in the car. It was freezing that night.

Once I got the car fixed I had to go to court. I had to run out of the court room to throw up. I had gotten a really bad cold from sleeping in the car, and I was really sick.

While I was in the bathroom, the judge called my name. Even when they told him I was in the bathroom throwing up, he put me back under arrest and doubled my bail. This pissed off the female bailiff. She told me to throw up on the judge the next time.

I was heaving so hard that they had to take all the women out of the cell with me because I was starting to make them throw up. They put me in shackles just to humiliate me in front of everyone in the courtroom. They treated me like I was some kind of harden criminal. Shackles are very painful to wear, too.

The next week when I went back to court, I told the DA what happened. I also told them that even the arresting officer knew that I wasn't guilty of anything and my doctor can prove I don't do drugs.

He went up and talked to the judge. The judge told me I was free to go after they set my court date. The people that worked there didn't believe me when I told them he let me go.

They said in all the years they have known this judge that he had never changed his mind and never reversed his own decision. They checked again then let me go. The police said they would drop my case but then didn't. They said if Tim would plead guilty, then they would drop it. It was his trailer.

My bail was so high that it took me a year just to pay Pete back. It really pissed me off because I stood up for all three of these people, because I really didn't see them with anything. Not one of them stood up to say I had nothing to do with this. They all just covered their own ass.

When I first got arrested, all the women in the cell ran up to me saying that they could tell I didn't belong there and asked what happened. Two very pregnant girls threw their mattresses on the floor and told me to take their beds. Just like the last time I was arrested, everyone there instantly knew I hadn't done anything. They even shared their snacks with me they had bought.

When the judge put me back in jail, the girls there told me that he only did that because he hates meth people, and I was in there on meth charges. It made no difference that I wasn't guilty. They said that he liked coke and now that everyone was doing meth, no one could find coke and this pissed him off. This statement I can't prove. Everything else in here, I stand by.

Early one morning after the judge had put me back in jail when I was sick, the whole building started shaking. Everyone woke up screaming and freaking out. I didn't even open my eyes. I just calmly said, "That was a small earthquake ladies. I was in a few of them in California." I said, "That was a tiny one and the most you will feel now is a tiny tremor an hour or two from now, but you got nothing to worry about."

They all went back to sleep. Later they all thanked me. They said that just me saying that calmed them down. Like I said, sometimes all it takes is the simplest thing to make a difference. One girl that was in there I didn't talk to much the first time. This time she told me what she was in there for and that she was still waiting to go to court.

I told her who to ask for and what to do to make sure they took her back in front of the judge. She did it and got the court date that they had repeatedly denied her. I truly believe that everything happens for a reason. I was put back in jail to calm these women down in the earthquake and to help this girl get her rights back.

Ike was still on probation and his probation officer asked him to drug test and he refused. She had him arrested, and I had to bail him out.

She superseded the warrant and had him arrested again. He finally had to do nine months because he wasn't supposed to be around these kinds of people while he was on probation and he knew that.

Ike made me go to court to say that he had a problem urinating to try to get out of it. I only agreed to do it because it was true. He had a surgery for it when he was little. He could drink all day and not have to go. He constantly yelled at me for going too much. His mom even sent me a letter about the surgery. I took the letter to court, but they refused to look at it.

Just after we had all gotten arrested, that same couple came out to my land. I reminded Ike that he could go back to jail just for having them there. The two of them and Ike kept telling me that since I had never been on drugs that I had no idea what it was like. Ike kept saying don't knock it until you have tried it.

All these years I had not given in to pier pressure, but I finally told him I would try it just to shut him up. I only took one puff. I didn't like it and told him that I didn't see what the big deal was. Now that I had tried it. I said I now had every right to stop him from bringing it into my home.

I told him that I thought a pot high was better and much, much cheaper and lasted a lot longer. I never met anyone that got violent on pot. Not even Ike. A few days later, I came home to find two used needles thrown out on both sides of my drive.

That same couple even left a note on the door to say they had come out and we were gone. They shot up drugs, threw their dirty needles out, and stole my flowers and the planters they were in. They never came back. I liked those planters, but it was well worth getting rid of them.

I heard that she and another guy got lots of jail time because they had killed a teenage boy. I heard they wrapped him in barbed wire and left him in the ditch. Such nice people he chose to hang out with and bring into my home, huh?

For weeks after that Ike cussed me like a dog every day. He would scream that he always knew that I was a low life lying drug whore. He said that I was screwing all his buddies for drugs behind his back all this time just like Brandy did.

Ike got nine months in jail for probation violation. If they had bothered to check his record in Ohio, he would have gone back to prison instead.

I begged Chris to please move somewhere with me while Ike was in jail. Any other state would be fine with me. He didn't want to leave this girl he was in love with, and I couldn't leave him unprotected against this man when he got out.

Even though Chris had heard all the things Ike said to me, he had never seen that look in his eye. I knew he wouldn't feel he needed to protect himself if Ike walked up smiling. Chris was also trained in self defense. He had been a security guard and they trained him to defend himself and how to disarm someone.

He trained in karate with his friend's father when he was in high school, and he was trained to subdue patients without hurting them when he worked taking care of mentally challenged patients. He didn't see Ike as a threat yet.

One time when we were watching CSI, they said the dead guy had no defensive wounds trying to defend himself. Ike said, "You can't defend yourself if you don't know you are being killed." Then he smiled and said, "That's how I roll." He meant it. I was glad he stopped watching this program.

It only gave him more ideas to tell me how he was going to kill me and my sons. He would go on for hours about how he was going to kill us and cut us into pieces.

Ike told me once that he was going to cut up cat's whiskers and make me drink them because it would cause an undetectable heart attack. It turned out that they were talking about a tea called cat's whiskers. Thank God he never figured that out. He would have tried it. I never let him fix me a drink or a meal. Not that he ever made the effort anyway.

When Chris moved back in with me I found a letter from a psychiatrist he had seen. I asked him what was going on. All these years he had heard and seen what Ike was doing to me, but he didn't say anything. When I asked him why he didn't say anything, he said that he felt I had enough to deal with so he didn't want to ad to it.

I told him that I thought I had kept it from him. He looked at me and said, "You walked around with bruises from head to toe all the time. I could see this man's actual fingerprints on your skin all the time. I am not an idiot, mom."

He said that when he moved out he suddenly started waking up in the middle of the night hearing Ike screaming and threatening us even though he was miles away from us at the time. He started passing out and his friends had to take him to the hospital several times.

They said he was having panic attacks and had post traumatic stress disorder and had to see the doctor. It turned out Chris was sleeping with his door locked every night and kept Brian's metal bat under the bed. Without my permission, he was put on Xanax and other hard drugs.

Chris also told me that when Ike first moved in, when Chris was twelve, Ike kept giving him cigarettes. Chris told him he didn't want to smoke. He said Ike told him to grow some balls and be a man. After he got hooked and asked Ike for cigarettes, Ike told him he wasn't his daddy, that he needed to go out and steal his own cigarettes like everyone else. I didn't like this at all.

Earlier I told you moms to not ignore those instincts. I also found out that when I thought something was wrong that one summer, Chris was cussed and ran off from everywhere he went because my name was in the news. I hadn't done anything. Chris sure as hell didn't do anything. Now I was starting to get pissed all over again.

Chris was walking the streets hungry. Sleeping in the ditch or cars he could find open all summer rather than be around Ike. I really wish he had told me. I loved those girls, but I would have found a different way to take care of them. It would not have been at the expense of my family.

When I first met Ike, I asked to see a mental health doctor because I needed someone to talk to. She just sat there shaking her head with her mouth open saying she had no idea how I put up with this man and all without taking drugs. Thank God for the calm Swedish side is all I can say.

She never did anything to help me, but when Ike found out I was talking to her about him, he wouldn't let me go anymore. They tried to put me on drugs too, but I don't react to pills like everyone else does so I never took them.

While Ike was still in jail, I used Chris's car and I found a free dentist through the church. They pulled my top teeth. These were the ones Ike had broken up so badly and they gave me dentures. They started filling the bottom ones. Chris went to get a couple teeth pulled too.

When Ike got out of jail, he had all his teeth pulled. Chris and I still had some work left to be done, but as soon as Ike was done with all his work, he stopped us from going back.

While he was in jail, I ended up having five back to back surgeries to remove cists and to fix other problems Ike would never let me go to do.

While Ike was in jail, I asked the people next door to please not give Ike any drugs when he got out, because every time he did drugs he tried to kill me. As you will see, it was a big mistake to trust that these people had anybody else's health in mind.

Adam had come to stay for a while during this time too. Brian came to see us and gave me and Chris his old computer.

We were just getting it hooked up when Ike got out of jail. My back was giving me a lot of problems. It seemed to take an hour just to lift myself off the couch. I had to keep moving different directions until it hurt less so I could lift myself. Adam is such a sweetheart. He always tried to help, but I had to stop him, because his trying to lift me just hurt worse. I love that he kept trying.

Shellie from next door came running over to us one day to beg Adam to protect her from her husband. I let her stay for a while but told her Adam wasn't going to go beat her husband up on just her say so. If I had any idea of what her and her husband were going to do to us later, I would have kicked her ass right then.

147

While Ike was in jail another women in the neighborhood that I had sort of befriended came to cry on my shoulder. She said she felt so bad that when she had gone to get drugs with Ike one day, that she had no idea he was going to take her far from home and tell her to put out or get out. Again, not a surprise. She said he went after her sister and her cousins really fat wife too.

I did see Ike in jail at first because visitation was during the day and Pete would take me. All Ike still did was scream at me and threaten me. Then Ike got into trouble trying to smuggle cigarette butts back into jail.

They changed visits to the evening. Pete's car didn't have lights, so I quit going even before this woman came to tell me what he had done. After she talked to me, I wrote to tell him what she said. Then I stopped writing.

Ike kept writing to me. He said he didn't know why he had spent all those years telling lies about me and beating me. He said I was the sweetest person he had ever met and that I didn't deserve what he had done. He said that when he got out, he was going to spend every second of every day making me the happiest woman on this earth. After I stopped writing, the threats started again.

Ike told me he had a fist fight with a guy that had HIV while he was in jail. He said the fight was over me, but I don't believe it. When Ike went to jail, a man from the Sheriff's department came to see me, Officer Dawn. He asked if I was ok.

He said that so many of my neighbors had called to tell them that Ike talk so much and so matter of factly about killing me that they made him come out to check on me. He asked if I wanted Ike arrested. I told him Ike was already in jail. He said to call him when Ike got out. When I called, I was told that the officer no longer worked there.

With all these calls, to the police they were well aware from everyone what this man was doing to me but still he was never arrested. That probation officer that kept having Ike arrested ended up losing her job when they caught her with a lot of cocaine. I still want to thank her anyway because at least we had a short break from his cruelty.

Shayne Kotter came out when Ike was in jail and asked me if he could search. He said someone told him Ike was cooking again and he had to check it out.

I told him to go ahead but whoever said it didn't know what they were talking about because Ike was still in jail.

One year earlier Ike took my birthday money that Brian had sent and said he was going to buy me something nice with it. He took off with my birthday money and a truck I had borrowed from a friend when Ike tore up my car.

When he didn't come back, someone came by to tell me that Ike was having an orgy and cooking meth three doors down from me. He bought all the stuff he needed to cook meth with my money.

He went three doors down with the guy that lived there and two married women from the neighborhood while he cooked. One of the women's husbands showed up that day and Ike told him nothing was going on. The guy came after Ike with a crowbar. Somehow Ike talked his way out of a beating, and the guy still came to see Ike even after his wife left him.

That guy's wife later came to tell me that during a party at her house just before she left her husband, she walked into her bedroom to find Ike and another couple going at it in her bed.

When I didn't react she said, "I don't think you understand what I am saying. Ike was with the guy, not the girl, she was more or less just watching." I told her that I had seen and heard so much about this man that nothing surprised me anymore.

Then I told her that I could already see that he was going to have a lot of diseases long before this was done. So I didn't have sex with him anymore anyway. She said she was leaving her husband because he was with that woman too. She looked at me and asked, "Is there something wrong with us that our old men would want to screw something that fat and nasty?" I told her that it was their short comings, not ours.

Ike is an idiot. He loves to brag about everything he does. A lot of times he will do things in front of people just to prove a point. I always told him that all he was doing was making sure he left lots of witnesses.

The guy that sent Shayne to my house was the guy from the orgy. He got busted later with Ike's meth lab so he was trying to snitch on Ike. A little too late though. The guy had gotten a year in jail for Ike's lab. He called the police on Ike after he got out. He didn't know Ike had gone to jail.

I know of at least four people that got stuck with Ike's lab because this is something he bragged about many times over the years to his buddies. In a small trailer you here things whether you want to or not. If I heard about something before the fact, I would always try to talk him out of it. It never worked but I had to try. After the fact there was usually no reason to mention it.

All I can explain to you about having to deal with this every day is that I had to live the old saying of keep your friends close and your enemies closer. I had no choice.

Chris and I always tried to be nice to Ike. We always hoped he would decide to stop threatening us and hurting me. That never worked. In his mind, on drugs, we were the enemy no matter what we did. It took Chris a little longer to see that than me. He always saw the con man side but didn't want to acknowledge the evil side.

Ike started telling me some of the lies he had told people about me. I just looked at him and said, "These people have to think you are a real idiot. What kind of man would stay with a woman if she did all the things you say I did?"

I had hoped that was enough to get him to stop, but it didn't. By this time the drugs have obviously done too much damage. Ike told other people not to do these drugs because they are poison. Too bad he wouldn't listen to himself.

Ike used to physically drag me out of bed, usually by the hair, before day light and force me to go to Pete's to get him cigarettes. I never smoked but I had to go out in the cold and snow to find them for him. Then when I got home, I was screamed at because he said I had to be having sex with someone to get the cigarettes.

I was charging them at the store and then paying it when I got paid. I told him this, but it didn't stop him from screaming at me or trying to beat me for it. There was never any end to any of this with this man.

He kept screaming at me that I needed to go out to get a job because my disability wasn't enough for him to live on. This man hasn't tried to find work to help me, but he tried to beat me into finding a job. If I had found a job he would never let me out of his sight to go to work. I still got screamed at about it for a many years.

One time this girl that was at our house and asked how we stayed together for so long. She was smiling and looking at Ike. She really wanted to know. He got really mad and got in her face. He pointed at me and screamed, "I hate that bitch but I am never going to let her go to be happy with someone else." It scared her so bad she jumped up and left. I didn't see her for a while.

Brandy kept telling me how nice Ike always was to her. I see now she just lied to get rid of him. I can understand that part of it, but she never should have left those girls to fend for themselves against him.

When Ike would get high, he would yell at everyone that passed us and say that he knew they were TBI and cuss them for following him. He would drag me out of bed in the middle of the night and make me look out the door and ask if I saw the TBI in the trees.

Then he would insist there were dwarfs riding little ponies all over the front yard. I would know then that it was only a matter of days before he would try to kill me again. He would look out at the moon and swear it wasn't the moon. It was some kind of satellite the feds were using to watch him with. Sometimes he wouldn't go outside for days. He would just stare out the window.

I used to wonder that with all he did to me and other people how he could sleep at night or look in the mirror. Then I realized he didn't sleep. He only took a power nap as he called them here and there. The only time he looked in the mirror was to shave. I heard Ike brag many times that he was awake for twenty eight straight days once with nothing to drink or eat. Just high on meth.

I have heard that not sleeping can actually kill you. It can seriously mess up your brain too.

Before Chris moved back in, one of Ike's friends Robby Lane started coming by real early in the morning to see me. I let him in a couple of times until he hit on me. Then I threw him out. He still came back a few times, but I didn't let him in. I started locking the gate at the end of the drive so no one could get in the drive. I gave Chris a key for the gate when he came out to visit.

Later Ike would wrap chains around the gate and put several locks on it thinking he was keeping me from leaving. We didn't even have a working car at the time.

So many mornings, on the rare occasion that he fell asleep, I would grab a bag and leave. I kept a bag packed and in the closet at all times. I hid it under things so he wouldn't see it. I never got very far away when I realized that he would either find me or find Chris. Also it always pissed me off because it was my place, not his, so why was I leaving? I would very reluctantly go back home.

All this time I didn't tell anyone what he was doing to me, other than the times I really thought he was going to kill me and I told the police. I guess I just didn't want to face that he had gotten away with doing this to me. I have never taken any crap from anyone in my life, ever.

On one trip to Ohio, he told his grandma that being with him the girls had turned into little ladies. He said it was all because of him. He didn't even want to see his grandma. His mom made him go.

She told him he had to see her because she was going to die, and she owed them money. I got mad when she said that and told him if he didn't see her and she died, he would always feel bad. Thinking back on it now, I don't think it would have bothered him. You have to have a conscience first. Ike was only trying to get more money from his grandma.

I showed my sons and Ike's girls pictures everywhere I went. Most people told me that in all the time they knew him he never said he had kids. Just like me, they had just become a paycheck to him. I was a free babysitter and a punching bag too.

I showed the girls picture to this one woman, and she said she knew them. She said that their mom had broke down in her driveway. Brandy asked her if she would watch the girls while her and her boyfriend got the car fixed. She said a week later she had to track her down to return the girls to them. She had never even seen these people before.

I still find it hard to believe that all these cops listened to Ike. I would be standing there bleeding from him dragging me through gravel with my cloths half ripped off. I would be tackled and my hands twisted up behind my back as soon as he would say that I was a kick boxer.

I saw through his lies as soon as I met the man. How could they not see it? Unless they just get off on beating women too.

Ike loved to brag to people about how he manipulated the police into punishing me or anyone else for him. He thought this was so cool. Ike also bragged to everyone he met about how he would steal my car and leave me stranded time after time.

He bragged that he left me with no money, no food, nothing to drink and no possible way of leaving. As I asked before, who could possibly be impressed by this?

As soon as Ike got out of jail, he went next door and got drugs. Then he took over the computer Brian had left for Chris. It cost me a lot of money to get the internet hooked up so Adam and Chris had something to do. Ike wouldn't let Adam or Chris even get on to play games.

One day Adam had had enough. As I said before, he was at least twice Ike's size but not a violent person. He just stood up and simply turned off the computer.

Ike ran next door and called Adam on the phone to threaten him.

I heard Ike say he was going to cut him to pieces and send him out in body bags. A threat Ike had said to me about my whole family many times. All Adam said was, "Well grow some balls and come get some."

I did tell you that when I met Ike, Adam was here recuperating from a wreck. What I didn't tell you was that when Adam was four, he was hit by a big, old heavy station wagon.

He was coming back from the ice cream truck. I saw him laying under that car and jumped off the porch. My feet never touched even one of those steps. My sister's boyfriend picked him up before I could get to him, so I shoved them both into my car and sped to the hospital.

When we got there, they said, "Don't tell me, he was hit getting ice cream, huh." They told me I was the lucky one.

They said that this happened all the time and that Adam had been the only child to survive out of all of them. They banned ice cream trucks soon after that. His head was swollen and he had a broken leg and had to be put in a cast up to his hip. After they told me Adam was okay, my knees went weak and I sat down and cried.

I always seem to hold it together while the crisis is happening but fall apart later. They yelled at me and said that I should have waited for the ambulance. I told them that he was already done being cleaned up, ex-rayed and in a cast when my sister told me the ambulance had just gotten there. They all stayed clear of me the rest of the time Adam was in the hospital.

Adam was so hyper that I had to take him for a new cast every week. He would wear it right off.

I had to carry him and his very fat baby brother up eight flights of steps every week to get it done. Having children, especially hyper children, will definitely keep you in shape.

Thirteen years later Adam had a friend in Alabama that had his birthday the same day as Adam.

He and a bunch of their friends went out on the mountainside to sit by a campfire and have a few beers.

I always told Adam not to go out there in the dark and that he needed to tell his friends that he was a very sound sleeper. He didn't listen. My mother called me and asked me to please sit down. She then said that first of all he was still alive but that he had fallen one hundred and fifty feet off the mountain side.

Adam had fallen asleep. When they were ready to leave, they thought they woke Adam up and he helped them put out the fire. When they all started to walk back to their cars, Adam walked the opposite direction and all they heard was a thump when Adam hit the bottom of the bluff.

My mother told me that when she saw him, she almost passed out. She said he had a huge gash in his forehead and that she never knew that a person had that much meat to their forehead. She told me that they told her that they would have to do plastic surgery to fix it. His head had hit the rock cliffs on his way down.

My knees buckled under me as I hit the bed. I looked up and said to God, "You caught him didn't you." He has a scar going down the middle of one of his eyebrows. That is the only way you could tell he was ever hurt.

When I got to the hospital, Adam had on three ID bracelets. Two of them said John Doe and one had his name on it. I asked them why. I was told that because of where he fell, the paramedics tagged him John Doe because in all of history no one had ever survived that fall.

They said when he passed out in the emergency room and they were told where he had fallen, they tagged him John Doe.

They said they couldn't believe it when they took x-rays and found that he didn't even have a broken bone. By the time Adam got to my house he was solid black up to both hips. He had fallen feet first. They never found one of his shoes. They said they believe it was buried in the ground on impact.

Adam said all he remembers was the feeling of falling and thought he was just dreaming so he said he just rolled over and went back to sleep. He said he remembered waking up briefly in the helicopter and the emergency room. He was pissed that they had cut his new clothes off of him and that he lost his new shoes. I told him God has something very special planned for him.

In the newspaper it said he fell sixty feet. My mother knew exactly where he fell. She said she grew up there and that this was her playground. She said it was one hundred and fifty feet or more. I called the news paper and I asked them why they said that. They told me they were trying to down play it so no one would go up there to look where he fell.

When my neighbor watched the rescue film with me, she gasped and looked at me when they were talking about what medicine to give Adam and said, "Oh my god, that's enough morphine to kill a horse. They wanted to flat knock that boy out." It didn't work. Adam was calling for me.

It took several hours to rescue him. It was a straight drop to the bottom. They had to scale down the rock wall and hoist him up on a stretcher. I thank God every day for the men and women brave enough to do this in the dark. I always wanted to hug their necks for saving Adam.

Two years later one of Adam's friends that had been with him that night took one of his other friends up there to see where Adam fell. Everyone said he was looking over the bluff and said, "How could anyone fall from here?" As soon as he said that, his foot hit some gravel and he fell off the same spot. He was messed up so badly that they had to have a closed casket.

The state finally blocked the place off and no one is allowed back there anymore. Adam felt really bad about this. He kept saying that if he hadn't survived that this wouldn't have happened to his friend.

Two years to the very day after Adam fell, he went to a friend's house for his birthday and fell asleep playing computer games. The guy woke Adam up and told him he needed to drive home.

Once again, Adam was not awake. He got almost home and woke up to realize he was driving off the road into a very deep ditch. He said he stiffened up for the impact and heard a snap. He said he was hoping it was the seat. He pulled himself out of the car but couldn't stand up.

The ditch was too deep for anyone to see him from the road, so he drug himself up the hill. The snap was his back. He had to have surgery and still has a rod in his back. The impact of his car was so hard that it shattered every window, including the sunroof, and shattered every rim on the car. They say there wasn't one inch of metal that wasn't crunched up and damaged.

Other than the broken back, Adam had three small scratches on his lower back and nothing else. Here again I was told that no one knows how he survived it.

I finally got mad and told Adam to stop this nonsense. I told him he really wasn't invincible. I told him I was going to kick his ass if he ever did anything like that again. He said he had learned his lesson and would be more careful in the future. So far I think he has.

When he had to drag himself up to the road the doctor said all those little bone fragments were cutting into his sciatic nerve. It never healed properly. Adam was too hyper to just lay down and heal. All my fussing at him didn't make him stop getting up and trying to walk around.

He has no feeling from his hip down in his left leg and foot. He has foot drop in that leg now and ends up stumbling from time to time, if he isn't paying attention to how he sets his foot down. He was told then by our doctor to file for disability. Adam said if he could walk, he would rather work.

The state told me at the time that they would pay me as his care giver. They said this would save them from having to pay for him a nurse. I was supposed to be paid for one year. Surprise! I never got a dime. With the way Adam eats, I really could have used it.

Knowing all Adam had gone through, I wasn't about to let Ike near him to try and hurt my child. Adam said his friend back in Crossburg wanted him to move in with him and that he could get him a job where he worked. I started packing his things.

All of a sudden Ike shows up with his buddy Shayne Kotter. Ike told him Adam had threatened him and demanded he arrest him.

The other cop with Shayne took one look at Ike and said to me, "I've seen that look before. He just got out of jail and is pissed off at the world, right?" Shayne heard this and told Ike that he could see Ike was the problem and that he was the one that was leaving.

Ike smiled and stepped up to Adam and said they just had a misunderstanding, that they were buddies and there was no need for anyone to leave. Ike stepped up to hug Adam. Adam put his hand up to keep Ike at a distance and said, "I am not your buddy." I asked these guys to keep Ike busy until I could get Adam and his things to the car and take him to live with his friend.

I borrowed some money and paid Adam's rent for a month to give him time to get on his feet. Adam didn't have a car and Ike wouldn't let me go anywhere in mine. All I could do was call him when Ike wasn't around so I could see how he was doing.

My child was only thirty minutes away and I couldn't go to see him. Heart broke again.

When we all got our teeth pulled, we were all given pain pills. Chris didn't want to take pills either, so we both threw ours away. Ike found the pills in the trash and said he would sell them and buy what he needed to build Chris a room on the back of the trailer.

Ike had the pills he had gotten too. He said he made about $2,000 just that one time selling them. He spent days telling us how nice that room was going to be and how he would put Chris his own private entrance in to make it special.

Chris went to town early one morning to see Adam and one of his friends. I got up to find all of Chris's things in the living room and Ike was putting a wall up where Chris had been sleeping. There had only been a blanket nailed up as a make shift room until now. Adam had been sleeping on the couch before he moved.

For a moment I thought Ike was going to make that into a small room for Chris until he could add a big room onto the back. When I asked Ike what he was doing, he said he was building himself a computer room. It wasn't even his computer. I asked what Chris was supposed to do, and he told me that he had discussed it with Chris and he was moving to town with Adam.

When Chris came in, he looked very surprised and asked what was going on. Ike told him he was moving. He hadn't discussed it with him at all. I told Chris that if he wanted to stay that I would call the police to take Ike out of there.

Chris told me not to say anything, that he would just go. I was ready to put Ike out right then, but Chris asked me to let it go. I just went back to doing my puzzles in my room. Ike succeeded in running my family off again.

I forgot to mention that Ike had probation when he got out of jail. When Chris needed his car to go to see a friend, it suddenly wouldn't start, but the next day when Ike needed it to go to probation there was suddenly nothing wrong with it.

Just like my car when I wanted to go to see my family. it would either not start or it would have several flats. But later he would fill up the tires and they were fine when he needed it. We were once again his prisoners, and it was getting old.

I would pray every night when I went to sleep hearing him screaming and threatening me for God to please not let him kill me in my sleep. When I woke up to him still screaming, I would put my hand in the air and ask God to give me the strength to not kill this man.

I would be fixing dinner and turn around and be face to face with this man. He would stare at me so coldly and say, "I could kill you so easy." Sometimes he would just stare and say nothing.

Sometimes before I could turn around, he would run two fingers across my throat and say, "It would be just that easy, bitch." Like I said, I endured mental, emotional, and physical abuse twenty four-seven for thirteen years while the police protected him.

The neighbors I asked not to give him drugs started calling him over every morning to do drugs. They started lying to him and he would came home angry and wanting to kill me every night.

When that didn't make me run away, they started telling him lies about Chris too. Ike would come home and threaten to kill him too. I told Ike that I could see that they were doing this on purpose for some reason, but he only had hurting me on his mind, so he didn't listen.

People told me later that Billy and Shellie Todson would laugh and brag about him screaming at me all night and the fact that they caused it. They sat over there listening and laughing about it every night.

Once when I ran out the door to keep Ike from beating me, I saw Billy Todson sitting on his front porch just doubled over laughing at seeing this. When I fell, hard, I looked up and saw him sitting there. He went inside when he saw that I saw him.

One night Ike barricaded the doors again and followed me for eight straight hours. Every step I took to try and get away, he was on my heels with a loaded shot gun telling me how he was going to kill my whole family and then make me beg him to kill me.

Ike's mom bought him this old Oldsmobile when Chris moved. He was supposed to see the dentist for a final check up and to get more pain pills. It was a two hour drive to the dentist. Fifteen minutes before he was supposed to be there, I called the dentist and asked if we could come the next day because we couldn't make it on time. They said that was fine.

Ike runs in really geeking and says, "Let's go." I asked where, but he didn't answer. We got a block away, and I asked where we were going again. He didn't answer.

I then said that I had changed his dental appointment to the next day because we would never make it on time.

Ike slammed on the brakes and started to grab me. While he was screaming at me, his face was red and the veins in his neck was popping out and the foam that had gathered at the corners of his mouth from the drugs was going everywhere.

Most of the time when he did this, he looked like a rabid pit-bull and he looked this way a lot. My back was still out from his last attack, but I got out of the car and tried to walk back to the house.

Smoke started rolling off the tires where he was holding the brake down and had the gas pedal to the floor. When I looked over my shoulder, he looked me in the eye and screamed, "Time to die, bitch" and let off the brake.

I could barely take baby steps I was in so much pain, but I had to jump the ditch to keep him from running me down with this big old car. As I jumped, I felt the exhaust heat on the back of my leg. He barely missed me. He drove up and down the street trying to get me to get in the car. When I got home, I had to sit out in the woods again until he calmed down.

Adam moved back to Alabama. He had spent months working with his friend but said there was no point in staying if he couldn't even see his mother. Chris came to see me when he could. He was busy working. Adam, Chris and their friend all worked at the same restaurant.

Every time I see my sons I give them a hug and a kiss on the cheek. Ike told me that him and his friends decided that this was sick because their mothers weren't that nice to them.

He said that if I didn't stop hugging my sons, he would kill all of us. I told him to stop trying to come between me and my sons because it was never going to happen as long as I could take a breath.

Every Christmas, Thanksgiving and Birthday Ike would go way out of his way to make sure I had a miserable day. Then he would cry and ask me why I started with him knowing how miserable his holidays were as a child. In his mind everything he did to me he would twist it around and convince himself that I had done something to him and that I had to be punished.

This one Christmas, Chris came out to spend a couple days. Ike decided we were all going to see his mom. His mom only invited Ike when she needed something fixed, and as soon as it was fixed, she would tell me to get him out of her home and never bring him back. She would say she hates all boys and would point at him and say, "Especially him." She meant it.

Since the girls weren't there, I told him I was never going back there. Chris even said he could take his car if he wanted. Ike started throwing things and told me that he would cut our throats and burn the trailer down around us if we didn't get in the car.

He forced me to go several more years pulling that. When Chris wasn't there one time, I said I still wasn't going. Ike left for a while and came back to tell me that he had hired someone to kill me for him as soon as he left and had an alibi.

Ike said Billy and his wife Shellie were the ones that told him to cut my throat and set the place on fire and that they promised that they wouldn't tell the police on him.

Ike went on another one of his rants where he followed me around shaking his loaded shotgun at me.

After eight hours of this I walked into the living room to tell him to shoot me and get it over with. I had been begging God to make him leave my home or just shoot me because I couldn't live like this anymore. Yes, he finally broke me.

Ike had passed out and was laying on the couch with this loaded shotgun right under his chin and his hand by the trigger. I don't know how long I stood there, but I know there was one hell of a battle going on in my head about if I should put his finger on the trigger or not. I finally just went to another neighbor up the road where Chris was staying to get away from Ike.

I have sat many times and tried to remember even one pleasant memory of this man, and I can't think of one. I gave him so many chances to try and be nice. It just wasn't in him. I still find that so sad. Drugs and his family really screwed this man up.

He tore up his own car once to keep me from going to my daughter-in-law's baby shower. I told him I would walk if I had to, so he told me to stop and get the car fixed on my way to the shower.

The guy that fixed it said it had to have hit something really hard to rip off this piece. He said he had never seen this come off on any other car because it was factory welded. Like I said Ike never does anything to help but, he will bust his ass to destroy.

Ike kept insisting that I go to the scenic overlook with him to take pictures for his family. He also insisted that we go before anyone else got out there, early in the morning. It just happened to be a hundred and fifty foot drop. No way in hell, I knew better.

When I walked up to that woman's house, Chris and her son took off to visit friends. This woman and I talked so long that we both fell asleep sitting up on the couch. When I got home, Ike was standing in the living room with the shotgun in one hand and an open can of gas in the other.

Of course we argued, especially when I realized he had all the phones and some of my personal belongings in his car. He was going to burn the place and claim I did it because my things were gone.

Ike always walked around the house with two loaded shotguns in his hands. He said they were to kill all the cops that would show up to help me. The judge in that town had a brother in the

Sheriff's Department.

The judge's brother stopped out in the road and said someone called him and said that they had seen us fighting. He asked if everything was alright. I started to shake my head no. When I saw the reflection of Ike walking up behind me I didn't say anything. Ike walked up smiling and said everything was fine.

The guy got in his car and pulled away. When Ike came up beside me, he put his arm around my shoulder and the knuckle of his thumb in the middle of my throat as a warning. As we walked back up the drive, he smiled and waved to the guy and said, "You do one thing to make him step on his brake and you are both dead." I decide once again to act like this didn't phase me so I went to start laundry.

The washer wouldn't come on, so I went to the breaker box to check the switch. It had been turned off. Ike came screaming, "Nooooo" as he ran down the hall. He went in the bathroom for a few minutes. Then said, "Okay turn the switch on."

Later he told me that he had pulled wires out of the water heater so that when I came home and flipped the switch on, the wires would spark the gas fumes and explode with me in the house.

That's why he had taken all the phones. The problem was that he was still in the house so he stopped me. Ike was an electrician, a mechanic and did plumbing and carpentry, etc. There wasn't much he couldn't do. It always bothered me that he always used his knowledge to destroy, never to help anyone.

When his next to the youngest girl, Angie was about three she walked into the room one time, put her hand on her hip and said, "My dad is so lazy he won't do anything for anyone. Not even me and I am his daughter." Feather got upset and said, "Angie stop that." Angie said, "Why, it's the truth." She stomped out of the room really upset.

Ike and Billy got into an argument one day. A few days later, the judge's brother was walking up the drive with a piece of paper in his hand. Ike grabbed his shotgun, took the safety off and went to the door. He rested the gun by the door and kept his hand on the barrel so he could grab it to shoot this guy. I stood a few feet behind him and was going to kick it out of his hands if I had to.

It was a court summons because Billy was going to sue him. Ike stepped out and got the paper. When he put the safety back on the shotgun, he said, "That's one lucky S.O.B. That wasn't a warrant, just a court summons.

I risked my life twice for this guy in a matter of days and not once did even one of these cops try to protect me or my sons. As a mater of fact when I tried to tell this same guy once that Ike was on drugs and the war path again, he was the one that told me to go home and get my ass beat. He said that he wasn't going to do a thing to help me.

So glad to know my tax dollar is paying for such a forth right bunch of officers, huh. I did go to sue Ike once and couldn't afford the court costs.

Chapter 9

My brother called me to tell me my mother was basically sent home to die. That there was nothing else they could do. Ike wouldn't let me go to see her. He insisted we were all going to see his mom.

It was still Chris's car we were using. We thought that once we saw his mom, Ike would let us go to see my mom. He insisted we stay longer at his mom's every time I even mentioned calling to see how my mom was.

When we got home, I already knew what had happened when I saw my brother's number on caller id. Before I could even hang up the phone to tell Chris what had happened, Ike started swinging his fist at me and cussing me. He was saying I had better not even think about taking Chris's car from there to go to a funeral. He said for me to start walking if I wanted to make it to the funeral.

Brian called to say he was on his way to get us. I never had a chance to tell him what Ike had done. My mother had been at my other brother's in Kentucky. We had to drive through Kentucky to get back home from Ike's mothers. If I had been able to call, I still could have seen her before she died.

Ike kept calling me on my cell phone the day of the funeral screaming at me to keep me upset. He told me once that he did this on purpose because he knew I would have no time to enjoy my time with my family that way.

He said he knew that I would be so upset over what he did and said that I couldn't think of anything else. He wasn't going to give me a break even long enough to grieve. My mother died two days before her eighty fourth birthday.

As soon as I got back home, Ike started telling me what he was going to spend my inheritance on. It took several years to get the properties settled and the money divided. Ike was relent less about staying on me about it all the time. He constantly told me how it was taking too long for him to get his money.

Chris came to visit after work one time and mentioned that a guy at work was just arrested for slapping one of their patients. He told Ike that there was so many crimes against the elderly and disabled that the new law was that you could get up to twenty years in prison for even yelling at someone you knew was disabled. This freaked Ike out.

He always knew I was on disability. Ike stopped doing drugs for a short time and stopped trying to beat me. It didn't last very long. When he first started back on drugs, he started asking other people to beat me for him.

He told them he wouldn't pay even one grain of meth unless I was beat down so bad that I couldn't walk or talk for at least a week. That's how he usually did it. I couldn't even swallow my own saliva for a week when he did it because he would choke me until I pried his fingers off my throat and nose and mouth.

This one couple was there when he said it once, and the man got really mad and told Ike he needed to shut up. Then he looked at his wife and told her to not even think about it. Later that night his wife came back alone. She scooted up real close to Ike to rub up against him and said, "Is she asleep yet and do you still have that gram of meth?"

She looked up and saw me standing there with my arms crossed just looking at her.

She backed away real quick and asked if he wanted to sell her the meth. Ike didn't answer so she left. Those two never came back again. I wouldn't have backed down, but one of this woman's legs made two or three of my whole body.

Chris had been renting a room from these two so I didn't tell him. I knew he would be really upset with this woman. Chris wasn't aware they were on drugs until later. He moved as soon as he figured it out. Chris said he figured it out when he came home one day and she said someone had broken in and robbed them.

Chris said he started looking around and realized the only things missing were all of his games and electronics. Things that could easily be pawned. None of their things were gone.

He saw this behavior in Ike all those years and now recognizes it in others.

Then Ike started asking guys to beat me and say that it had to be done well so that I was really beat down. I reminded him in front of these people that I am a professsional kick boxer and that I wouldn't just sit and take it. I wouldn't be the only one getting hurt.

Most of the guys he asked had crushes on me. I don't think they even considered it. I couldn't be totally sure about this because if an addict is jonesing bad enough they will consider just about anything.

Just before Adam moved out, when he got into it with Ike, he made the comment that two of the girls that came there were kind of cute, but they were married so Adam would never even try to go there.

Ike told Adam that those women were so desperate that all he would have to do is be nice to them, and he bet Adam that he would have both of them sucking him off within the week. Adam told him that was disgusting because they were married. Ike said he would prove it.

Adam moved, but Ike still had to prove what he said. He started looking at them and smiling a lot. He laughed at everything they said and started giving them more drugs than the other people including their husbands.

Ike knew the one girl was pregnant with her second child at the time. This made no difference to him.

In a matter of days these girls would walk right past me to get to his computer room without even saying hello to me.

Ike said he had to get a few things done around the house one day. The one girl ran out to get his tools and followed him around like a puppy for two days helping him. She did this right in front of her husband and little girl.

I couldn't believe he was this willing to break these peoples marriages up just to prove his stupid point. I finally got pissed and told him to stop his s---, right the f--- now.

With Ike if I didn't cuss and take off my glasses to prove that I was willing to tie up and fight over it, he didn't take it serious. Those people left and didn't come back for a while. The other girl I ran off myself. I told her I knew she was sneaking off with Ike in my car while I was asleep. I told her if she ever set foot on my land, she would have to deal with me.

I was already pretty pissed at this woman anyway. I got up one morning and Ike was gone. I was out of laundry detergent. I had to walk to town about twenty miles or more away. It was summer. The walk was so far and the pavement so hot both my feet were blistered when I got home.

As I said this was mountain roads, no sidewalks, up and down hill. Then I found out that Ike had spent that entire day driving this woman around to find morphine pills while I had to walk to town.

Ike screamed at me for days saying that I just walked so I could meet men. I was so sore I could barely move, but I still had to fight him.

I called the last number Ike had dialed on my phone one day. It was a drug dealer in Sun. Ike was still there. I called the police and told them where he was and that he would soon be coming through their town with drugs on him. I told them when he got home he would try to kill me. They laughed and said it wasn't their problem and that they wouldn't do anything to him.

One time this guy was going to tow my car to work on it, we tried to get it on the trailer. We couldn't get it on there by ourselves. I saw a police car coming so I ran down the drive to ask if they would stop and help. They slammed down the gas and whipped around the corner without even stopping for the stop sign. They gunned it to get down the road as fast as they could.

The guy that was trying to tow my car started cracking up and said, "I have never in my life seen the police run like that from anyone. What did you do?" I had to explain to him that as they got closer I could see that it was Land County Sheriff.

They were over there illegally once again. They ran because they knew they weren't supposed to be there. I really didn't like that the cops were afraid of me but sometimes I do get a chuckle out of it.

I get so mad when everyone tries to tell me Ike doesn't mean anything by it when he attacks me and that he is just trying to get to me. Every time I would try to talk to Ike and tell him neither of us were happy and ask him to please just leave, his eyes would instantly turn white and as cold as ice. He would throw me on the floor and try to choke and smother me.

He would say, "Time to die, bitch." The one time he sat on my chest and held my arms down with his legs. It took me awhile to get my hands lose to pry his hands off me. I almost blackout more than once when he was doing this. He would lean over and coldly stare me in the eyes the whole time.

Once I kicked him off me and got to my feet to defend myself he would start crying and shaking and say it wasn't him, it was the drugs. He said he would never do that again. One time as I walked away, under his breath he said, "At least not while you are awake."

I said I heard what he said and he swore he didn't say a word, that I must be hearing things. That night I woke up to him sitting on my chest holding my arms down with his legs and choking me and smothering me again. It took even longer to get him off of me then. I knew it wouldn't be very long until he succeeded. How silly of me to not see this as a joke, huh.

We had a fifty five gallon barrel in the ground for a temporary septic tank. Brian sent me the money to put in a real septic tank with. Ike had a friend dig the hole, and I ordered the nine hundred gallon tank and field line.

They came out and set the tank in the hole and stacked the field line against the trailer. Ike said he would put the field line in and then said a few days later that he couldn't do it. Ike screamed at me all day saying I was just coming out to see the men putting in the tank. I just got tired of hearing it and went inside. Ike called me out to see the tank when everyone left.

He asked me to come up on top of the tank with him. When I leaned over to look in the tank he grabbed me and held me over the hole yelling that he was going to bury me in it.

He said no one would ever find me. He said, "No body, no crime. Then all this will be mine."

For months he kept telling me how that would be my tomb and that he would get away with it. He said he would be the only one, LIVING, on that land in the end. He would lean over and really stress the word, living. I started having vivid nightmares about it, but I never told him or anyone else.

One day Ike got really high and decided to suddenly be honest. He told me that I was a stupid bitch because all these years I didn't notice he was beating me for what everyone else had done and that I had never done anything to him.

I said I knew that and I had always said, "I'm not those people." Then he told me that ever since the day he met me he has made up horrible stories about me and my sons and told them to anyone within ear shot. I said I knew because people had told me some of the stories over the years. I had even repeated the stories to him many times.

Then he said that most of the stories were so bad that most people would ask where they could find me because they were going to either beat me or kill me. Then he looked at me and said, "Yeah, why aren't you dead yet? Well, I guess I will have to make up worse stories next time."

I asked him why he would do this to me and he said, "So when I kill you, no one will care enough to make the police look for your killer." That's why he was so willing to make it look like he was the victim. He said that if they even looked at him for it, he would run to Ohio or claim he was crazy and get away with it. He insists that Ohio wouldn't send him back, even for murder.

I didn't say anything; I just went to my room. My knees went weak and I practically fell on the bed. I started shaking and crying uncontrollably. I kept thinking that after all these years of having to sleep with one eye open to protect myself and my family from this man, there were a thousand other people out there wanting to kill me for things I never even thought of doing.

This was starting to get too hard to keep taking from this man. I still have never done anything to him ever to deserve this.

He would constantly walk up to me and say, "God really hates you. Why else would he have given you a prick like me." After so many years of this I started wondering if he were right when he said God hated me. I wondered why God wasn't letting the police help me get rid of this man. I started to wonder if I were ever going to be free of this evil man.

All I had ever done is try to help this man and his children. All he has ever done is try to destroy me and my family. He had no reason to do this but I could finally see this man truly hated me. He really was my worst enemy.

As soon as I bought the trailer, I had to start fighting him to even go to the store to buy him food. Then I had to fight to get back in my own home, with the food. It still, according to him, always took longer than he allowed. Once I carried everything in to the house, he would dump the bags out on the floor.

He would start throwing cans and jars at me saying I didn't buy anything for him because he didn't eat that crap. Later that night I would get up to find most of the food I bought for the month lying on the living room floor, half eaten. He would swear he had no idea how it all got there.

I went thru this every month for years. Fight to get out, fight to get back in, having food thrown at me, then him waste it all for fun.

He would throw full two liter bottles at my head and laugh about it. After that, he would waste all that food and drinks. I had to go wait in line for hours at the church to get a few cans of vegetables to keep myself from starving the rest of the month. I knew he was doing this on purpose.

After he would waste all my food, I would have to go clean all the garbage out of his car. There were more food wrappers and soda bottles than one person could eat and drink. He was leaving me home to starve while he was out feeding someone else.

When I would fix dinner and bring him a plate, he would throw it at me and try to beat me because I didn't put enough pepper on it. He would throw a whole, hot pizza and pizza pan at me because it didn't bake exactly to his liking.

I had to dodge bowls of milk and cereal being thrown on me. I hated to come home anytime I had to leave for any reason. I knew I had to come back to hell. This was my home, not his. The police should have done their job and made him leave. This wasn't right that they did nothing against this man. I would have fought like hell to defend their rights, so why weren't they fighting for mine?

Everyone has the right to live in their own home without fearing for their lives from anyone. Isn't this why we pay the police? For them to protect us, not the criminals.

One day I was at the store and as I bent over to get some hot dogs, I notice four different people I hadn't seen in a while. I thought that I would go see what they had been up to. When I stood back up, they had all disappeared. I walked that direction quickly to see if I could catch them. No one was in sight. They had to have run to get away from me.

I started noticing people I had known for years would look the other way like they hadn't even seen me when I passed them on the street or in a store.

In case I haven't mention it I have long bright red hair, so it isn't likely that anyone has ever not noticed me. Most of the places I have gone I was the only redhead around. I mean carrot top red. When I was young, I hated it so bad that I dyed my hair every color, from white to black. Then I bought wigs to wear all the time. I even had an afro wig in the seventies. I finally got used to the red.

I cried all the way home from the store the first time I realized that this was because of all his lies. I couldn't understand why everyone was so willing to believe this man without even asking me if any of it were true.

Then I was pissed and thought, well obviously they never were my friends. I had to let it go because I didn't want him to see he won or that it bothered me in the least.

One time I stopped for gas and the woman behind the counter asked, "Is it really that bad? I have watched you for years and you always had a big smile and friendly word for everyone. I haven't seen you smile in years. Is it really that bad?" Sadly, I had to say, "Yes, it is."

Ike said he and Robby Lane were going to the river one day. I thought that with other people around it may be safe to go along. Ike said that

I could go with him later, but that this was the guys time. I knew that meant he was taking someone else, but I didn't care.

The next day Ike had his hand in his pants scratching like crazy. I said as a joke, "Did she give you crabs when you went to the river?" He jumped up and tried to make me look in his pants.

I wouldn't look. He said he had little blisters all over his crotch and that they burned like hell and itched real bad.

Ike had just told me a day or two before this that Billy called to tell him he had shingles. He said it is a form of herpes that form blisters that burn and itch. This told me without even asking, that when Billy told me Ike was sleeping with his wife Shellie, he was right.

About a week later, the girl they had taken to the river called me to tell me that Ike had tried to romance her. She told me that he had been bringing her drugs and movies he had pirated for at least six months. She said Robby was trying to get her too.

She said that me and Robby's girlfriend were idiots to put up with these men. Then she said to me, "Ask around, people will tell you that I am no prize. This man spent six months trying to romance me. If he wanted to have me that bad he will sleep with anything."

I wasn't mean enough of a person to tell her that I was already told about her. Everyone that tried to tell me how fat and ugly they thought she was would start to gag. When they tried to tell me how bad she smelled, they would have to excuse themselves to go throw up.

This was said and done by several different people. I just agreed and told her thanks for calling. She said she would send me a picture of her and Ike together at the river, but she didn't.

In a few days Ike and Robby got into it. Robby, his girlfriend and his girlfriend's son told me that Ike came screeching up their driveway and told Robby to come out to let him beat him for trying to take this girl away from him. Ike didn't know the girlfriend and her son were even there.

Robby had taken that girl back to the river without Ike. Ike still denies it all. Ike never said anything to Robby about him hitting on me. He just tried to beat me for it. He said that I wanted it or I wouldn't have let Robby in.

Chapter 10

I bought a bunch of trees to plant on the land. Some of them were fruit trees. I thought that when my grandchildren get older, I would bake pies and make other desserts for them. This wasn't easy to do either. This clay soil was like trying to dig into concrete.

Ike had a fit as usual. He said that I should start putting money into his land because he didn't want to live on this corner lot. He said he didn't feel it was private enough for him. I told him he didn't have to help me that I was going to plant them myself anyway. He said that he guaranteed that nothing was ever going to grow there.

Ike didn't mow very often, but every time he did he would mow down everything I planted and tell me he just forgot they were there. One time his buddy Ronnie Dawn was there drunk and said, "You lying sack of s---. You asked me to mow last time and told me to run everything over because you were proving a point." If Ike says something, he will do whatever it takes just to prove his point.

I went out and bought a refurbished lawnmower. I told Ike I would go out to mow. I had been mowing my own lawn for many, many years. He ran outside to do it. I kept hearing this grinding noise, but I didn't think much of it. It sounded like he would grind for a minute, then lift it up, and then he would grind it again. This went on for a while.

Ike suddenly came in and called Ronnie and said. "I just went out and spent a hundred bucks to buy a lawnmower. That lazy f"ing Chris just broke it on purpose so he won't have to mow the lawn." I told Ike to stop lying.

Chris hadn't even been there for months. Ike said, "Well, I am not stupid enough to say I broke it on purpose." He said that he "accidentally" ran over a stump and it broke a plastic piece in it and he wasn't fixing it. He knew how to, but he was refusing to do it.

Another time I spent a couple dollars to buy a tomato plant. Once again I got beaten down and told I was an idiot for spending my money. I planted it and took care of it anyway. It grew twice as tall and twice as wide as that end of the trailer. I believe it grew so well because that is where I had been dumping all my ash from the wood burning stove all these years.

Ike started bragging to everyone that came in that he had bought it and took care of it and look how big it grew. He started telling everyone to take tomatoes. They took so many that I never got even one tomato from the plant that whole summer. I found a smashed one at the end of the year that I saved seeds from. I plant a couple of those seeds every year now.

One time that Ike went to his doctor, he came out and told me that there was something wrong with his blood test and he was dying. Ike did stuff like this a lot to see if I would react, so I didn't.

I had a feeling he was trying to make me feel sorry for him so I might sleep with him. After all the times I saw him share drug spoons and saw the women he was with, no way in hell.

All of a sudden our doctor called my name. I didn't have an appointment. I went to the same doctor but at his other clinic. My doctor told me to take a blood test. I asked him why. He said even though Ike lived with me, he couldn't tell me why.

I told him Ike had already told me about the blood test. He then told me that Ike had just tested positive for herpes, hepatitis c, and when he said, "And" I said, "AIDS." He said, "No, it isn't full blown AIDS yet, but that is just a matter of time."

For the twenty years this man was my doctor, he would ask permission to touch me for any kind of exam. So when he grabbed my hand and pulled me face to face with him and said, "Imogene, please take this as seriously as I am saying this. Any exchange of any body fluid with this man will kill you. Do not eat or drink after this man. Sterilize anything he touches." I had to take him seriously. He then said, "This bears repeating, so you understand," and he repeated it.

He said, "Zero alcohol and zero sex." He said, "If you drink you will forget you can't have sex. You are my patient and I have an obligation to look out for you." The doctor that we had that had already quit as Ike and Feather's doctor was one of this doctors assistants. This was my regular doctor and he was still treating Ike and me.

I went to take a blood test. I was told I had to wait a week for the results. After Ike tried to beat me and kill me everyday for over a year because of the neighbors, Billy and Shellie suddenly turned on Ike instead of making him torture me and Chris.

I guess they finally figured out that him beating me wasn't going to run me off. Ike went next door after the doctor visit to see them. Ike didn't come home.

The next day Billy called me to tell me he took care of Ike for me. He said Ike came in and told them that my nasty ass had screwed so many guys that I had AIDS and that they needed to find him a women because he was never touching me again.

Billy said he took Ike off to some trailer park out in the boonies and left him with one of the women Billy sees. He said he had an open marriage. He said he and his wife both agreed to see a lot of other people.

I never understood this. If the love is gone, just leave. Billy said the woman he took Ike to stay with looks and walks and talks just like a man, but he said he knew Ike didn't care.

He said that when Ike called him to pick him up because the girl had already left him, he told Ike that I was really mad and I had called the police on him and they were looking for him. I hadn't done anything.

Ike started calling me leaving threatening messages on my recorder. Different people had come by at different times while he was calling and heard the messages.

Billy was making all this up. I never called the police until the threatening phone calls started. I was glad he was gone and prayed he would stay away. When he called, he would say he knew Shayne Kotter was with me and that this is why he turned on him that one day. He said he was going to kill us both.

I told Billy and Shellie that Ike was the one that was sick. Billy got really mad when he realized that Ike had now infected one of his girlfriends. Billy then told me that he called the police and told them that Ike was hanging out with drug dealers and sent the police to these people's house to raid it. He then told Ike that I had sent the police over there.

I didn't even know where Ike was at and now drug dealers that I didn't even know now thought I sent the police to their house!

Billy had Shayne Kotter's personal number and gave it to me. He said he called the guy and told him everything he and Ike and Shellie had been doing including all the drugs they had all been taking. He told Shayne he was going to shoot Ike if he ever came back.

I called Shayne to tell him the truth about what was going on. I also told him about the phone threats and that if Ike was on meth, he would try to kill me. Shayne told me not to worry that he would talk to Ike. Billy and Shellie asked me to come over. I could still barely walk from my last fight with Ike, but I was curious to see what they wanted.

Shellie told me that when they introduced Ike to that girl that he told her he was going to buy her a diamond ring and buy the land across the street from mine so they could torture me together. Ike was waiting for his disability to go through. I figured this was bull s---.

I had just told Shellie that for years Ike told me when he got his disability back pay he was going to buy me a diamond ring and buy my land for me and buy me clothes to replace all of mine that he had ripped of my back. Just before he left he said he was going to buy the land across the street for me.

For many years now Ike never complimented me. If he liked what I was wearing, he would rip it off my back. Then he would rip it into pieces and tell me no one would ever see me in that. He ripped up coats and purses too. I could see Shellie was just repeating this to me to hurt my feelings. It was obvious to me already she was hurt that Ike had taken off with this girl.

Ike said he would pay to put in the septic field lines since he had stolen the money Brian sent to put it in with. He said he would buy me a car too since he had destroyed mine so many times. I still wonder why she didn't try to throw that in my face too.

Shellie then told me that to get even with Ike that I needed to sleep with her husband and sign my land over to them and move far away. She said the only thing she asked is that after I enjoyed the hell out of her husband, she wanted to be there when I told Ike all about it.

Billy drove me home. He said that Ike told him to sleep with me and that I should sign the land over to him and give him all of Ike's tools. He called me the next day to say that he was leaving Shellie because as soon as I said Ike was the one sick that she freaked out and made him go with her to test for AIDS the next morning. As the saying goes, "Hoop there it is."

They had Ike torture me and my son purposely for over a year just to steal my land. I laughed and said, "I quit sleeping with Ike years ago because I didn't want his diseases. You just told me how you and her sleep around and you think I am stupid enough to sleep with you?" I also told him I was never giving up my land to anyone. I didn't hear from those people for a while.

One night I heard a noise out back and figured it was a stray dog. My back door was about four steps up off the ground. I figured I would just open the door real quick and yell and it would spook the dog and it would run.

I opened the door to find myself face to face with a huge bull. He had wandered over from across the street. This startled us both and he went back across the road. I called the owner and said I was afraid he would get hit crossing the road. They said he did get hit, but it only hurt the truck that hit him. This was a big bull.

Ike showed up after a week and tore the phone wires off the pole and broke in. I had just hung up the phone from telling Shayne Kotter that Ike kept leaving threatening messages and that he would try to kill me. I picked the phone right back up to call my son and it was dead. I knew Ike was there even before I heard him screaming in the back door.

Ike dared me for days to call the police so he would have a reason to kill me. I told him that Billy had told me everything. He denied any of it ever happened.

He said he had just gotten stranded at a friend's house and the guy didn't have a phone for him to call for a ride.

I still had all the threatening phone calls he made to me on the recorder.

One day when Ike started threatening me, Chris very calmly said to Ike, "You are obviously upset with me and taking it out on my mom. I have had enough of it. You and I are adults, and we need to talk about this."

Ike said he wasn't talking about anything and started out the back door. Chris said one more time, "Let's talk about this Ike." Ike stormed out to the shed. Chris was upset and said he was going to go see a friend of his.

Ike didn't know he was going to leave, so he didn't have time to disable his car like he usually did. Before Chris even got out of the drive, Ike ripped open the back door and screamed, "I'm going to kill you, bitch." He punched the walls all the way up the hallway.

My back was still out from the last fight. I tried to run but all I could do is take tiny little steps, very slowly. I got to the middle of the front yard. Ike grabbed me by the hair and body slammed me to the ground.

I could see Chris's tail lights as he went down the street. I had the worst sinking feeling that this was going to be the last time I ever saw him.

Ike grabbed me by the throat and started dragging me. He had such a tight grip I couldn't breathe. I saw a knife in his left hand as he used it to point around at everything while he was telling me that after he cut me up and buried me out back that all this would be his. He then said, "When your kid gets back, I will take care of him too. Then his car will be mine."

Ike had just said a few days before this that if Chris took off in the car after he had fixed the brakes that he would pay for it. I bought the brakes. It took Ike all of twenty minutes to put them on.

Now he is willing to kill him for his car. He drug me over stumps and through the gravel. I tried to reach back to trip him by pulling his pant leg so I could breathe, but I couldn't move. When we heard the neighbors come out to tell this couple that was visiting goodbye, he tripped over a stump.

When he lost his balance and lost his grip on my throat, I let out the most blood curdling scream I have ever heard. It even startled me for a second. I screamed that he was trying to kill me. He grabbed my throat again.

This time he dropped the knife and grabbed my shirt with the other hand. Now I had his hand, my shirt and my bra choking me.

The couple that was leaving drove by slowly and Ike couldn't get me in the woods fast enough, so he picked me up and started brushing me off saying, "Oh honey, did you fall? Let me help you." He was afraid that they would be witnesses.

I know Billy and Shellie heard me. When they were quietly saying goodbye to their friends, I could here them like they were standing next to us. They never came to help or called the police.

I couldn't even walk when Ike picked me up. I was in more pain than I had ever felt before.

Ike wouldn't let me go to the doctor. I lay in bed wanting to just scream I was in so much pain.

I constantly roll from one position to the other to try and find one that hurt less. There wasn't one. Ike was afraid I would tell what he did so I lay there for weeks in almost unbearable pain.

Ike knew though that if I missed my regular appointment that my doctor would call, so he took me for my appointment and walked in the room with me to make sure I didn't say anything. My doctor's assistant immediately sent me for a MRI. She said that she knew me long enough to know that I could take a lot of pain and that she could tell by the look on my face that this was unbearable.

Ike had shattered several vertebrate and the bone fragments were grating on the sciatic nerve. I saw a surgeon a week later. It still took another month for them to schedule my surgery.

Ike screamed at me everyday to buck up and take it like a man. He wouldn't even bring me water to take my medicine with. It took twenty minutes to turn different directions until it hurt a little less, so I could roll off the bed and drag myself to the kitchen.

Then I had to keep changing positions until I could pull myself to my feet without screaming, to fix myself a sandwich and get a drink to take my meds. They were basically aspirin with a mild muscle relaxer. Otherwise Ike would have had them gone already.

Ike would come to my room to tell me how when he was in a car wreck and broke his back, his then girl friend didn't help him. He said that was why he wouldn't help me. In just a few days he was screaming at me and calling me names saying I didn't help him when he broke his back.

He was so high he thought I was his ex girlfriend. I knew it would be just a day or two until he is dragging me out of bed to beat me because she didn't help him.

Suddenly he crashed from all the drugs. He laid on the couch screaming for me to wait on him. He would even lay there and scream for me to go get his mail. I couldn't walk, and I had to go down steps and walk down the drive to get his mail. I did all this with a broken back.

Early one morning Ike kept staring out the window at Billy's house. He got a phone call from Shellie telling him Billy had finally left for work. I was very quietly saying "ow, ow, ow." to myself because it hurt even to slowly drag myself to and from my room. As I was dragging myself on my stomach back to my room, he walked by and kicked me out of his way.

He told me to shut the f--- up. I was saying this so quietly to myself, face down on the floor he couldn't have possibly heard me. He said, "I'm going next door to f--- the neighbor because she appreciates me. Her and her friends are all over me all the time." Yes, this is after she was told about all his fatal diseases.

I turned over on my back and held up my fists and said, "Come on asshole I've had all I can take." He kept walking. There was nothing near enough to me that I could have pulled myself up on. I couldn't have stood up if I tried, but I honestly had had enough. I would have tried like hell to fight him.

Chris called to tell me he wanted to go to Oklahoma to meet his dad. I told him I had to have surgery but didn't tell him what had happened. I needed help, but I needed him away from Ike more. I told him to be safe and have fun. He called when he got to his dad's.

Ike screamed at me all the way to my surgery that day. So high the foam was spraying every where again from the corners of his mouth.

He said he didn't know why he had to waste his time taking me for surgery. After all, he wasn't getting paid for this.

All the years I paid his way and raised his girls obviously was nothing to him. Let alone the fact that he broke my back.

Ike cussed me so much that when he went to the bathroom, the nurse said she was going to have to tell him to leave if he didn't shut up. She said his mouth was upsetting the entire staff and all the other patients. I told her she could tell him to leave anytime.

Before they took me to surgery, Ike threw my purse at me and said I was going to give him all my money or else, so I did.

I had bought a car from my brother after my mom died because she had left him two. The next thing I remember was waking up face down in the back seat of my car soaking wet with sweat and in a lot of pain.

Ike was shopping with my money. This car had power windows and he had the key. This was summer time and I was burning up out there. I rose up to see that I was way too far from the building to even try to walk to it. I passed out.

When he finally came out, I said, "Please don't stop anywhere else. I am hurting." Then I wake up and spent ten minutes trying to get out of the car to get to the bathroom. He was in the gas station flirting with some under aged girl behind the counter.

By this time I was in tears. I begged him to please get me home. He just screamed that I embarrassed him in front of this girl.

I noticed that the back seat ash trays of the car were full. I cleaned the car completely when I got it. This meant that he had once again been stealing my car when I went to sleep and ran the roads for drugs and women.

I just went back to sleep. Once again I woke up drenched in sweat to find him in the drug store. When I asked him what he was doing, he said he had forgotten his medicine. I found out from my doctor later that it was the pain pills my doctor had prescribed to give me for my surgery.

I never got even one of them. After that, every time I got pain pills, he would take the prescription in himself, fill it and then sell them to his buddies.

I was in a lot of pain one day and made it to his room to ask for one of my pills. I don't like pills but the pain was getting really bad. He looked up and laughed and said, "What pills?"

As I turned to go to my room, he put some of my pills in his grinder and asked the people sitting there, "Who needs another line?" He just kept laughing about it.

Even though I had just had surgery, when his attorney called him about his disability claim he made me go with him. This was just a day or two after my surgery. He screamed at me when I had trouble walking to the building and up the stairs.

He wouldn't even get me a wheel chair when I went for my MRI because it embarrassed him. Now my walking slowly was embarrassing him.

He made me go to his doctor appointment too a day later, and he was there for over eight hours.

It was too hot for me to stay in the car, and I couldn't sit down. I slowly paced the floor the whole time just waiting to go home.

He said he wouldn't leave me at home to have someone over. I could barely move I was in so much pain all the time, but he thinks I want to stay home to screw someone? I think what upset me the most at the time was the fact that I now have an open surgical wound and he is the only one there to help me change bandages every day.

I would pour alcohol down my back and tell him to put the bandage close to the wound and guide my hands to press it on.

Ten days later on my birthday, I had to go to get the staples out of my back. I got screamed at all the way there and back. He had made thousands of dollars selling my pain pills, and this still wasn't enough to keep him off my back.

My doctor said that he had never removed such a large bone fragment out of anyone's back before. He said the nerve was so roughed up from this huge piece of bone that it may not heal.

This time I filled my prescription and hid the pills.

Ike asked Billy's brother and his wife if they wanted to go out to eat with him for my birthday. Just a few days before this, I caught Ike peeking at her though the crack in the bathroom door. He thought her husband was too high to notice, and I was sleeping a lot to ignore the pain.

He left with them. He told me they were giving him a camper for the pills he had sold them. I said no. I told him that I knew this was his way of thinking that he could get away with cooking meth on my land. I told him I would kick his ass and call the police if he tried to bring it on my land. Plus I wasn't going to give him my pills.

All of a sudden I see a total stranger walking out of my shed with my brand new $500 chainsaw. This one I bought. Ike said he had to have it to cut us firewood. He never once used it. Now I see that I could have just gone out and bought the wood for a lot less. Hind sight, right!

I had already had to buy the chainsaw back from the pawn shop when Ike pawned it to get Billy and Shellie high.

I told the guy to put it back or I was calling the police. The guy starts calling me names and started threatening to beat me. Ike walked up and unlocked my door, then stepped out of the way to hold the door for the guy to come in to beat me.

Remember, this was only ten days after my surgery. I still couldn't walk, but I have never backed down and wasn't about to start now. When he stepped on the porch, I said, "If you are over eighteen and think you can take me, then step into my house."

The guy told me if I wanted a chainsaw that I needed to get a job and buy one. I told him that he obviously didn't understand because since I was the only one with a pay check, that it was my saw not Ike's. He gave Ike a dirty look and turned around and left. But he left with my chainsaw. Ike gave him a receipt as if I sold it to him.

Ike then told me that he was selling my pills to everyone at the party next door. He said if I was stupid enough to call the police that they would all swear I sold them my pills and I would go to prison for it. He went next door.

When I looked for my pills, there was nothing but the empty bottle left, so I called the police.

When they came out, they said once again that it was domestic, that their hands were tied.

I said it was ok because I could tell they were all getting pretty high next door and I really didn't need a bunch of meth addicts coming after me as soon as the cops left.

I didn't hear any sound from the trailer while I talked to the police out in my driveway but had a feeling someone was watching me. When I went in the house I realized while the cops were there, Ike had snuck back in and stolen all my phones and unplugged everything he could reach in a hurry.

That meant to me that he was planning to come back and beat me or kill me. He wanted to make sure I couldn't call the police. Happy Birthday to me, huh! Ike must have gotten too high to come after me because he didn't make it home that night.

Ike had tried to pull that camper with my car and the transmission went out, so now once again I had no car and I had to hitch hike to find my car. I drove it home very slowly with the transmission slipping in and out the whole way. I could barely sit upright to see over the steering wheel, I was in so much pain. Sometimes I really hate to be that stubborn Irish woman that just can't quit.

Ike told me he was going to buy five acres a couple of lots down from mine. He said it was for us. He even made me go with him to get it. When we walked out of the office after he signed the papers, I said, "If it is our land why is it only in your name?"

He said not to worry that he was going to have an attorney draw up papers to say that it was mine if anything happened to him. He said he didn't think I could have two deeds in my name since I was on disability.

My goal the last few years was to try to make him a better man for his girls. I knew that one day they were going to want to see him. When I told him to take the five acres up the street that he had bought and fix it up for the girls, he told me that he already raised his kids and that "Those girls" were no longer his responsibility.

That's when I knew I had failed when I told God I would make him a better man. I thought that was why God had made it so hard for me to get rid of him. It hurt me so much to realize this man truly did not even care about his own children after I fought so hard for all of them.

After a few days Ronnie came by to tell me he didn't feel Ike had a right to do what he did to me. He then started telling me, word for word, what Ike said to me when he broke my back that night.

My mouth just fell open. I said, "Oh my god, has he started bragging about this already?" Ronnie said, "No, one of my friends was out here poaching deer and saw and heard the whole thing."

This man told him he heard my hair rip out of my head when Ike grabbed me from behind and heard my bones pop when he body slammed me to the ground. He said the guy thought he had watched him kill me when my body went limp and he started dragging me by the throat.

He said he thought about shooting him, but he was too afraid to move or even breathe because he didn't want Ike to know he was there and come after him.

He said he saw my body bounce off the ground with every stump, ditch and gravel he dragged me over. He said that my ass had to look like raw hamburger after Ike was done. And yes, it was cut up and solid black for weeks.

I asked him who it was. He said he couldn't say because the guy was afraid of being arrested for poaching and that Ike would kill him.

I felt relief. After all this time, I finally had a witness. I told the police and they said again that it was domestic that there was nothing they could do until he actually killed me. They said again that if he succeeds in killing me that they would take care of it.

I still don't think I realized he was being protected. One day when we were in town we ran into Shayne Kotter at a sandwich shop. He was there with his wife. I asked him what happened to him talking to Ike. He just laughed and said, "I knew you would work it out." I still could barely walk from my surgery. This is how he thinks we worked it out?

I was pissed. I wanted to storm out, but I could still barely walk. As I walked away, I heard Shayne tell Ike that he had just gotten busted with five working meth labs in his house and that they made him quit his job instead of being arrested. He said he went a block away to the city police from the county and went right back to work.

By this time I was really getting pissed. It was these men's jobs to protect me and my sons and all they were doing is breaking the law themselves and protecting the criminals of this county. There is seriously something wrong with this picture.

Ike made me go to his lawyers again when he had his disability hearing. He said all the way there how he owed me everything and how he was going to repay me as soon as he got his money. He said he would definitely pay off my land for me first of all.

He had been telling me this for years even in the letters he sent me from jail. He told me how I never deserved what he had done to me. He said when he got out of jail he was going to make me the happiest woman in the world. This is what he thinks makes a woman happy?

His attorney told him that even with all his physical problems from all his car wrecks that he was getting this disability for his mental problems. She asked if he was seeing a doctor and taking his meds. He said, yes. This was a lie.

He got a small check and of course bought drugs with it. When he went to the doctor, they took another blood test. His doctor then told him he was taking Ike off of all his drugs and putting on the computer that he would never get any more drugs in this state again. The test not only showed meth in his system, they proved he had none of the drugs he was prescribed in him.

Ike stopped seeing the doctor when he asked him to take a liver biopsy to see if he could be helped with the hepatitis C and HIV. He refused and never went back. He said he never planned on living forever anyway.

Ike pulled down my pants and was on me before I could say anything one day. I call him the minute man, there was no time to fight it.

When he got up, I told him that was considered murder because of all the fatal diseases he knows he has. He got mad and said he was wearing a condom so I couldn't do anything. When I asked my doctor, he told me that wasn't true because condoms break and they don't cover the entire infected areas. He repeated, "Zero alcohol, zero sex."

I told Ike what the doctor said and told him that if I ever tested positive, I was going to sue. I also told him that all these women he was still sleeping with, that it was still murder. He laughed and said, "Do you really think I am giving these women anything they don't already have?"

"Besides by the time they figure it out, I will be dead, so what can they do to me?"

Before Adam left the last time he came into my room and said, "Where's my mom?" I said, "Right here, why?" He said, "I want to know what you have done with my mom? My mom would never take this s--- from anyone. Where is my mom?"

I told him that when I was done with all this I would explain everything but for now to just accept that it had to be like this. Once again he asked if I wanted him to snap Ike like a twig. I asked him to just let it go. I really hated to do that. I wanted to break this man in half myself. How could I keep telling my son to leave him alone?

Chapter 11

Chris called from his dad's. Ike suddenly decided that Chris had just gone there to get me and his dad back together. Ike started screaming at me and said he wasn't going to put up with this and I had better get him home. I missed my son, but as long as he was away from Ike, I felt he was safer.

Ike got on the phone and told Chris to hurry home because as soon as he got his back pay, he was going to start buying houses and remodeling them. He told Chris he would teach him every thing he knows about houses and Chris would be his partner.

I would never be stupid enough to let Chris go off with Ike to use power tools. Ike was a big enough threat when he was without any weapon.

I tried to let Chris know that I didn't think Ike was being honest, which wasn't easy with Ike sitting right there. Chris told me he was wanting to come home anyway. So he headed home. When Chris got home Ike told him that he didn't mean right away. Then he told him he wasn't going to stay with us, so Chris moved back to Crossburg.

Ike was always doing this kind of thing to Chris. He would say or do things to constantly piss him off or hurt his feelings. I hated it and jumped all over him as soon as Chris left every time.

Chris got signed up for college. Brian had to hire some people under him at the bank he worked for. He told Adam and Chris that if they had any computer training that he could have hired them to start working for him at fifty dollars an hour. This was enough incentive for them both to go back to school.

For three years, I tried to get Chris in college and a woman at the main campus kept hiding his paperwork. I finally went over her head to the Dean and got his paperwork found. She hid it at the bottom of the stack, down in the basement. As I said our last name starts with an A.

I can't prove it but I think it was because of everything that had been in the paper about me. We had never even met the woman. Again, I wasn't guilty and Chris had nothing to do with any of it. I think she owes him three years lost income. Ike constantly screamed at me for trying to help Chris get back in to college.

He said that he never went to college and he turned out okay. That made me fight even harder to get Chris back in school.

Billy bought a trailer and moved a block away with a younger version of his wife. Not long after that we heard that Shellie was arrested for animal cruelty. She had a horse and the horse had just had a colt. You could see this poor animals bones it was so thin.

I called and told her that someone wanted to buy both horses. She refused. She let both of them starve to death and left them just laying in the field to rot. She said no to selling them, then just let them die.

When we were putting in the septic tank, a wild pig wandered into the yard. It was playing in the mud by the tank. I couldn't even be mean enough to run it out of the yard. I just let it play. Plus it was a really big pig.

I got a letter in the mail that said I had won 1.6 million dollars three years earlier and that they had been trying to reach me all this time. I got in touch with them. They said it was for real.

This guy called me everyday for two weeks asking me what I was going to do with all this money and telling me there was no catch.

He said the money was coming by bonded courier, and all I had to do was give them two pieces of identification, and the money was mine. He said I would have to pay the taxes on it. Ike got on the phone immediately and started telling all his drug buddies and his mom he was going to be rich.

When Adam called, I told him not to count on it but I may have some money coming. Ike came in my room and started screaming at me saying I had no right telling anyone about this. I called Brian and asked him if he could go on line and check this out for me. He called back to tell me that if this was from another country that it was illegal to cash the check and I could go to prison.

Ike kept asking me what I was going to do. I said, "Nothing because I don't know if it is even real." He came running back to my room a little later and told me I was going to put him a large amount of money in the bank for the first thing. He came back later telling me that I was going to buy him at least two to three hundred acres of land. Then he came in to tell me that I was going to buy his girls a couple acres a piece.

Then he came back and said he would "consider" letting me buy my sons a cheap car a piece. He never once said I could use any of my money on me. Every time he came to my room over the next two weeks he got madder and madder and threatened me more and more.

When Chris called me I asked him to come out and sit with me to see if the guy really did send me a check. I started to see that Ike was thinking about killing me for this money.

Ike really blew up, telling me that he could see that I was going to kick him to the curb and spend all my money on my sons. He said he wasn't going to let me do that. That he would cut me to pieces and bury me first.

When I told him that Brian said it may be illegal to cash, Ike told me that I was going to sign it over to him, and he was going to go to Canada and cash it. He said he would come back and marry me later so half the money would legally be mine.

I said, "Well, then I could go to Canada to cash it." He said no because you have to live in Canada for at least six months before you can get a bank account. I said that cashing it anywhere may send me to prison. He said he would wait for me, then we would be rich.

Surprise! The check never came. The guy called me back the day after it was supposed to come to say that it was his fault because he forgot to have me send him $550 to cover the courier. I laughed and told him he definitely had the wrong sucker. I sent the paperwork to the Better Business Bureau.

This man that keeps saying he loves me was going to murder me over a bogus check. He made my life hell for weeks over this. Then he was mad that I didn't get the check and said I must have done something wrong to lose this money.

If there is no problem he makes up a problem in his head and punishes you for it as if it actually happened. Most days I truly wanted to just beat my head against the wall. I started to hate the sound of his voice. He never had anything nice to say, ever. There were days that he bitched at me so much that I swear my ears felt like they were going to bleed.

I just kept telling him that he was so lucky I was such a calm person. The Pope and Mother Theresa would rip this man apart before the week was up. I had to take it for thirteen long miserable years.

Just think about it, 1.6 million dollars. This should have been the happiest days of our lives, but he chose to make me miserable over it. He bitched on and on about it instead of letting me make my choices. I could see that after all these years he knew absolutely nothing about me.

When I lived in California, Chris's father was a bartender in a local country bar. When I was at the bar and I saw someone sitting alone crying in their beer, I would go talk to them. There were usually a few people crying in their beer so before the night was through, I had all these people sitting together talking and laughing and having a great time.

This frustrated the bartenders to no end because no one wanted to leave at closing time. The nights never ended early for me because I usually ended up having to drive everyone home. I go way out of my way to make everyone around me feel comfortable, wherever I go. I love to make sure everybody around me is happy.

I have always said life is too short to sweat the small stuff. Grab life by the balls, hang on tight and enjoy. That's how I lived my life.

Even when someone does me as wrong as Ike did, I try to make them happy. He didn't have to threaten me into doing things for him.

Sometimes I get mad at myself and ask God why he had to make me the bleeding heart nice guy. I didn't want to be nice to this man. It was just built into my DNA. Shortly after meeting me most men and women poke me in the arm and say, "You're alright for a girl."

I always liked the fact that most women didn't mind me hanging out with their husbands and boyfriends. They said they knew I wasn't the type to be interested in someone else's man. This helped a lot, being a tom boy.

I was always more comfortable being one of the guys but being a mom, I could also hang out with the girls. I am a small stature woman so all my life everyone around me always tried to protect me. That is, until I met Ike.

One night this guy got a little too close in my face flirting with me than I was comfortable with. Before I could even step back to warn him to back off, I saw this look of shock and fear come over his face.

A big arm came down across the bar next to me and I hear someone say, "Are you really stupid enough to mess with my baby sister?" As the guy backed out the door, the guy told him to never show his face in that bar again. My protector was Jack Youngblood from the LA Rams.

He usually had to duck to walk through the front door of, well, anywhere. I said thank you but actually I was thinking that I was capable of taking care of myself. Now I wish there were a few guys like him in this state. It would help if there were a few cops in this state like him.

Even after all Billy and Shellie put me through, when I heard screams coming from their house one night I called the police to help.

It turned out someone had taken the corner too fast. The woman had ran through their fence and had wedged her van in between the last two remaining trees in their back yard.

She got stuck trying to get out her window. She was in their back yard screaming for help, and I seriously doubt they bothered to call for help.

Ike said he got a job running a grocery store and restaurant for a guy whose wife got sick and the guy had to go to the hospital all the time. I knew this was just his excuse to hang out and meet women, but as long as he was gone, I didn't care.

People kept coming by to tell me he was hitting on everyone, eight to eighty. I still didn't care. Ike came in one night and told me Billy came in bragging that he had just killed a guy. He said he laughed about the fact that the FBI were looking at his mother for it because it was her drugs the guy took.

Ike said that Billy said he knew from all the drugs the guy said he had already taken that what he sold him would seriously screw him up for life or kill him. It killed him. Everyone including the mother of the guy that died knows he did it and the police refused to investigate.

The mother of the guy even called Sheriff Redletter to her place of business and told him if he didn't do anything she was going to put a bullet in Billy's head. It was never investigated. That is when I first started seeing that it wasn't just a case of them being too lazy to do their job, they are protecting the criminals.

Billy told me later that his doctor told him that if he ever got into trouble to call him and he would get him out of anything by telling everyone he is crazy.

Ike had this grow light hanging in the shed one time when I went out there. I told him to not even think of putting any plants in there. He said he would never do that to me, so I told him to get rid of the light to prove it, and he did.

I kept seeing him take his friends down this worn down path to look at something past the shed.

I went out there to see what he was up to. I found this pot plant growing in a planter. I told him to get it off my land. He said since it was in a planter it didn't count. I told him I didn't care and that he had to get rid of it. He said he did.

A few months later he moved it in the house instead to keep it warm. Late one night Linda Espier came by and said she was coming right back. She didn't come back or go home. The next day the head Sheriff Donnie Redletter showed up looking for her. At first this seemed odd to me.

Then someone came to tell me when Ike thought I had called the law on him, when in fact it was Billy that did. Sheriff Redletter was the one that went out personally and told them that they were about to get raided. That they needed to stop their traffic.

You really can't trust anyone these days. In case you didn't get that, he was the main sheriff, the one that was voted in by the people.

When the sheriff showed up looking for Linda, I threw a blanket over that plant Ike had brought in the house and rolled it up. I didn't know then the guy was crooked. Ike was so mad he tried to beat me with the plant. There were leaves in every room of the trailer.

He knew the guy wouldn't come in because he was his buddy too. I wish I had known. It would have saved me being screamed at for days.

The day Ike's lawyer called to tell him his money was in the bank he told me to get in the car.

He screamed in my ear all the way there that this was his money and that I would never see a dime. He screamed at me at the bank and when we stopped at the drug store. He screamed that he wasn't paying for my medicine.

He has never paid for my medicine. He just wanted to embarrass me in front of everyone. He screamed at me all the way home. I said I didn't want his money, that he should pay off his land and move there. He screamed that I wasn't getting rid of him that easy.

He said that he hated me so much that he would never go away and let me be happy with any one else. I told him that the sad truth was that when I left him it wouldn't be for another man, it would be to just get away from him.

Of course just like that small check he had gotten, he spent most of the money on drugs. He did finish putting in the septic because he knew we would lose the land if it wasn't finished properly. And because he had stolen the money Brian had sent me to finish putting the field line in with. He knew that eventually Brian would ask why it wasn't finished.

He fixed my transmission that he had messed up and told me I was giving my car to his parents. They bought a car before mine was finished though, so I said I was giving it to Adam.

Ike had Brian build him a gaming computer, and he gave Chris back the computer that was supposed to be his in the first place. Ike acted like we should kiss his ass for giving us back what was ours to begin with. Then all the threats started again that he was going to bury me in the septic tank and no one would ever find me.

When Billy was trying to keep us fighting, he told me that when I went to sleep at night Ike was talking kinky to under aged girls all over the world on the internet. I told Ike I wasn't paying for the internet anymore for him to risk me going to jail for his s---. I turned it off. Ike called and got it hooked back up and started paying the bill. First thing he had paid for, ever.

Ike told me that since twelve was legal in their country for them to marry that it wasn't illegal for him to talk about sex with them. He had learned how to pirate movies. He started selling them out of the store he was managing. Then he went to pirating CDs and computer software.

Then he put up a web site with an illegal radio stream. It was for people to get the pirated movies from him to sell to other people. The MPAA and Perverted Justice said they couldn't do anything until the police got involved, and the police said they didn't know what to do about it.

Ike started taking people's prescription pain pills in trade for movies. This should be federal since the state pays for these prescriptions, but no one will do anything.

Then I heard him making deals to sell these people's pills for cash for them and charged them a fee. I knew by then there was no point in telling anyone, especially the police.

Adam came to get the car I gave him. I wanted him to stay, but Ike started getting angry again so I told Adam to take some clothes back to Alabama for my niece because I was scared for his safety. I really hated sending him away.

When I found out Ike was seeing two married women, one of which had small children, I did try to tell them about the fatal diseases he had. One of the women he was seeing we heard on the scanner that she had just got arrested. I went to see her while she was in jail. She laughed and told me that Ike had already told her this crazy woman would say that to her to break them up. He said not to believe me, so she didn't.

In a fight once I asked Ike why he kept trying to beat me, saying I am a snitch. I told him that I didn't talk to anyone about what he had done to me. He laughed and said he always knew I was too stupid to tell anyone and that he had always counted on that.

Since he was gone all the time now at the store I started calling my brother and telling him all the things this man had done. I realized that if he did kill me, no one would ever know what he did.

My brother wanted to beat him, so I told him about the diseases. I told him that somehow I was going to take care of this. Ike stole so much from the guy at the store he fired him and closed the store. His wife had died while she was in the hospital.

When Ike was seeing the one girl I talked to in jail, everyone said they had nowhere to go to sleep together because she went from one man's place to another. I knew I wasn't going to let them do it at my place or so I thought.

Ike laughed in my face so many times about how he purposely kept me from my mother when we knew she was dying and how he got me so upset that I forgot it was Adam's birthday when he came to see me that one time. He is always so proud when he destroys people's lives.

Ike told me he had hired someone to kill me once because I had quit smoking pot with him. He said that was all we had in common and since I quit, I needed to die. He always came up with some stupid reason that he convinced himself of that justified my having to die.

Chris started coming out more often so I asked him if he wanted to move out there and let me take care of him while he went to college. Ike had slowed down on the drugs a little bit and wasn't blowing up as much. Short lived, but it was a break.

Ike didn't like it, but he finally agreed. He said he wouldn't bother Chris if he went to get food stamps so Ike wouldn't starve. In other words they were for Ike, not us.

I put a mattress in the living room floor for Chris. We stood it up by the window during the day so Ike couldn't say it was in his way. When Chris moved in, he gave me a butterfly knife to throw away. He said someone gave it to him and he didn't want to hurt the guy's feelings, but he knew they were illegal and didn't want it.

Ike picked it up and said, "These are illegal. I'll take it. Anything illegal appeals to me and you know it."

I woke up from a bad dream one night trying to scream but nothing came out. I told Ike I dreamt his one friend came to borrow his shotgun and that when he brought it back, he shot me with it. I said I really didn't want him here anymore.

Sometimes my dreams will happen exactly how I dreamt them. I had also heard that this guy stalked and raped women all the time. He had even bit one woman's nipples off. He is still out on the streets stalking and raping women. The police know what he does and ignore it.

Late that same night I got up, and I noticed the gun was gone. Ike said the guy I had just told him about borrowed it to go hunting. I said, "Even after I just told you about him shooting me in my dream?" Ike just flashed an evil smile and said, "Yes, I know."

Ike had started hanging out with this new couple. The guy turned out to be the brother of the guy that stole my chainsaw. I heard them talking about drugs including pot. I didn't mind the pot. He didn't try to kill me when he was on pot.

From the conversations I was hearing, Ike had started selling large quantities of pot for him. The couple he sold pot for is Tom Espier and Linda Espier. The same ones Sheriff Redletter was protecting.

When Ike got his money, he bought a car. I gave my car to Adam, and Chris's car quit.

After Ike had stolen and tore up our cars so many times all these years, he suddenly refused to let me drive Chris to college. Chris had to start walking twenty miles to school every day even in the rain and snow.

He had to walk home sometimes in the dark on old winding roads with no street lights or side walks. He said he not only had to dodge cars but he had to fight off dogs too. This really upset me.

When Ike would do something against Chris like this and when he would say and do things to either upset or piss Chris off so he would leave, I would just put my hand up and go to my room. You know the gesture like when you would say, "Talk to the hand." I never said anything. I just give him a look. Ike knew by this that I was really pissed and had enough.

This gesture actually worked on him. Ike really, really hated it when I wouldn't speak to him.

To him this was me being mean.

When Chris got his college money, he gave a big chunk to Ike hoping it would make him happy enough to stop giving us constant crap. I had hoped maybe happy enough to let me take Chris to school until he could buy a car. It didn't work.

Chris went to buy a car to get to college in. I asked Ike to go with him since he was a mechanic. He cussed me for asking. He sent his friend with Chris even though he said the guy had ripped him off on a truck.

When Chris came back and said he bought a car, Ike had a fit. He said he wasn't going to help him with anything anymore. He never did ever help him, but he was making another one of his stupid points.

The car died on the way to the house. Ike not only didn't help him, he wouldn't let anyone else come to help him either. Chris is not a mechanic, but he went out to put a timing belt on it by himself anyway. It took several weeks because he was still walking to and from college.

Ike wouldn't let me get it towed so someone else could fix it either. This went on for months. I realized he was trying his best to force Chris into quitting college. I told him that I was going to get my son through school even if I had to move away to do it.

I had Brian tow the car to be finished. I knew Ike wouldn't try to stop him. When Chris went to pick it up, the motor blew up. Ike wouldn't even let me drive six miles to bring Chris home from the garage, so he stayed in his car that night and it was cold.

Chris said the police came to ask him what he was doing there and told him he had to be gone by morning. Chris called Pete to take him to his doctors the next day and spent a couple days at his house to stay away from Ike.

One of Ike's friends said he was about to lose his truck. He told Ike he would take what he owed on it and give him the title. Chris loaned him the money even after Ike went out of his way to not help him.

My inheritance money came in, but I had no way to cash it, so I sent it to Brian and told him to come up and just pay what I needed paid. He agreed. I also knew Ike wouldn't challenge Brian on how he spent the money.

In the mean time Ike told Chris that if he gave him enough to get this truck he would help get him a laptop computer that he could take to college with him. Chris had already just given him lots of money, but he said ok to make Ike happy.

When I saw the truck, I said I liked the color and the fact that it had a back seat, because I don't like putting groceries in the bed of a truck. Ike said, "Since you like it, it's your truck." He only said this so he could take my inheritance to fix his car and the truck.

I told Brian to stop in Alabama and pay a month's rent for Adam before he came to see me. I paid money down for Chris's laptop and paid off what Ike owed that company so he could charge the rest. This way Ike could make payments instead of paying out his cash.

I bought a lot of food and cigarettes for Ike and Chris. All the rest of my money went to fix Ike's car and to fix what was supposed to be my truck.

Brian has had his own money since he was eight years old, so he didn't want anything. At eight years old Brian started selling toys and scooters to his friends for a friend of mine. Then he started buying, selling and trading baseball cards and comic books.

When we moved to Tennessee he started playing in "Magic" card tournaments to make money. Later Chris got into this game and played tournaments and sold cards to make money. I think Brian and Sara had their children's college fund in the bank long before they were even born.

After all that, Ike still refused to let me take Chris to or from school. I couldn't use either vehicle after spending all my money to repair them for him. He still bitched at us constantly. Not only did he not thank me for doing all this, he cussed me for days saying that I had led him to believe there was more money than that, and he said I had told him all the money would be his when I got it.

I know I never said that. I didn't feel he should be entitled to any of it. He kept getting in my face insisting that there was more that I didn't tell him about. I think I told you already that I don't drink or do drugs, so I know I would remember if I ever said that. He made me miserable before I got the money and after getting it. He got almost all of it and still wasn't happy.

Ike said himself one day that if you handed him a gold bar that he would punch you in the face and tell you it should have been platinum. Ike cussed me over Chris giving him money. He said Chris only did it to make Ike feel like he owed us.

He screamed that he owed us nothing and that he was going to prove that to us both. Again, this money helped him. He should have been happy. Nothing was ever enough for this man.

Chapter 12

I told you he went out of his way to make holidays the worst. The day before Thanksgiving, Chris and I, Ike and this kid that was friends with Ike were watching TV. Ike went in his computer room to do something. He was in there over an hour. He came to the living room and started screaming and throwing things. He said he was only gone five minutes and someone changed his channel.

No one changed the channel. The show he had been watching went off. I saw him starting to escalate in his bad behavior. I knew he would hurt us both just to prove he owed us nothing. I went to call 911.

I heard a scuffle going on, so I hung up the phone and ran to protect Chris. I saw soda spilled next to where Chris had been sitting and asked Ike if he had put his hands on my son. He said no.

The guy that was there got so scared he ran out in the middle of the night without his coat and it was snowing. Chris had went up the street to his friend Rick's house.

Ike then trapped me in the bathroom and started throwing all my towels and wash clothes at me, Still insisting we had changed his channel. When he had nothing else to throw, he picked up my heavy duty dryer to try and throw it at me. When it caught at the vent hose that was still connected, it slide over and broke the toilet tank.

By the time he stopped the water that was going everywhere, he was too tired to fight anymore. Yes, I mean a full size, heavy duty, clothes dryer. Ike picked it up and tried to throw it on me.

The next day when Brian brought his new baby girl to see us because it was Thanksgiving, Chris was still too upset to come back, so I sent Brian to go get him. Of course it was a bad day because we were afraid that Ike would go off again.

When I told my brother what was going on with Ike, I asked him to not say anything to either of my oldest sons. They knew I wasn't happy, but they didn't know why.

Brian came to me as he was leaving and said that my brother told him that I needed his and Adam's help to get out of this situation but wouldn't tell him why. Just that I needed help. He said, "Anytime you need me, just call. I can be here in four hours."

I had a big sigh of relief as I hugged him because after all these years I could finally see there may be an end to this hell.

My sons always have been and always will be my life. Even when people asked what I did for a living, after helping to run big businesses for my friends and rubbing elbows with the rich and famous at the movie studios I always said, "I am a full time mom first, model second."

I showed everyone my sons' pictures everywhere I ever went all the time. People would say that my eyes lit up like diamonds when I talk about my sons.

I would have done anything to not put them through this with this man. After everyone left, once again, Ike cried and asked me why I had to ruin another holiday for him. He said that I knew how horrible his holidays were as a child and how dare me do this to him.

It took some time and some talking but Ike finally ordered Chris's laptop. He had built up one or two small mail order magazine accounts.

He fought against it right up until I picked up the phone and said I would order it if he didn't.

People still kept coming to tell me who all Ike had been seeing at the store he ran and that one of the girls he never slept with because he was too cheap to rent a room. After all he couldn't waste his drug money. Someone would tell me every other week about this girl. I still didn't think anything of it at the time. That's coming soon.

Two days before Christmas, Ike started on his rampage again. This time Chris saw it coming. He said since Billy had left Shellie that she asked him, as a friend, if he wanted to spend a couple days with her. She was my enemy, but he would be away from Ike, so I hugged him goodbye and asked him to be careful.

When Ike found out where Chris was at, he blew up and started his usual threats. He said he would make him pay for seeing his worst enemy. He said that he hated Billy and Shellie and that he was going to kill both of them and Chris.

He then drug his loaded shot gun out and screamed that he was going to blow my whole family away as soon as they came for Christmas.

To prove he meant what he said, he trapped me in my room punching at me, and then held me down on the bed and tried to push my eyes out of the sockets with his thumbs. I got his fingers out of my eyes, so he punched me and split my lip open. Then, he put his thumbs back in my eyes to push them out again.

I finally got away from him. I remember thinking that even if I had escaped not getting HIV and Hep C before, I probably had it now from this split lip and his fingers in my eyes. It pissed me off that he got that last shot in like that because I usually had faster reflexes. But I am getting older. Much too old to have to deal with this crap on a daily basis.

I also remember thinking the next day that Christmas day never seemed to end. I sat there waiting for him to burst out of his room with his gun and shoot us all.

I looked down at my baby granddaughter and said to myself, "I won't put you through this. Somehow this ends, now." I didn't know how though because Chris still wasn't seeing this man as a threat, and that is more dangerous than you can imagine.

This time when Ike cried and asked me why I had to ruin his holiday again, I almost lost it. I just looked at him and told him he was one of the biggest asses I had ever met and went to my room. He knew I was really pissed, so he didn't try to talk to me for a while.

A few days later, Chris told me he was moving next door with Shellie. He seemed mad at me. This shook me for a minute. I found out later that Ike had convinced him that I had spent days bitching at Ike because Chris was with Shellie. He told Chris I was the one ranting and that I was threatening him.

I did pull Chris aside when he said she had slept with him and told him she had been with Ike, so she has everything he does. He said he always wears a condom. I told him that my doctor said that still doesn't cover everything. He said he was an adult and promised he would be careful.

She isn't a very nice person, so it didn't take long for Chris to see that. They got into a disagreement soon after that, and he came home. Chris said he knew better than to believe anything Ike said, but Ike is a very convincing liar. Ike has had his whole life to hone this skill.

I took off my glasses and went over to tell off Shellie. One of the girls answered the door.

I told her I wasn't going to start anything in front of her kids and asked her to step outside. I said that she should have told Chris that she had been with Ike. I said that she was now killing everyone she slept with and didn't warn them first. I told her I would be back to kick her ass if my son ever tested positive.

I also asked her how could she put me through that year of torture with Ike just for my land, especially knowing she had to fight Billy all the time. If a woman knows how this feels, it seems to me that she would do anything to keep other women from this pain and humiliation. Some people just have no conscience I guess.

211

She swore it was her husband not her and that she couldn't stop him. Everyone that has grown up with her said that was a lie, that she was just like him. They say that those two aren't satisfied with screwing someone over; they have to screw them over hard.

I had to look down at her just to talk to her. I kept thinking, why would someone this small want to try and piss people off at them. Just like Ike they say she gets a crazy check.

I also looked at her and thought she and Ike would make a perfect match since her husband was gone. They could drive each other crazy and no one would care. I almost said that exact thing to him when I got home, but it would just give him a reason to try and beat me.

Ike sold his shotgun for drugs shortly after that. For a short time, I felt relieved that he had no way to shoot me. That relief was short lived. I have never allowed guns in my home, not even when my parents came to visit. They both carried guns with them at all times and slept with them under their pillows at night.

When I was pregnant with Brian, Adam walked into where I was doing laundry and said, "Hands up mommy." I just laughed and continued doing the laundry. Then I thought, "He doesn't have any toy guns."

I turned around to see him pointing a loaded pistol at me. I asked him to set it on the table carefully and back away. My mom had snuck her gun into my closet thinking I would never know. She and I had a few words.

I told you that I sat in my room doing picture puzzles, trying my best to ignore Ike and his parties. I have a really large collection of puzzles now. I glue them to card board when I am done. They are pretty pictures. It's kind of funny that when I look at the pictures I don't think about all the misery I had to endure to do them.

Ike sold a lot of pirated movies at that store, so now all those people were coming to the house to see him after the store closed down. Since it was a small trailer, I heard things even when I tried to block them out. He was definitely selling pot for Tom. Linda came a lot too. She tried a little too hard to be my friend. I should have known something was up.

I heard Ike tell one of his buddies on the phone that Linda was bringing him the pot this time and meth and pills too. I told him if he did any meth that I was walking out for good because I was tired of him trying to take my life every time he did meth.

He took so many pills that night that he overdosed. Not because of me, just because she handed them to him. I heard him tell someone that he snorted twenty different pills at once. He put them all in his pill grinder at once. He fell out in the living room on the floor.

I had to carry him to his computer room and prop him up in his chair. I pushed him back against the wall sitting up. I knew if I called the police I would have to fight him, so I just went to bed. Chris got on his laptop computer and sat next to Ike and watched him all night to make sure he was ok.

The next day Ike called his buddies and said he thought he had a small stroke because his chest and left arm hurt and he could hardly use it. He swore he would never do that again. Two days later he did the exact same thing, with pills from Linda again. I sat him up against the wall and went to bed. Chris watched him all night again.

As I walked past the kitchen to go to my room, I started remembering how I was taking my medicine one morning. Ike was pissed about something and slapped the counter and yelled as I was swallowing this huge capsule. It turned sideways and stuck in my throat.

He saw me choking and said, "I hope you choke to death bitch." He went in the living room and sat down and listened to me choking on this pill.

I was slapping myself in the chest and slamming myself against the wall. He just sat in there laughing. I almost passed out. I made one last attempt and slammed myself against the wall as hard as I could. When I started breathing again he got mad and said, "Too bad I wish you had died."

Sorry, but by this time all my sympathy for this man was beaten out of me. I think I prayed he wouldn't be breathing when I got up. I felt badly, briefly, for feeling like that.

A couple days later he told several of his friends that Linda was coming over again. He said that every time she came she would rub up against him and tell him not to tell her husband she was coming to see him.

Then Ike said that he could tell by the sound of her voice that she was finally ready to give up the p----. I was still home and Chris was asleep in the living room so I thought, surely this man isn't stupid enough to do anything with us here.

A short time after she got there, Ike came to my room to talk to me. He kind of shyly played with my toe asking me what I was doing. Then he went back to his room. He came back to my room about twenty minutes later. I asked him what was going on. He said, "Nothing is going on." I said, "BS, you wouldn't leave anyone alone in your room especially her. What is going on?"

He said that she was in there smoking meth and that he was so proud of himself for not smoking with her, and that he left to let her finish it.

I stood up to go toss her out the door. He told me he would take care of it. After another ten minutes, I started in there again to take care of it. He stopped me and said she was going to finish it out side.

I started out the door to tell her to get off my property with the s--- and never come back. She was backing out of the drive already.

Ike was upset because he said I was going to screw up his pot guy. I knew he had smoked meth with her because when he first does it, he gets quiet, almost guilty acting. Shortly afterwards, the rage starts. Chris told me he heard it all including them smoking together. I told him then that he had never seen Ike in one of his meth rages and that they weren't pretty.

I would have done anything to spare my son from this, but we both agreed later that it had to happen this way for him to finally see for himself the evil in this man and to say enough is enough.

When I got up the next day to do the grocery shopping for the month, Ike was already going off and throwing things around his computer room. At first I thought this was just him going off like he had every month when I had to go to town. I woke Chris up to go with me. I wasn't about to leave him there with Ike.

At first, he said he would stay there to calm Ike down. I told him when Ike is on meth there is no calming him down. I said since the food card was his, he had to go anyway. Chris then remembered he had to get his medicine for the month at the drug store that was right next to where I was going, so he got dressed.

We went out to the car to leave, and Ike came out threatening us. He said we weren't going to run all over town in his car. He stood in front of the car screaming, so we went back in the house and sat down on the couch.

Ike came in and told me that I was never going to call the police on him again because he had put stuff on mine and Chris's computer sites.

He said if he went to jail they would take all the computers. He said Chris and I would go to prison for what he put on them. At the time I knew almost nothing about a computers. Chris had just started school to learn about them, so this didn't worry me. I knew he was just ranting.

Ike suddenly bowed up like King Kong and charged at Chris. He was calling him names and daring him to stand up and fight.

Neither of us had even said anything to the man. I took off my glasses and sat them on the table, so Ike backed off. He still kept ranting on and on. As soon as I put my glasses back on, he charged at Chris again. I threw my glasses on the table this time and started to stand up to fight.

I didn't want to have to do this in front of Chris. This always upset him. Chris said to me once that if I didn't fight Ike that maybe it would change the outcome. I tried that and no, it didn't work. My not fighting always made him angrier.

Ike backed off again. Chris went outside to cool down and to call Pete to see if he would take him for food and his medicines. He thought this would make Ike happy. Ike started screaming out the door at him. When I heard Chris say, "That's it m----- f-----, I have had enough" I knew it was time to end this. Chris was finally angry enough to fight. I dialed 911.

Before I could say anything on the phone, Ike came after me swinging. I held up the phone and said, "It's 911, they want to talk to you." He didn't believe me, so he grabbed the phone. He was still coming around the bed swinging and grabbing at me while he was talking to them. Smiling, saying everything was fine, that they didn't need to come out.

Before he hung up the phone, he said to me, "You called the law on me bitch. It's on now." He thought he had hung up. But he hadn't.

He called them back and told them not to come. I think they asked for me because he came in the living room and told me if I didn't call them that he was going to beat the hell out of himself and swear me and Chris attacked him for no reason.

Then he said we would go to prison, not him. He had gotten away with this so many times before, and I was starting to see they were protecting him, so I called and said we were fine.

I sat down next to Chris. I saw him rub between his eyes, then I saw a bump and bruise there. I asked if Ike had hit him.

He said he hit him with the door when he was coming in to talk to him just before he came after me. He said he cut his arm up with the door when he did it too. The chicken shit hit him with the door, then ran to my room to attack me.

For a split second I saw red. I always told him to never make the mistake of laying a hand on one of my sons. At that moment, I seriously wanted to go in there and tear that man apart with my bare hands. Then I thought that Chris didn't need to see this.

I grabbed Chris by the arm and took him to my room and put his things in a bag. I pretty much shoved him out the back door. I told him it was time to call his brothers and tell them everything this man has done to us. I told him to bring the police and Brian to get me. We are done with this.

Brian had already planned on coming and buying Chris a car to get to school since his blew up. So Ike didn't say anything when I said he was meeting his brother to go look at cars.

Ike ranted all night, I didn't say anything. He then told me that after he sold the shotgun that he bought a pistol from Tom. He said, "I bought the pistol specifically to force you to watch me slaughter your whole family. Then I will make you beg me to put a bullet in your brain."

Every time Ike got mad at me, he would play this song in which the guy screams, over and over, "Put a bullet in your head." He would crank it up and play it over and over for days. When he stomped off to get the gun to prove to me he meant it, I grabbed my keys and my phone and I walked to Pete's to see if Chris was still there.

Chris had already went to Crossburg to wait for his brothers. While I was at Pete's, I called the Sheriff. I told them what had happened, and of course, I was told once again they couldn't do anything until he actually shot me.

When I got home, he was still ranting and waving the gun, so I ran through the briars again and sat down behind a tree to keep from getting shot. I pulled my house coat over my head to keep warm and called Chris.

Chris said he felt like an idiot sitting at that restaurant with all his things in bags waiting for Brian. It was getting late, and I told him I was outside and safe for now, so they could wait until morning to get me. Brian wanted to bring a truck to move me right then. I said no, but to make sure the police pulled in this driveway first in the morning.

Ike kept yelling out the door that he wasn't mad anymore. He said that if I came in to help him move his computer that he would leave peacefully and never bother me again. He said he would leave me everything. How generous since it was all mine anyway.

I have fallen for this line in the past only to be barricaded into my own home.

I tried to go in the shed to keep warm, but he had put two new locks on it while I was outside to make sure I had nowhere to go. I waited for him to pass out, and I snuck in the back door and got some sleep. I slept on the floor, so he couldn't see me. By the morning he was mad at Chris again and said he was never coming back to his home.

He said that I needed to sit Chris's things out on the curb for him to pick up. He was forcing me to climb up and down this ladder with heavy boxes full of books and things getting everything out of my shed. As I took my son's things to the curb, I also put my coat and purse and a couple bags of my important paperwork out there too, when he wasn't looking.

Ike told me to tell Brian thanks for his new car. He said he would smile real big while he was driving it everywhere. I said he hadn't even bought anything yet.

He said it didn't matter, that as soon as he did, it was his. He acted like he was driving a car around like a low rider. I finished moving my son's things out. I was determined that he wasn't going to sell or destroy Chris's things like he did the last time.

Ike screamed that Chris owed him the car because he didn't pay him for the ten dollars he spent to buy his website for him. This was the one he said he bought just for me and Chris, just to make us happy.

So for ten dollars for a site that Chris never asked for, Ike was going to steal his five thousand dollar car as soon as he got it. This was no joke. Ike meant every word of it and would have done it just to prove his point.

I never spoke another word to the man, and I hope I never have to again. Ike called the police and came outside, so I could hear him. He told them that my sons were coming to beat him up and since he was disabled that he was going to have to shoot all of us. All he was aware of was that Brian was coming to get Chris a car.

Then Ike said, "Oh, so you say I have every right to do exactly that. Well thank you very much." I knew that this is exactly what he planned to do. He was setting up his defense right before my eyes. He still had no idea that we were going to even tell Brian about any of this. He was going to shoot us for a car that hadn't even been bought yet.

I'm not sure if I mentioned this, but when he broke my back and said it was so he would have my land, I stopped making land payments. When I got the notarized letter to move or pay I thought, "I worked hard to get this land where it is livable, why am I letting this man run me off?" I went to the office and told them what had happened and said I didn't want to lose everything.

The manager said he would use the money I had in it as a down payment and he would have to start it as a new contract. He said he would only put it in my name. He said if I ever wanted to add anyone else that I had to do it after it was paid in full.

I wanted to put Adam and Chris on it. They said no. I had added Chris to the last one after Ike insisted on putting himself on it. They said redoing the contract would add back a few more years' interest so it will cost me more money. I agreed.

I told Ike for years that the land was no longer in his name. He just said it made no difference, because when it was all said and done he would be the only one LIVING there in the end.

It was his buddy Sheriff Harry Dawson that showed up with my sons. Brian had even went to pick up Adam. I told Harry what happened and told him that Ike told me he was going to move. I said that if he does just move, I won't do anything. Chris got out and told him to tell Ike if he moved and never came back that neither of us would press charges.

I told Harry that since it was my house that I gave him permission to search for the gun.

When I called later, Harry told me that Ike told him that he was moving as soon as this guy showed up to buy the truck.

On the way through town Brian wanted to stop at the courthouse and see what I could do. They told me that since I left, I couldn't go back and that I had to evict him. I said I would wait to see if he moved like he said he would. I did however stop at the electric company and phone and water and cable. I told them to turn everything off. I wasn't going to get soaked for his bills like the last time.

I told them I was having him evicted if he didn't move so for them to not hook back up if he called. To get everything turned on in the first place, I had to pay out a lot of money and bring in all kinds of proof that it was my place.

I couldn't believe they all reconnected him just because he said the place was now his. The electric company told me that they couldn't disconnect while he was there. And that since he was the last one there, he would get my deposit. They did agree to wait until I proved in court that it was my land.

This kind of pissed me off because when I first got it turned on, they made me put it in both our names. Ike and I both said no because he didn't even work. They insisted that it was their policy. I did get stuck with his electric bill when it was all done. Ike always wins.

I was going in to see an attorney and the electric company called and told me that since my bill was past due that I had to come in immediately and pay my bill, or they were turning it off and it would cost me a lot of money to get reconnected.

I said that he had moved right next door and gave them the address and said, "You already know it's his bill. Send it to him." They replied that it was in my name so I was responsible. "Ain't this a bitch?" They flip flop on the rules when it's convenient for them.

I emailed Ike to tell him I was evicting him and said to not sell my truck because that was now going to be the judge's decision. He wrote back to say that I deserted him and my land for no reason.

He said that his grandmother was getting him an attorney and they would tie the land up for years and that when it was done, everything would be his. He also said he had a doctor to prove he never did any drugs. He said my taking him to court was a joke.

When I was told that he reconnected all the utilities, Brian took me to file for the eviction. Chris and I spent the next month with Brian, his wife Sara and my granddaughter.

The first week I had to stay in my room away from everyone because I had a really bad cold from sitting in the cold that last night. Ike told everyone I was up the street with a guy he said I had been seeing, Pete's son Ron.

This was one of the guys he had asked to beat me for drugs. I didn't even date for eleven years before I met him and hadn't even given anyone a second look in the thirteen years. I went through hell with this man. Why would I ever want to date anyone?

Ike kept driving by Ron's house yelling at him and honking his horn. Ike was still convincing himself that I had just sent my sons away and would end up having to move back home.

I was at Brian's about two or three days when the new head of DEA Ike Wrench called me.

He told me he had heard what happened and not to worry. He said he had so much evidece on

Ike that he would personally put him away. He told me he had such an air tight case with a huge file that he didn't even need me to testify. He said he had been after him for over thirteen years.

He said he would camp out on my land and wait for him to screw up, then he could arrest him and bring in all the charges he had.

Two weeks later Pete called to tell me that the day after I left, Ike had changed my locks and moved Handy and one of her friends in. This was the girl from the store that I had talked to in jail.

I found out later that the night I was hiding behind a tree all night Ike called the police and lied and told them I was out in the middle of the road screaming threats at him and he insisted they come out to arrest me.

He thought if I was arrested, he could have Handy there while I was in jail, and he could pretend to me later that nothing happened. He thought that since I had no one to help me that I would spend a couple nights in jail, then have to go back home. He thought I wouldn't involve my sons.

He thought that since he had turned everyone else against me that I would have no choice but to come back home and continue taking his crap.

I found out about his call from a woman that works at the sheriff's department. She helped me get the 911 calls put on CD for court. I knew when she told me what he did that he did all this on purpose, just like the last time, just to have a place to screw another diseased low life.

Since I had left, Handy stayed the month with him. Ike kicked her out the day before our first court date. He still thought I would have to come back home. She wore my clothes and slept in my bed.

He knew all along that I could die from the blood and other fluids she left on my things. When she left, she stole a lot of my things and keep sakes from my mother.

Pete told me he counted at least a hundred cars going in and out of my home the last two weeks. I was told it was wide open orgies and drugs. All the neighbors tried to get the police to stop it, but no one ever came out. He said some of the neighbors considered stopping him on their own, it had gotten so bad.

I left a message on Ike Wrench's phone about what I was just told. I asked him why they did nothing. He called to tell me that he had just been too busy to get out there and once again for me not to worry, he would handle this.

I told him Brian just offered to pay an attorney to sue Ike for attempted murder and that he said he was going to hire an investigator to find out who was protecting Ike and to prove why he got away with so much for so long. I left a few messages after that and the guy never called me back. As no surprise either, nothing ever happened.

They flat out lied to me to keep me from doing anything against him. They were helping him steal my land, my trailer, and everything I owned.

Ike's mom emailed me and told me that I needed to move on and get a life. She said if I didn't leave him and his girls alone she would make my life a living hell. I wanted to call and tell her that thanks to her, he had already done that. I chose to take the high road instead. They were already miserable excuses for human beings. There wasn't much I could add to that.

He moved two lowlife's into MY home. He was destroying my home and selling all my belonging's for drugs. And she is telling me to move on and go get a life? No wonder he is so screwed up.

After he did this the first time I did see that I could replace some of my things. But in reality I really liked my possessions. I wanted to keep all those souvenirs from my travels and keep sakes from family and friends. To me these things were irreplaceable.

I was born under the sign of Cancer. We value family above everything. Possessions come in a close second. He tried repeatedly to take even my family from me. And that is beside the fact that he had no reason and no right to do this to me. I also forgot to mention that he was almost ten years younger than me.

When I left my home this time, I took one last look around and decided that none of it was worth risking my life for.

Chapter 13

Ike started selling my things off for drugs right away. After all, he got away with it before. Since it was my home this time, he also started tearing my home apart. Brian bought Chris a car for school, paid off his last years tuition, and rented us an apartment close to the college.

Ike doing all this to us just cost Brian over ten thousand dollars. And that was just the minimum to get us on our feet. Now every holiday, he tries to replace a piece of furniture that Ike stole from us.

We came back a day or two before court. Once again I was sitting on the floor of an empty apartment, while Ike was selling my things for drug money. When we went to change our address, we had to drive past my place. I saw Shellie's truck in my drive. I wanted to stop and throw them both out, but I decide to do this the legal way. Neither of them were worth going to jail for or dying for.

Just a few months before the blow up, Ike said he bought the web site for me that I had asked him for years earlier. I decided since I had no one to tell about all he was doing to me that there had to be thousands of other women going through the same thing, with no one to talk to.

I wanted a site for women only to just get on and tell their problems to each other. Just getting this off my chest all those years, I think would have helped me deal with it better. With other women telling their stories too, I definitely wouldn't have felt so alone going through it.

For one thing he signed his mother and daughters on there before he ever even mentioned that he had it running. He was still controlling it, and he had them on there, so I couldn't talk about him or my problems. This defeated the whole purpose from the beginning.

Ike acted like he was doing this just for me. He bought Chris a site too. That was what Ike felt we owed him ten dollars each for. Chris wanted to put games on his for people and have a Christian format.

Chris had talked about going to ministry school after college. We were both really excited to have our sites on line finally. Before long Ike started yelling at us that we weren't building up our clients as fast as he thought we should be.

I heard Ike say on the phone one day that he had gotten another guy a site and as soon as he had a thousand clients that he was going to sell the site out from under him to make a profit for himself. I told Chris what he said and we both quickly lost interest in our sites. It was never for us, it was for Ike.

When I first got to Brian's house, I went on line and had Chris put all my forums from my website on a flash drive to save them. I deleted everything from the site Ike was still controlling.

Before I could take my name out and delete the title, Ike caught it and blocked me. Later I found out he had sold my site to over twenty porno companies. I know Ike found this hilarious. My company wasn't even open, and he was ruining the name.

Brian went on line and bought me and Chris our site names back but on a different site. Once I have enough money, I hope to get it on line so I can help other women in the same situation. I hope I can fight the state to make them start protecting the women and children of this state. No one will tell me where to go to do that. I keep asking.

I can get really loud for a little woman, and I am persistent as hell when I know I am right.

Not protecting these women to me feels like they just pimped us out to these men and that's not right.

What I was told is, that by law if you have sex with a man, he can do pretty much whatever he wants to you, and the police can't get involved. What kind of law is that? I want to know who thought this up.

Just before all this happened, Ike's daughters started e mailing him. He just ignored it. To him it made him angry they were bothering him when he was on there to make himself money. I answered back and told them when they turn eighteen that I would make sure to give them my address and phone number because I love them and have missed them so much.

Just after Ike Wrench called me the first time at Brian's, another guy from the Sheriff Department Mick Lamby, had called me. He asked me what happened.

When I told him, he asked if I wanted Ike arrested for assault against me. I said yes. He said he would see what he could do. When I got back, the night before court, Mick called and told me Ike was in jail and that he would make sure he didn't get out before court the next day.

He said he wanted Ike marched in there in shackles.

I asked him if I could go over to take pictures of the damage for court. He said, "It's your place, you do whatever you want." When I got there the door was unlocked and that kid that had run out without his coat that one day was there. He said Ike told him to stay until he got out of jail.

He said Ike had just bought a five hundred dollar bag of pot and asked if I found it, would I give him some. I said if I find it, I am calling the police. The guy left. I went to Pete's and asked if his nephew would help me change the locks back out. The guy waited in my driveway while I went to buy new locks.

While he was changing them for me, I started looking around. I noticed some of my clothes on the bed. Then I noticed a lot of my clothes and shoes missing so I thought maybe they were in the washer. I looked in the washer and it was empty. I looked in the dryer and found some towels waded up.

When I went to take them out, I felt something hard in the middle of it. It was a canister with a big bag of solid buds, a bunch of baggies, and a big bag of pot seeds. I told the guy to hurry with the locks because Chris had a job interview and I had his car. I had to get home.

I left every thing like it was. I touched nothing else. I went home, so my son could go on his interview. We had only been home a day, and Chris already had a job and was signed up for college.

While we were at Brian's, he told Chris how he put himself thru college running the college computer lab and working at Papa John's Pizza. That is also where he met his wife. He said he made a lot of money delivering pizza. Chris took his advice and went to work at Pizza Hut.

After his interview I asked Chris to go with me to the trailer and I told him what I found and that I was going out there to call the police. I was never in the trailer by myself that whole night. You will see this is important later.

I called to tell Mick Lamby what I had found. He had said before that he had searched and found nothing earlier.

He was searching for the gun too, but I was pretty sure Ike had gotten rid of it as soon as I emailed him that I was evicting him. I am sure Harry Dawson told him what I said too.

Harry should have charged Ike when I told him what he had done and that he had my permission to look for the gun. He didn't do anything.

Mick Lamby had already finished for the night. I told the dispatch girl what I found and asked her to send someone. I told her I had my camera there to take pictures of the damage, and I was going to take pictures of the pot.

A few minutes later she called to say someone was on the way, and they said to not touch it. I told her I had already taken pictures of it, and she said okay but leave it where it is. I said that is what I did.

After all that had happened, I knew Ike was never going to just let me move home in peace so while we waited for the officers, I started packing my TV from my room and a few other things.

I grabbed Chris's computer, the one his brother had given him. I grabbed some of my clothes and a few small things that would fit in the car. I was going to come back later and get as much as I could. While Chris was out packing things in the car, the phone rang again. The caller ID said it was Wanda Butt. She was the other woman Ike had moved in with Handy.

I told her I was going to kick her ass for stealing my and my dead mother's things. She said she was too big to fit into my things, but that she had seen Handy take them. Including my makeup, shoes and jewelry. Handy was too big for my things too. Maybe she gave them to someone else.

She told me that after they moved Handy had stolen her husband and that if I wanted she would take me to her and help me kick her ass. I know they all have Ike's diseases now, so I told her I would let the police handle it. She then told me to look on my camera. I saw it behind me, so I did. It is a digital camera, so you can see the pictures right on the camera.

The pictures were of all the women that came to party with Ike while I was gone and pictures of them having sex in my home on my mattresses. She said that every woman that came there Ike told them that if they would suck and f--- him and let him take pictures that he would put them on his own personal porno site.

Officers Landon Bagley and Ernest Lamby, I believe he's the brother of the officer that arrested Ike, came in. The first thing I showed them was the TV Ike had mounted above his computer and showed them he had a camera facing the drive, so he saw Mick Lamby when he came earlier and had plenty of time to throw the pot in my dryer.

They took pictures of the pot and asked if they could search. They asked where he might hide things. I told them he slept on the couch on the rare times he slept. They found his scales under the couch cushions. They giggled like little school girls when they found the scale.

They said with the large amount of pot, the baggies and the scale made it felony resale. The big bag of seeds made it cultivation for felony resale. Then they told me that they found a small plate with a white resin on it and took pictures, but it was too little resin to have tested. They said they also took pictures of all the stems and seeds they found all over the house.

They knew like everyone else that I had just gotten back in town. I was gone a month. I told them about Wanda calling and handed them the camera.

They knew everyone on the camera by name. They even mentioned that one of these girls had brought her mother to join in. They were laughing about that.

When they got to the sex pictures, they said, "Doesn't he have AIDS?" I said that it may be full blown by now but I wasn't sure. They said that this was obviously unprotected sex and asked if they could take the camera as evidence. I said sure because I sure as hell didn't want the pictures.

They pointed at Ike's computer and asked why I wasn't taking it too. At the same time Chris and I both said, "Because that belongs to Ike." Before they left, they told me that for some reason someone had let Ike bond out. I knew he was probably on his way to the trailer, so we left as they did. Here again I was never in the trailer alone the whole time.

Ike had already damaged my place and had trash thrown everywhere, but most of my things were still there. I had really still hoped he would do the right thing and just peacefully walk away.

It turned out Ernest was the one that rousted Chris when he had slept in his car when he broke down at the mechanics. So he already knew part of the story about Ike always being a prick to us both.

Unless you have been through it, no one could understand the cruelties this man has done to us. I haven't gone into details because I don't want to bring you the nightmares Chris and I have had because of it. For all the gory details you will have to wait for the movie.

I took all my paperwork to court with me the next day. Brian paid for me to have my day in court or so I thought. The judge kept putting his hand up every time Chris or I tried to say a word. He looked at Ike and smiled and asked him how he was doing and asked him what was going on.

I would like to know in what universe this is legal. I was suing him, not the other way around. This judge was already on his side.

Ike said, "Well, now all the lies are going to start. They are going to lie to you about me so they can take my land. They broke into my place last night and stole my s--- and my camera." I said I only took my clothes and my TV. I started to show the judge my paperwork where I had paid for everything. He put his hand up and told me to be quiet.

It wasn't until later that I realized Ike had just told the judge, in open court, that I stole his pot. The judge got really rude with me, when I tried to show him my land contract, Ike said it was all forged copies and that I had a copier to fake all the paperwork with.

I didn't have a copier, but Ike did and I had no idea how to do that, but he did. I only check my email because my son has it set up where I hit a couple buttons and I am at my email site.

I asked for an order of protection for me and Chris because he threatened us with a gun. Ike said he never owned a gun. I said I had seen it and Chris said he had seen it too because Ike showed it to Chris himself a few months ago. We both described it. The judge told us to shut up.

Then Ike told him I was a professional kick boxer. As usual this was to make it look like I was this mean woman, and it worked again. The judge said since Chris wasn't Ike's son that he wasn't giving him an order of protection and that I had to file paperwork to get one for me. He told Ike he would give him a few more weeks to bring in proof that everything was his. I couldn't believe it.

Are you comprehending this, ladies? For the second time this man has run me out of my home to save my and my sons very lives. He has run us out with nothing but the clothes on my back both times. Remember, he tried to do this many other times too.

Both times I was in court with three or four huge bags of receipts, all my cancelled checks and this time with my land contract and receipts where I paid for my trailer and land. For the second time, Ike was standing there with not even one scrap of paper, and the court was giving everything I worked so hard for, to him, again. "Wow, what a justice system we have, huh."

I told the judge about him breaking my back and trying to kill me to take my land. I even tried to hand him my paperwork from my surgery. I had a huge envelope with paperwork from my doctor's office about all the injuries he has done to me over the last thirteen years. He put his hand up to shut me up, and then he ignored me. He acted like me and Chris weren't even there.

I was told later by an attorney that the judge should have charged Ike with attempted murder right then. Since he didn't, it was illegal that he didn't. I was told then that I only had ten days to appeal it. It was more than ten days before I found this out.

Everyone in the court room was whispering about how rude the judge was to us. You could tell by all the whispers all over the court room that no one there was agreeing with what Judge Mavis just did to us. When we went out in the hall, a woman approached us and said to follow her and that she would get our order of protection.

She made some calls and then asked Chris to step in the judge's secretary's office to be sworn in. We had to swear the statements were true. She was from the battered women's shelter and said that when the judge got so short and so rude with us, it got her attention.

She said she was in the back of the room talking with a client. She said she dropped what she was doing and watched carefully the rest of my case. After his rudeness got her attention. She had never seen me before, but when I told the judge about him breaking my back, she said she remembered getting recordings from me that Ike had attacked me and tried to kill me.

I made those recordings after Ike said he counted on the fact that I was too stupid to tell anyone. I wanted someone to know just in case he had succeeded. I was told once to come in and pick up an emergency cell phone from them, but I never got away from Ike long enough to do it.

She asked us if we wanted to press charges on the judge. She begged us to please sue him. She said that I wasn't the only one the judge has been doing this to. She wanted it to stop. She said that what he did to me was so wrong and that there were a lot of witnesses in that courtroom that agreed it was wrong.

We said no, that eventually we would have to live in that town again and that we didn't need them as enemies. It is almost impossible to sue a judge, and I knew that. Here again though, I had lots of witnesses.

Chris was upset and said the law and the justice system in this town really sucked. He said he would wait in the car. A guy standing there turned to go after Chris and said he was going to arrest him. The woman from the battered women's shelter threw her hand up to stop him and told him he wasn't doing any such thing.

She wanted to cuss him, you could tell, but she simply said that he had no idea the trauma this man had done to us for years. I was getting ready to say something when she did. I wouldn't have been as nice.

They were going to arrest Chris for having an opinion but refused repeatedly to arrest Ike for actual crimes.

The order of protection hearing was set for the day Ike was supposed to bring proof everything was his. I brought all my paperwork again. Once again, he showed up with nothing.

Pete came to the court to tell me he had seen Ike moving all my things out the night before and that he had destroyed my place. He said Ike moved in with Shellie right next door. Pete said he would wait and tell the judge all of this too. Pete is almost eighty. He could barely breathe after coming up all those stairs, so he said he would wait in the hall for the judge to call him.

The judge waited to call us last or so he thought. He heard all the whispers before and didn't want a court full of witnesses like before. Most courts go in alphabetical order. My last name begins with A. We should have been first.

He wouldn't look at any of my papers or listen to either of us again. Just like before, he listened only to Ike. He refused to call my witness in. I told him Ike had stolen all my things and that I was pretty sure he had booby trapped my place.

I was told later, by several different people, that Judge Mavis hates women. They said that in any case he had if someone had to go to jail, that nine out of ten cases he sent the woman to jail, not the man. He did this no matter what the circumstances.

He was the judge, so no one could fight it. I believe he is the only judge in that small town.

Ike came to court without one scrap of paper in his hand again. He said he didn't know that the judge meant to bring it "this" time.

I had gone to the land company and brought a notarized letter saying I was the only name on that land contract. The judge told Ike to get his computer only and leave and never set foot on my land again. You could tell the judge didn't want to do this, but he knew more than one person was pissed about what he did to us.

When I said again that there was nothing left, the judge got mad and said, "You got your order of protection. Just be happy with that." Since they let us both file he had no choice but to give O.O.P to us both and that pissed him off. He stood up and walked out while I was still talking. Just like the last time.

They had to run after the judge because there was still one case sitting there he hadn't heard. He thought he had cleared the court, but in fact, he left these three witnesses sitting there and the woman from battered women.

I knew the law was protecting Ike, but the judge too! This was definitely more than Ike just being a snitch. I couldn't say anything because I still had to go in front of this judge for the assault charges.

I somewhat understood what Judge Stevens did. He was covering his own ass. He did it illegally but I did understand. I have never been in this court before for any reason. Judge Mavis had no reason to do this to us. If he hates women, then he should have let someone else hear these cases.

The judge said to send an officer with Ike when he got his computer, so we went across the street to get an officer. We were told they didn't have the time to waste on us.

We told them the judge ordered it, and they said they would send someone. When we got to my land, shortly after Ike, the officer was there talking with Ike. Ike put only my barrel of crushed cans on his truck and left.

Ike had put my original lock back on the door. I told the officer what the judge had said and asked him to please go in first to see the damage. He came out and said that Ike had taken everything and that the place was destroyed.

I asked him to please make a report for me to pick up so I could sue for damages. He said no problem and that he would be glad to go to court with me to say what he saw. He never filed a report and never showed up to court, not even when I paid for a subpoena. You try to ignore a court subpoena sometime and see what happens. Nothing happened to any of these people.

When Chris stepped into the trailer he said, "The lights aren't working." I went around the trailer and saw that the meter was still there. I said, "Don't touch anything he has booby trapped the place. We closed the door and went home.

As soon as I got home, I called Pete to tell him what happened. Before I could say anything, he said in a panic, "Don't turn on the electric. He has the place rigged to blow up on you."

I said I had already figured that out. The problem was, if I hadn't figured that out, I would have already turned it on, and Chris and I would be dead. Maybe even the cop.

Pete said that this guy Jed Stuart came to him and said he couldn't let Ike do this to me. He said he helped Ike move my things next door and he was there when Ike rewired my shed.

He watched Ike put holes in my roof to make sure it would burn hotter and faster and wired the back door shut so I couldn't get out. He said that Ike's exact words were, "If the judge doesn't give everything to me in the morning, this will blow the bitch up and burn everything down." Jed said he would go to court to testify if Ike was in jail and couldn't get out to come after him.

I went to the police and was told Harry Dawson was the only one that could investigate these kinds of cases. I told Harry what had happened and asked him to please come check it out for me. I asked him to do that several times over the next few weeks. He always told me he had been too busy.

He finally told me to get an electrician to undo it and he would take it from there. I even told the DA what he had done and they ignored it like everything else. The DA kept saying that she was going to really stick it to Ike on the assault charges.

Ike didn't show up to court on the assault charges. That should have been a hold without bond warrant for not coming and a bond revocation. It turned out Ike had bounced a check to bond out to begin with. When I asked the judge's secretary, she said that a warrant was never filed.

She said that somehow someone came in and wrote in pencil in her book that there was a new court date set. She said she didn't write it and that in all her years there no one else had ever written in her book. She was quite upset. She said she was going to talk to the judge about it.

When Ike finally came to court, the DA said it would be better to drop the case because Chris had already left when Ike threatened me with the gun, so there were no witness. She said Chris didn't take pictures of his injuries and that officer Dawson never filed an incident report when he came out.

It turned out that he had never filed any reports against Ike any of the times he was called out.

The judge said he couldn't hear what happened without the officer or his report being there.

I didn't want to drop it. Our lives were still in danger and no one cared. Chris was really pissed about the justice system after that. I knew letting Ike get by with this was only going to make him worse next time, but no one would listen. Chris said to let it go and let God handle it.

Then the DA said that this judge wouldn't put Ike in jail any way, that he would slap him on the wrist and send him home. He was going to kill my whole family that day and many other days, and this was a slap on the wrist charge! When did human beings' lives become so unimportant?

They finally told me that if I dropped it that they would put in my paper work that he was never ever supposed to be anywhere near me or my sons ever again. They said this was like a permanent O.O.P. They told Ike, and he said he understood.

He was also asked if he understood that this meant forever. He said yes, he understood. None of that was ever put on the paper work I got. It just said he agreed to terms. What a surprise, huh.

I had to file more papers for everything he stole and damaged. I paid for four subpoenas for my witnesses, including one for Harry Dawson because he never filed a report. I figured he could just tell the judge what happened when he came to court.

The same thing for Johnny Reels, the other officer that saw all the damage and stolen things. Another subpoena was for Jed Stuart, the man that helped Ike steal my things and who watched him booby trap the place to kill me, and one was for the electrician that undid the booby trap for me.

Tab "Cowpoke" Dominguez, the electrician, told me that yes, this is exactly what Ike was trying to do. Cowpoke pulled the floor of the shed up. He showed me where Ike had twisted the wires back together on purpose and put a plastic cap over the end hoping no one would notice.

He said that would re-route the current back into the trailer. He said that not only would there be a lot of sparks but the sound would be so loud that it would scare the hell out of all my neighbors. And he could see my neighbors didn't live close by.

Cowpoke said Harry knew him and knew where he lived. He said he could come by anytime to talk to him. I also told Harry that Jed was the other witness. He knew him too. I told them at the courthouse that Jed usually stayed with Pete. I gave them the address and directions there.

Neither officer picked up their subpoenas. They never even tried to find Jed. They said there was no such address. Everyone around there knew where Pete lived.

The only one served was Cowpoke, and he said Harry was the one that served him. Harry never asked him one question about the case. Cowpoke said he tried to talk to Harry about it, but he told him he was in a hurry and couldn't talk.

When I went to get my money back because they weren't served, I was told that both officers were told they were there but didn't pick them up.

They said they couldn't find the other address, so I couldn't get my money back because they tried to serve them. They checked and said I had even put down directions but they said they couldn't find him. I had written, "The first driveway to the right past Barnett Bridge." Does that sound like hard directions to you?

I asked Pete and Jed if they would write a notarized letter for me to take to court. They said yes.

Jed said that he would only say Ike rewired my shed in the letter and that he would specify it was to kill me when he had to go in front of the judge. He was afraid Ike would come after him.

He also said in the letter how Ike had bragged to everyone after court about how easy it was to lie to the judge and get him on his side instantly. He joked about what an idiot he was to believe him.

I took the letters to the court to be put in my file so the judge could read them the first thing. I told no one about this. Someone from the courthouse told Ike. Early the next day Ike jumped Jed. He threatened him and said he knew for a fact he did this. Since it was daylight and they were outside, Ike didn't do anything but threaten.

Jed moved to another state. Since he now gets disability, it wouldn't be hard to find him if anyone ever arrests Ike.

Since I couldn't turn on the electric, I went to the trailer from early every morning until dark to clean everyday for a week and move what little he had left. It took another whole week just to take everything he had torn up to the dump.

I stopped to tell Harry everyday that I would be there. I would ask for him to come out and investigate, so I could turn my electric back on. He never came.

Ike had torn up all of my father's keep sakes and most of my mother's keep sakes and left them there for me to find. He had taken the expensive cookware I had bought from my mother before she died, also a keep sake, and bent all the handles in and beat the bottoms of all the pans.

Ike had also taken an axe and beaten this big quarry rock to pieces. He had put pictures of us and his girls on this rock and varnished over it. He left his girls picture behind too just to make sure I understood he just did this out of rage. He was still trying to control me.

Ike was only there for six weeks on his own. In this short of a time he and his friends had boiled over so much food on my stove that after spraying it several times with cleaner, I still had to soak and scrape the rest off with a knife. I had to turn on the self cleaning oven part twice to get it clean. Again, this was done on purpose.

When I went to court on the theft and damages, Ike didn't come. It was a different judge. Judge Mavis had suddenly gone on vacation. The acting judge was a local attorney.

He said since he was Cowpoke's lawyer he couldn't hear from him for contrast of interest. This judge said I won by default because Ike wasn't there. He said just to keep it honest, he had to see my paperwork just to be safe.

He didn't even get half way through my papers when he said that it was much more than I was asking for. He said that he had to stop adding because he could only give me what I originally asked for. I said that would be fine.

Ike had traded my truck title for this other guy's truck title. Judge Mavis said that since they had already put the trucks in both their names that he couldn't do anything. I went to see another attorney and he said that wasn't true.

He told me to file paperwork for them to take everything of any value that Ike had in his name.

I did that. Then I had to file for the court to go out and take his truck and his car. This all ended up costing Brian a lot more money.

I also asked if I could tie up his land, the one he said he bought for me, but they said not until it was paid for.

After I paid all that money out for them to do this for me, they told me that even though I had keys they had to be towed. They said that the court would sell them for next to nothing and I would get whatever was left after they took out their fees. In other words, I get little to nothing for what I paid them for.

Ike still owed me for a judgment in Crossburg for the last time he stole everything. He never paid me. The tow truck really tore up the front of the truck and the back of the Geo Storm.

A friend said she was driving by when the tow truck and Sheriff showed up. She said Ike was screaming and kicking gravel and telling them they couldn't take his car because his mother had just died. They took it anyway.

I found out his mom really did die. Her and her husband both died the same day so I can only imagine that there was a car wreck. I felt bad, but he did this to himself. And never once felt bad about anything he did to us.

Every time I run into someone from out there, they run up and say, "I want to hug your neck. I am so proud of you for taking those vehicles. That son of a bitch deserved every bit of it." I was definitely not proud of having to do that to anyone, but I could see how much people there hate this man. They see him for what he has become.

When I went to pay the tow truck fees, the guy asked me to go to the sheriff with him because they never told him what to do with the vehicles. He told Mick Lamby what he was there for. Mick looked at the file and said, "When she pays you your fees, they are her vehicles." He asked him if he was positive so he couldn't get sued later, and he said, "Yes they are all hers."

I couldn't afford to transfer titles or get insurance, so they both sat out in front of the apartment for a year. I just went out to start them once a week. I looked out everyday expecting to either find them gone or torn apart. Everything I get was now going to pay rent, utilities, and food. When I got my stimulus check, I put the truck in my name finally.

I decided that since the judgment in Crossburg, for when he stole everything ten years earlier was about to expire that these vehicles were about the amount he owed me from then. So as far as I am concerned Ike still owes me the judgment from Wartville. I have ten years to collect.

The day after I picked up the car, two big guys knocked on my door and said it was their car and they were taking it. They demanded that I give them my keys. I asked for proof that it was theirs. They gave me a card for a repo business. I called the number, and the guy said Ike had borrowed money on the title and didn't pay them.

He said that they had to notify Ike, and if he came and paid off the car, they would have to give him the car. This was Ike's doing. He was trying to make them do his dirty work for him.

After I explained why I had the car, they told me that if I paid them that they would send me the title. The fees were almost as much as the car was even worth, but I paid it anyway. Ike owes me more money than what these and fifty other cars are worth. I wasn't giving them back.

A few months later, I heard that Ike has tried all this time to kill Shellie too. He even started attacking her on the toilet they said. They said she told Billy, who was living with someone else now, but he went to her rescue any way.

He told Ike he wasn't going to let him do this to the mother of his children. They said Ike picked up a metal bat and started beating Billy in the head with it. I told you that I saw him escalating to this.

Ike knows it normally only takes one or two blows to the head to kill someone.

The other guy that was there, Rick, said Ike hit him five or six times before he could get the bat out of his hands. He said Ike fought hard to keep the bat.

Rick grabbed the bat and ran to keep Ike from getting it back. Billy and Ike then fought all over the house. They were both beat pretty bad and lost a lot of blood.

Ike was arrested for beating her, but then they arrested Billy and Rick for assaulting Ike. They had to prove they weren't trespassing. I couldn't believe it. Ike tried to kill these people and they got arrested, not Ike.

Billy laid on his couch for weeks he was beat so bad. Billy told me that Shellie wanted to see me to ask me to help her in court. After what they did to me, I didn't want to help her, but if it would get Ike off the streets, hell yeah!

When I went to her place, she showed me where all the blood was still there on the floor. She said there had been three times that amount on the bed. I noticed that it was my sheets and covers and pillows on her bed when she pointed to where the blood had been. I had to order these sheets special out of a magazine. You can't get them at just any store. They were definitely mine.

I told her again about all his diseases and that the only way to get rid of it would be to bleach everything. What few things that were left at my place, I bleached it all. I washed down every surface of that trailer too with bleach water.

She again insisted that he didn't have anything and that she made sure to ask his new doctor.

I asked her to give me his keys to both vehicles and the title and plates for the truck. I could have it all transferred with my court paperwork, but getting the title would save me money and a big hassle.

She didn't want to at first, but I told her the court had already given the vehicles to me. So she gave it to me. I asked her if she had seen my one folding double chair too. If it had still been in the bag, I would have chanced taking it back.

She pointed and said that she did have it sitting right there but it had gotten broken, and she threw it out. I saw all my other stuff sitting there in her living room but didn't want anything these two had their hands on. I said I would go to court with her, but I had to get home because I had Chris's car and he had to go to work.

When we got outside, she said that none of those things in her house belonged to me and that she could prove her father had left her everything. I hadn't said anything about my things. I didn't want any of it back. This was a case of guilty conscience talking, and it was lying right to my face.

She said she would never let him bring my things into her home. I had already proved in court all these things were mine and Jed notarized a statement that he helped them move everything over there.

When her father died, many years earlier, most of these things hadn't even been made yet. I let it go.

She showed me where she had put a few boards and a chain up over the back door to keep Ike out. I had to laugh when I saw it. I just said she obviously had no idea of what this man was capable of. This wasn't going to stop him.

I also told her that the day he moved in, everything there in his mind became his. I told her when he left that everything would be taken or destroyed just like he did to me so many times. This man has no respect for anybody or anything. He has no boundaries. Whatever he wants, he takes, no matter who he has to hurt to get it.

She said the only reason she let him move in was because she couldn't afford the cable and internet, but that ended up the only thing he ever paid for. She should consider her self lucky that he chose to even pay for that.

I also told her and Billy that they both now have Hepatitis C, herpes and HIV. She looked at me a minute and said, "How the hell did you take him all these years? I had enough after the first month." Trust me a week with this man is more than enough for anyone.

Billy told me that Shellie gave a bunch of Ike's stuff to him. I told him the big box of CD's he had were mine. There were easily two thousand dollars worth of CD's in that box.

Billy gave them all away to his friends and never offered to give any of them back to me. I truly have no idea who is the worst excuse for a human being. Ike, Billy, or Shellie.

Billy said that he and Shellie both took Ike's computer and her computer to Landon Bagley. They told him about Ike's illegal sites. Billy said they both would make sure Ike went to prison. I went by the station and told Landon that I had the key to open the computer. That way he didn't have to break it open.

Landon came out to tell me that Billy had stripped everything off of it before he brought it in, including the power unit. He said that they had no idea what to do with it. Landon said since the last place he had seen it was at my house, that it was mine and for me to take it home.

I told him I didn't want it. He said that maybe he hadn't explained it very well to me so he sent Ike Wrench out. They sat the computer out there for me anyway. They both told me that if they kept it that I would have to be charged with everything they found on it since they last saw it at my place.

I would have to prove it was Ike's. All that was left was the outside shell, the mother board and the dual hard drives.

When I asked what happen to the pot case against Ike, Landon told me that they had wanted to take it to the grand jury because Judge Mavis would plead it down to a misdemeanor and slap his wrist and send him home. They said they didn't feel Ike deserved a break. Not all the cops were crooked.

He said that Handy wouldn't press charges against Ike. The DA said since the house was mine that I had to be charged with the pot, and I would have to be arrested, and then I had to prove it was Ike's. He said they didn't feel that was right, so they dropped it.

They said they were told the same thing about whatever they found on the computer so they wouldn't pursue it. Landon told me if I sued Ike, to ask him to go to court to explain all of this and what he saw on the camera to the judge.

My Space emailed Chris and said that Ike was trying to hack his computer to find our address. They also called the sheriff and said that they caught Ike trying to hack Chris's computer to find us. Even though we had the O.O.P and asked the sheriff to pursue charges, they said they had no idea what to do. Again, nothing was done. My Space blocked him off our sites.

We had just moved in here and didn't have internet yet. The manager told Chris he could run off his wirelessly until we had ours hooked up. Chris helped him to do a few things on his computer. So this helped them both. If My Space hadn't blocked Ike off of ours, he would have broken in to attack our landlord, thinking it was us.

Chapter 14

When I would go to visit Pete, this girl that was there named Angel Rush, started telling me things she knew about Ike. She had worked with him at the store he ran, and she was friends with Ike and Shellie. She told me that Ike cut me down all the time at the store and said I was crazy because I never did drugs.

She said she thought it was cool that I never gave into peer pressure. She said Ike always said it like it was something detestable to him. Everything else he said was lies so evidently the lies didn't stop even at the end.

She talked about how Ike would brag about what an expert thief he was. She said he would walk around the store and tell her to watch him on the camera. She said he would then walk up to the front and put all kinds of stuff on the counter out of his pockets and out of his pants that he had taken, and she didn't even see him do it.

I never told anyone about that look in Ike's eye when he said he was going to kill me and my family, not even when people would tell me he was probably just kidding with me. I often wondered if they would take it as a joke if he tried to choke and smother the life out of them on a daily basis.

Angel told me that Ike had a hit list of the people he said he would make sure to kill before he dies. I have heard him talk about this list for years. Then she told me how his light blue eyes would turn white and as cold as ice when he talk about killing these people. She said it gave her chills just thinking about it and that she wanted that crazy man off the streets.

I walked around twenty four seven with his finger prints as bruises for thirteen years. They were all over my body, especially my face and throat. I was very well aware of that look in his eyes.

How silly of me to still not see it was all a joke.

Angel told me one day that Ike had taken her several hours drive from home and told her to put out or get out. She said she didn't do either. She said Shellie was with them.

She told me he bragged that when his daughter Feather came to see him when she turned eighteen that she had turned out just like him and that she just agreed to kill someone for him already. He said he was really proud of her for being just like him.

I told the DA and was told not to worry, that Ike was just trying to get to me. Ike had no way of ever even guessing that Angel and I would ever meet. This was not a bluff. I know for a fact he means exactly what he says.

It made me sad though that this man hadn't seen his daughter in all these years and talking her into killing someone is the one thing he talked about, and that he is now bragging about it. He is willing to send her to prison and ruin her and her unborn child's life just so he can have an alibi.

Then I realized that it may not be Chris and me he is sending her after. When they let her foster parents adopt the girls, he was mad that they took his paycheck away. I tried to find a phone number for the foster mom, but they are unlisted. I didn't want to scare the younger ones by emailing them, so all I could do was pray God watches over them.

Angel said Ike said he never felt a thing when his mom died and that he never shed a tear.

I knew when I went to court that day Shellie was going to drop the charges on Ike when she came out and rudely told me she didn't need me there. Ike kept coming out in the hall to try and get my attention. I ignored it.

I asked her to please not drop the case. I told her to think about the fact that he has already killed her with his diseases. Angel had told me that Shellie asked Ike if he wore a condom when he was with Handy, and he said he did.

I told Shellie that was a lie. I told her there was proof on my camera if she wanted to see it. Landon Bagley was in the court room at that time. I told her to ask him, she didn't have to believe me.

I also told her that thinking Ike would be grateful for her dropping this case was a big mistake because he doesn't think that way. I told her the next time he beat her would be worse because he got away with it this time. I told her next time he may kill her. She said she wasn't dropping it.

Minutes later Ike strutted out of the court room like King Kong, his arms all bowed out. She dropped the case and let him move back in. She is probably the closest I have ever came to having an enemy, but my heart sank for her anyway. She had no idea what she just did.

Before they left the courtroom, I heard Shellie tell Billy's attorney that this was all a big misunderstanding. That they were all going to work it out.

Later Angel told me that her and Sharon had to pull Ike off of Shellie. She said he had the phone cord wrapped around her neck choking her, while he was beating her in the head with the phone. She said Shellie was yelling, "Just go ahead and shoot me. I'm dead anyway." They found out later Shellie just tested positive for HIV.

Angel told me that Billy had found a picture of his thirteen year old daughter Brittany on Ike's computer. I asked Billy. He said that his friend said he saw it and she was only wearing pants and nothing else.

Billy said he reported this to Ike Wrench and that he said he would take care of it. I was told that two other thirteen year old girls are now saying Ike molested them along with Brittany.

I flashed back to when Ike told me the only reason he had spent so many years with this older woman in Ohio was because of her daughter. He said the woman paid his way and the girl brought all her high school friends for him to sleep with. It didn't hit me until that moment that these were underage girls. He has been doing this his whole life.

I was then told by Angel that when they were at Ike and Shellie's house at a party once. Ike stood up and put a pill in the end of his d---. He told Shellie to suck it out. She said no. She knows by now he has killed her with his diseases already.

Angel said an underage girl that was there dropped to her knees and said, "I can do it better," and did, right in front of everyone. He is now killing children and no one is going to even try to stop him. Not even Shellie.

Billy saw Ike and Shellie in front of the courthouse after court. He stopped and threatened them both when he figured out she had dropped the case. Billy went to court and filed for a divorce and custody of their two girls. It's already too late for that family.

They have a younger daughter too. She has already said she woke up to find Ike watching her and her sister sleeping. She said Ike ran when he realized she was awake.

Billy said a guy he knows came to tell him that he was with Ike and Shellie when they had set this whole thing up to get him over there for Ike to kill him.

They later found a woman that was there after it happened when Ike and Shellie were bragging about how they set him up to be killed.

Ike dropped the case against Billy and Rick, and nothing happened to Ike. Once again, he got away with attempted murder.

Now Billy says he is friends with Ike and Shellie again for the sake of the girls. Ike has murdered this entire family, and they are all now friends. Isn't there something seriously wrong with this picture?

I see this man escalating and no one believes me. He has succeeded in killing these people and knows nothing will ever happen. Mark my words, somehow I know in my heart that God will find a way for this to come back to those protecting him. Somehow someone they love will end up getting this man's diseases and they will regret not stopping these people.

Just a few months ago Billy swore he and his family were going to kill both Ike and Shellie for doing this. I was told by a few people that Shellie knew Ike molested Brittany. Other people say that she not only knew but that she was a part of it. They probably drugged these girls to do it.

Early one morning I got a call from a detective. He said that TBI had called him and that he needed to talk to me about my ex. I went to see him. He asked me if I knew about Ike's pornos and if I had ever seen them.

I told him I had heard he was giving girls so many drugs that they got so messed up that they didn't know what they were doing. Then he would have sex with them while Shellie filmed it. Then she had sex with them. Then they went home and sold it on his personal porno site. I said I never saw it and never wanted to.

I told him who I knew had seen it and knew the girls that were on it. He asked if any of the girls were underage. I told him I didn't know but that Ike wouldn't have a problem with that.

Both of these people know they have fatal diseases and are killing these girls. They don't even tell them after the fact so they might have a fighting chance to get treated and survive it. No one has been arrested yet. I guess TBI ignored it too. I heard Ike filmed from the neck down so whoever was in it wouldn't be recognized.

I went to see this one girl that said Ike and several other people were at her house when she over dosed on Ike's drugs. They said Ike left when she went into seizures. They all left her to die.

She said the worst thing was that they left her kids there to see it. She did almost die. Ike is well aware of how much of what most people can take. Angel said she thinks he tried to kill this girl on purpose. She is one of them on the film, I heard.

They said she won't say anything because she is married. I have heard her husband has leukemia and has to live in a very sterile environment, or he could die. I would hate to be in her shoes when he finds out she killed him for sex and drugs.

Every time someone drags Ike off of Shellie, he always says it was all her fault that he had to try and kill her. I have told these women to either go to Ike's old doctor or to the health department and tell them what he is doing. No one has come forward yet.

When Ike got away with trying to murder all these people, I knew it has come back to me to stop him. I tried to give it to God.

I have witnesses and the police refuse to investigate. The woman from battered women's shelter called Harry Dawson and asked him why he never did anything. He told her that he told me he wasn't pursuing it because it was hearsay. All these witnesses willing to testify and he says it is hearsay. He never bothered to ever call me back, so how could he have told me that?

I go by my trailer from time to time to check on it. I gave it to a family up the street, and they were getting ready to move it so their kids would have a home. I heard they lived in a tent. Since Ike is still right next door, he saw them take the skirt and steps off to move it. He went in one night and took every light switch, plug in and light fixture down and smashed them.

He ripped all the wires out of the wall and ripped down the ceiling. This was almost a year after I had left there. I haven't said or done anything to this man. Every time I go by I find something else missing or torn up.

I tell the sheriff when I see something missing. I also say that I can't prove it was him. I also said that I think they should know he is still going on my land after the judge told him not to.

Harry calls me on my cell phone one Sunday to scream at me. First of all he asked me why I hadn't called him right back when he called me. I told him I was just getting out of church. He started telling me I am a liar because church doesn't last that long.

I went to church in Crossburg which is an hour time zone difference. Plus I was talking to a preacher that was there from Wartville. I asked him if he would take the bill of sale for my trailer to the couple I was giving the trailer to.

Harry said that everyone there knows Ike has never done anything to me and that if I didn't leave this poor man alone that he was going to personally arrest me for filing false reports. I told him that I am now working with an investigator and that I was calling my investigator to tell him that he just threatened me.

I told him that Ike had stolen two gates and a bunch of fence posts and my mail box. He painted the mail box bright orange and put it and the post it was on, right up in front of his place. Harry screamed that it belonged to Ike and that they all knew it.

That couple didn't take the trailer. I called the sheriff to come out to make a report on the damage. They sent a new kid. Sorry but if they are younger than me, they are a kid.

When I pointed up at the damage while he was taking pictures, I said, "Well, maybe someone was just stealing the wires." Then I realized the wires were still there. I knew then that this was done purely for destruction.

When I sat and looked at the damage he did, I realized that it not only took hours to do this much damage, it also took one hell of a rage. He wants me to know he still plans on coming after me.

Shellie told me that when Ike said he was still going to come after me. She told him since I live in an apartment that there were too many witnesses. Mark my words, he will brutally kill me the first chance he gets. He has no reason to stop now.

I told her to tell him to bring it on. I told her that all my neighbors are armed, and we had two big pit bulls right across the street.

I told her everyone was warned that the dogs got out from time to time and had trapped a few people in their apartments or cars, growling.

When their owner came over to play basketball by the dumpsters, he brought the dogs with him. When I went out to take my garbage, they always ran up wagging their little stump of a tail and would jump up to be petted. This even surprised their owner.

One other time I saw one of their babies ready to run out into the road so I ran over to tell her. The door was cracked open and one of the dogs ran out and jumped up to be petted. I heard someone hit their brakes and a woman jumped out and yelled, "I got a bat if you need it."

I told her I was fine. She said it scared her to death when she saw the dog jump on me. She said she knew the dogs and didn't trust them. I have a cautious respect for animals, but I have never feared one. I hope I don't regret that someday.

Shellie had also told me that several times when she got up at night Ike wasn't home. She said when she looked out the window, she could see lights on at my place. She knew Ike was over there, but she said she was afraid to ask him about it.

I also realized that this was thought out first because there were no tools in the trailer. He had to bring at least a screwdriver to do this with. The young cop actually filled out a report and sent me copies of the pictures he took. I thought that just maybe I could get something done this time. I really should stop thinking, huh.

I went to the Sheriff Department and told Landon what had happened. He said he was starting in a new town the next day so he would send someone else out to talk to me.

All of a sudden a woman came out and said that Sheriff Redletter wanted to talk to me. I had already heard he warned Ike and the brothers they were going to be raided, but I still try my best to give everyone the benefit of the doubt.

I went into his office. This man is over six foot tall, and I am pretty sure he is over three hundred pounds. He demanded to know what I said to Landon. I said I told him about the damage to my place, and he said he was transferring so he was sending someone else to talk to me.

I very nicely asked if he would consider sending someone out to take fingerprints so I could prove it was Ike that did this.

He started screaming at me and pounding on the desk demanding to know who was involved in this and who I gave the trailer to. As I said, I don't intimidate easily. I scooted my chair closer to the desk, leaned over and put my arm on the desk and leaned my head on my arm and patiently listened until he was done ranting and threatening.

The woman behind him that was filing papers looked over her shoulder and started to laugh when she saw me scoot closer to the desk to listen.

I told him that I didn't know everyone's names and I didn't have any phone numbers because I gave it to the church, and the church gave it to them. He demanded that I go out and write down my new phone number or he would have an officer take me out to get it.

When I came back in with the number, I said, "Now just so I have this straight, you are refusing to send someone out to fingerprint and help me right?" He said, "There isn't enough left to fingerprint."

I still wonder how he could say that, so matter of factly, when he never even looked at the pictures I had taken.

That officer hadn't even printed out the ones he sent to me later. He started to rant that Ike has never done anything to me, so I told him that he didn't have to worry about anything other than the damage because I had an investigator for the rest.

He got really mad then and told me he wouldn't allow anyone to investigate anything in his town, ever, for any reason. I said, "So you are going to try and stop an attempted murder investigation that one of your officers wouldn't look into in the first place."

He screamed until I told him that the guy had already proved Ike tried to kill me so it was already over. I told him all I was waiting for was a court date. He calmed back down when I said it was over and I left. My investigator Don Kamar said it was their job to go out and fingerprint and prove it was him. He said we would bring that up in court.

Mr. Kamar was upset that they tried to intimidate me and said he thought about calling and telling them who he is and for them to leave me alone. I want them to wait and introduce them selves in court so I can see it. An ambulance was sitting in front of the sheriff's office a little later.

When Ike kept believing what Billy and Shellie said before, I had said, I tried to tell him that if I said anything about him to anyone that I would say it to his face too and he knew it. I am the type that if I have to call the police I will be standing behind them when they come to the door saying, "It was me m----- f-----." If I have a problem with anyone, I go to them face to face and ask what the problem is.

One day when I was out helping Pete, I called Billy and asked how court was going. I could tell he was really high. He was still taking the pain pills from when Ike beat him with the bat. Billy said to me that he was going to shoot me because I made Rick rent his cabin to the people I gave my trailer to and that he doesn't like them.

When that fight happened Rick moved out of the cabin that his mom who had just died had left him. He knew Ike would come after him. He said that he could tell Ike had been there already looking for him. People try to convince me Ike was just kidding, yet grown men run from him. Even armed grown men run away.

Angel was there at Pete's and asked if she could get a ride when I was leaving. I told her alright but I was stopping at Billy's first. She said, "Are you crazy girl? He just threatened to shoot you." I told her that was why I was going there. I was going to see him face to face.

No, I don't have a death wish, but I'm not a runner.

When I got there Billy's girlfriend said she thought he had passed out already. I went to his room, and I pulled up a chair and watched him sleep until he woke up and saw me there. I told him I had nothing to do with who that cabin was rented to and he acted like he didn't remember saying anything.

I told him that I told Rick those people had asked if I knew of any place for rent. I told him that I also told Rick that they asked if they could rent my trailer until it was moved and I said no.

Billy and his girlfriend both confirmed that Shellie had just tested positive for HIV. I still don't think it has sunk in yet that Billy is positive too. All I can do is tell them. I can't make them believe it or try to be treated.

Robby Lane came to me in a panic and begged me to help him get out of the trouble he had gotten into with A.T.F. Ike had called them and said Robby had blown up the local dump with dynamite. I found the guy that was investigating it and told him that if Robby had done this, that I would have heard him bragging about it all those times he came over drunk, or high.

I told him and Sheriff Redletter about the pistol Ike said he bought from Tom Espier to kill my family and me with. I already knew Redletter protected Tom's wife but didn't think about it at the time. I just wanted this man stopped before he could kill me and my family or anymore children. I really want to be here for my sons and my granddaughters.

Robby told me if I helped him he would talk to my investigator for me and tell him all he knows about Ike and the fact that he said he knows the reason Harry protected Ike. Robby said it was because Ike has been giving him drugs to look the other way.

He said everyone around there has known it for years. He said that is why no one goes against Ike because they know he is a snitch and pays the law drugs. "Hoop there it is." The other piece to the puzzle now in place. In my heart I think I always knew it but didn't want to believe it.

An hour later ATF not only dropped the case against Robby, but they also apologized and returned everything they had taken from him. When I asked Robby when he wanted to talk to Mr. Kamar, he suddenly had nothing to say. He swore he didn't know a thing.

God is already getting even with him. He is in trouble over meth charges and theft, and he and his girlfriend were just evicted by his girlfriend's parents. They are pretty much on the run now. He knows he can never come to me for anything again.

He is such a weasel that when he knew the police were coming, he ran and left her with his meth lab. She had enough sense though that she turned him in.

Not long after I told Sheriff Redletter about the investigator, I heard that Tom committed suicide. When I talked to Bea, she said that it wasn't suicide because he couldn't have shot himself in the head twice.

I was told that a few years back when one of their own sheriffs quit and was going to turn states evidence against the Sheriff's department, they found the man and his two small sons shot and the police said it was a murder suicide.

What wasn't in the paper was that the two boys were shot with a smaller caliber bullet and that gun wasn't there. I still wonder if they were trying to cover their tracks with Tom and if I was next.

Tom was a nice man. I even called him after Ike said I stole his pot and told him the police found it and took it. I didn't want him mad at me. He said he was fine with it and not to worry about it.

Living in an apartment seems to have a definite advantage. Maybe the police won't come after me either.

Bea said the guy running for sheriff now said he knows about the corruption and said he needs help weeding out the bad cops when he is elected. I told her to have him call my investigator.

I have also heard that the corruption is so bad that two surrounding counties want the Sheriff's department in Wartville closed down.

When I was at Bea's one day, this girl came in upset that her father just died. They said this one guy had done stuff against him for years and he finally got so fed up that the police did nothing that he set his own house on fire in protest.

They said when the fire department showed up, he shot himself. Everyone there said they think the police shot him and covered it up. Everyone in this town hates this Sheriff's department.

When I picked up the 911 tape for court the guy that made the CD said he was very concerned about it. He said that there was a long period of time between calls and there was no evidence that they ever called to check on me or sent anyone out. I said that was because they didn't do either.

He said their "only" job was supposed to be my safety and that they should be sued for not doing their job. Remember, Ike hadn't hung up the phone before he threatened me again. It was on the recording, and they still didn't call or send anyone out.

Chris and I both started looking for guns, but we can't find anything we can afford, not even at a pawn shop. We both want to get some training and get licensed to carry a concealed weapon.

I am determined that Ike never gets close enough to put his hands on me or my sons or granddaughters. I have traveled all over the world alone and have never felt the need for a weapon. I no longer have that luxury. If it comes down to him or me, it will be him.

I saw a friend of Ike's at the store one day, and I asked him to tell Ike something for me. He said no problem. I first told him to look at my face and make sure I wasn't saying this as a threat or in anger. I told him that I will be licensed soon and if Ike comes near me or my family that I will have to shoot him. He said he would tell him.

Since I couldn't afford a gun, I started working out a lot to get my strength back. I also lost some of those extra pounds I had put on. I don't think I had realized until then just how angry I had finally gotten.

Everyday I would start my routine calmly. By the time I was done a few hours later, I would be in tears, angrily doing my boxing routine thinking that I wish Ike was there for a practicing dummy. I dropped those extra pounds pretty fast that way, though.

I just flashed back to how I put on those pounds. When I was skinny and took care of myself, Ike always wanted to fool around. Even when I told him nothing would ever happen again. So I put on weight. I stopped showering when he was around and wore the ugliest, ripped up and stained up sweats I could find.

When he would leave for a while, I would shower real quick and put back on the old sweats, so he wouldn't know I had showered. That was also when I would call my family to catch up with everything. The more time I have to think about all he did to us, the more I realize he really is lucky I am a calm person.

The church had told me when I gave that couple with the kids my trailer that they would help me build a house on my land because I gave up my home to help this family. Now that they didn't take it because Ike destroyed it, I guess I am out of a home.

I asked Rick if he wanted the trailer. His cabin has no bathroom. If he moves it to his land right up the road, then he has an instant bathroom, kitchen and bedrooms. He said he really wanted it but couldn't find anyone to move it for him. I just wanted all those bad memories gone.

At first Brian was going to take over the payments on my land and keep it for his daughter, but we found out that in this state you have to be eighteen to have land in your name, and she is only two.

When Landon gave me Ike's computer and said they wanted them to charge me with what was on it, I took out the hard drives and sent them to Mr. Kamar. Since he is an investigator, he can't be charged with anything on it.

I asked him to see what was on it and to see if any of it could be used when I finally get a court date against Ike. He said someone is working on it. If they find anything with underage girls on it, which I know it is there somewhere, then TBI can use it.

Chris's computer that Brian gave us crashed soon after we got it back. Ike had put an illegal copy of Windows on it he had pirated. I threw it away. It was getting too old to fix.

One day when Ike was on his computer, I saw in big letters the name Teen P----, on Ike's screen. There was a bunch of pictures of crotches on there.

Ike said he had no idea how they got there. I really resent someone treating me like I am that stupid. But as I said, pick your battles.

Chris told me he no longer celebrated his birthday anymore because so many of them had been ruined in the past. I hope he doesn't mean by Ike. He ruined mine, but I didn't think he did this to Chris. Someday he will tell me when he is ready.

I went out of my way all those years to make sure Ike's girls had a happy birthday every year. I have always done that, even for strangers. I have always thought that everyone's birthday is special and deserves to be celebrated. Even if you don't think it is a special day, I guarantee your parents think it is special.

When we first got this apartment, Chris didn't talk to me much. He was upset over everything that was happening. I let him get over it in his own time. Now he comes in after work and talks to me about his day.

I can't wait for the day Brian is over it. I can tell he isn't quite there yet. He feels I deserted my family for this man. That kind of pisses me off because I saw what this man was from the very beginning. At first I was there to protect his girls. Then it was self preservation and to protect my sons. At least he brings my granddaughters to see me for the holidays.

Adam moved to Texas. He said there just wasn't enough work in Alabama to live on. He is now seeing that Texas isn't any different.

He called me recently to tell me he is right next door to Ft. Hood where that guy just shot all those people. Adam was at the Laundromat at the time. Life throws enough crap at you to deal with ladies. You don't have to deal with an evil maniac too.

Every time I tried to get on the computer when I was with Ike, he wouldn't let me. He told me my patent ideas were stupid.

Now that I have my own computer I turned in all those ideas I had, and I have one patent pending. When that one is done, I have three more to be patented. The patent pending I was told is gold and worth millions as soon as it is produced and sold. That could still take a few years. I have something to look forward to.

I now get free product in the mail from time to time to test, and then I get paid for my opinion of it. I even get new foods to try out. I play games that I have won money on and surveys I have gotten paid for. It doesn't pay a lot, but since my check all goeson rent and utilities it helps with the extras.

When Ike stole all my things the first time, he found some nudes that I had taken for Chris's father. I had a photographer friend take them for me. I never even showed them to Ike. Debney found them when she was destroying all my pictures.

She gave them to this other guy and told him to put them up on bulletin boards all over town for her. The guy kept them instead. He told me about it later. When I asked for them back, he swore he threw them away. I hope he did.

This time Ike started telling guys that he would start handing out nudes of me to them. Since I even slept in my clothes around him, I am pretty sure he doesn't have any. None have surfaced yet. I told them that if they don't have two small tattoo's then they aren't me, they are photo shopped. That, I wouldn't put past him doing.

It took me a year calling everywhere to find someone to take my case. One attorney here said he could guarantee he could put Ike in prison, but it would cost me five thousand. When you are on disability, he may have well said a million.

I was finally referred to a place called Police Abuse. The guy told me he would take my case for five hundred. I sold the little Geo Storm to pay the investigator. I still lost money on the car, but I think that makes it poetic justice, don't you? It was sold to send Ike to prison where he belongs.

I had started writing OPRAH and DATELINE NBC a few years ago about what Ike was getting away with doing to me and my son. I already said I am persistent as hell when I know I am right.

Police Abuse is affiliated with DATELINE NBC. When I first hired them, the sheriff and Harry Dawson hadn't threatened me yet, so I just told them to see why they obviously weren't doing their jobs. Now it is much more serious, but they did all this themselves.

I have had two on line audio tapes made of my testimony to Mr. Kamar, another investigator and several attorneys that were present at the time.

I have two witnesses that have said they will come over and tape their testimony too. They said they are more than willing to testify against the More County Sheriff's department too.

They already have all my paper work documented on computer that will put Ike away once I get a court date. All the paperwork Judge Stevens and Judge Mavis refused to look at too. Ike will go to prison even if he kills me first because all the information is out there now.

I also sent them a copy of the first rough draft of my book. It is basically my written testimony. Later I got Skype and did an online audio, video tape of the same testimony. I just hope this isn't a case where they are waiting for him to kill me so it makes a bigger story.

I also mailed a copy of the rough draft to OPRAH, DATELINE NBC, AMERICA'S MOST WANTED and 48 HOURS MYSTERY. Ike still may kill me, but now I can rest knowing he won't get away with it.

I am finally getting things done with my life and want to continue to do more. I have other women's rights in this state to fight for too. It isn't just my cause anymore.

A lot of women that had heard what happened to me came up and asked me to write a book. They said that it would help other women to see that there are still evil men like Ike out there. When Mr. Kamar asked me to try and write down in my own words what happened he said, "This is starting to read like an extensive murder mystery novel."

Writing it all down was not only very therapeutic, it really was becoming a novel. Hence, my decision to finish my book. This state needs to have their butts kicked for not protecting these women, not just me. I intend to be that butt kicker.

Chris went to Amsterdam to see a girl he had talked to for years on line. He liked her a lot. He spent about a month there. Since I was in a small apartment now I had nothing to keep my mind occupied, so I cried a lot. I missed all my children when they left home. I missed them every time they left home, but Chris was the last one at home. It was definitely much harder.

His experience worked out great for him but please be careful who you talk to online. My sister married a guy she met online and he later went to prison for molesting her granddaughter. My father's sister who was raising her grandson let him invite a couple of teenagers over to play video games that he had met online. Later my aunt and her grandson were found beaten to death.

Chapter 15

Just after we moved to this town, they had a huge coal ash spill just a couple miles away.

We kept hearing it on the news but really didn't think much of it. When we first started getting sick we thought it was a cold and went out to get cold and flu medicine.

Several weeks went by, and I started getting really dizzy. The room would feel like it was spinning before I even opened my eyes. I literally bounced off the walls trying to walk a few feet to the bathroom. And it wasn't going away.

I waited for weeks before I even went to the hospital. It got so bad I couldn't get out of bed. I started getting the worst leg cramps every morning. I jumped out of bed one morning to try and make the leg cramp go away and instantly fell back on the bed. I knew then that this wasn't a cold. I also knew I couldn't wait for my regular doctors appointment anymore.

After I went to the hospital, Chris started telling me his symptoms too. His were worse than mine, but he hadn't wanted to worry me. He said he started having lapses of memory. He said he would leave work and have to call back and ask them where he was going and how to get there.

He said he would slam on his brakes thinking he was about to run a red light, only to see the light was green. He had to drop out of one of his college classes because five minutes after reading, he couldn't remember what he read and he was too sick to go to class.

He has an almost photographic memory. He still totally remembers books he read as a child.

When he got the job at Pizza Hut, he got a map and remembered all the streets and how to get to all of them. We moved here specifically for him to go to this college and now he had to drop out.

When I went to the hospital, I told them that I wanted a blood test to see if the ash spill was causing this problem. The doctor told me he was going to rule out other causes first. They took blood but used it to see if it was the flu or allergies.

They checked my heart and did a cat scan of my head. The doctor came back after the scan and asked me to step into the other room so he could show me something. He showed me several other so called normal scans, then showed me mine.

I was told that my brain was shrinking. He then asked me if he could take another blood test to check for chemicals. They found arsenic, lead and mercury in my blood. Not high levels, thank God or it would have killed me. They said for me to go to my regular doctor and tell him what they found. My doctor said he had no idea what to do. He said he had never dealt with this before.

I went home and looked up online the effects of arsenic and other heavy metals on the brain and muscles. I read on line that brain atrophy from arsenic and other heavy metals can later cause Parkinson's, Dementia, and Alzheimer's.

When the price of food went up with the gas prices, I had to stop buying bottled water. Now I had no choice but to start buying bottled water again or continue getting poisoned. Even my plants were dying when I used tap water on them. TVA kept saying on the news that they were safe levels of these chemicals out there. And that the public had nothing to worry about.

Chris and I went to the next town meeting just to see what they planned to do about this. They said it wasn't their fault and that we all had to prove it was them. They said the water and air was safe because they checked them.

People were standing up and telling them that they now have unexplained serious diseases. They told everyone they had better have proof from a reputable source that they were at fault. They basically dared everyone to prove it and sue.

This really pissed me off so I emailed Erin Brockovich. She took our case. I was her fourth case. Now she has hundreds. I was on the news the night I met with her. They showed me talking to her, then they interviewed me later. I was a little pissed that they took what I said out of context, but what can you do? Erin took her own air and water tests and proved they were lying about all of it.

She found them trying to shred documents that proved they knew all along this was going to happen but didn't want to spend the money to fix the problem. Now a year later, TVA is on the news saying they are sorry and it was all their fault. Erin says to wear a mask if you have to go outside because this stuff causes cancer too.

Chris and I were most concerned with the fact that if it was affecting healthy adults like this, what is it doing to the children around here. The county said that if the school kids had gotten sick that they would have come forward. They didn't even check on them.

Most of our problems stopped when I went back to bottled water, but when it rains, I get nose bleeds and blisters in my mouth. It got worse when they started transporting the ash to places in trucks. They drove the trucks right past our building and right past the elementary school here on the corner. What were they thinking?

We can barely afford to live here. We sure as hell can't afford to move away from my son's job. Most of his classes are now done on line. So in effect Ike running us out of our home may have killed us after all.

I am worried about what the long term problems are going to be for me and Chris. Are we going to end up in wheelchairs drooling and wetting ourselves? Not remembering our own families? Or are we going to be in the hospital fighting cancer the rest of our lives? Even if they pay us, is it going to be enough to pay for our doctors later?

Just before the spill, the news station broke a story that TVA had given all their employees credit cards for their expenses. The employees had put over twenty two million dollars on that account for new cars, stereos and video games, just that year alone.

One guy bought himself six brand new cars. When they told us that TVA knew the spill was going to happen, they also said they were told that it could be fixed for twenty five million. They chose not to spend the money on the problem but spent it on their big boy toys instead.

Now TVA says that since they are a government entity that they don't feel they should be held responsible. The judge ruled they were wrong and is going ahead with the law suits filed against them. Erin says they can't file as a government entity anyway since their CEO makes more than the president of the United States.

They have already raised everyone's rates to cover the clean up costs so they aren't paying for it anyway. The public that they poisoned are. The spill covered over three hundred acres. It was in the nearby lakes. The dike failure released over 5.4 million cubic yards of fly ash.

I am hoping that my story ends with Ike going to prison. Now that Ike isn't around to torture us Chris has already weaned himself off of all those medicines he had to take. He is still working full time and going to college full time, and he just started ministry training. He quit smoking, too.

Brian just bought Chris a really nice guitar and case. He is thinking of starting to play with the church band. I wanted him to get back into his music. He writes music too. Chris and Brian had talked about making video games. Brian was going to go back to college to learn graphic design, and Chris was going to write the music for the games.

J 103, a local religious radio station here, gave Chris some concert tickets last week. I told him I was happy he got them. Then he said, "You mean happy we got them. You are going with me aren't you?" We sat next to his favorite D.J. way up front. The concert was great. Chris's favorite group there was "Skillet."

What I loved the most was watching Chris have the time of his life. I haven't seen him smile like that in years. The damage Ike did will always be there under the surface, but we are getting through it.

My family won't be safe until this man is gone. I'm not so sure that even with him in prison we will be safe. I hope that I can get a court date soon so all of this can be left behind, like a really bad dream.

Ike sits up every night thinking of how he can hurt everyone around him. I can't stress enough how this man has let the evil take over his life. He will even hurt his girls if he lives long enough to see the rest of them. If not physically, definitely emotionally and mentally. It has become his way of life. I'm not sure he can stop it anymore.

He loved to drive fast to scare the girls and drive close to the edge of the road on winding old mountain roads. He wouldn't just do it once or twice. He would keep them screaming. He loved it.

When my father said he had never met a stranger, that it was just a friend he hadn't met yet, I started seeing everyone so differently. I spent my life trying to live up to that. Ike was so evil he almost broke me. I started to hate everyone except my sons.

Ike cut my sons down so much that I know he was trying to turn me against them. He tried to turn them against me too. I told him that was never going to work, but it didn't stop him from trying every day.

For a long time I didn't think I was going to get over that feeling. For so many years, I thought I was never going to get away from this man alive. I still get mad when someone says Ike was only kidding, but I do realize that I used to think the same way. I actually stopped speaking to a close family member when he said it.

When I would meet women in the past that were in the same situation, I would think, "What an idiot she is to take that from this guy. Why doesn't she just leave or call the police? Maybe she just likes the abuse." Now I wish I had taken the time to help them.

The police abused me almost as much as Ike did. They stomped all over my rights time and time again to tip toe around the rights of a true criminal.

I truly believe Ike should be held somewhere with terrorists or the criminally insane. And unfortunately, that is no joke!

So many people said to me that they would talk to me again once I got rid of him. Now I think, "Were they really that stupid or were they just too lazy to try and help?" This really was beyond my control, and it may be beyond these other women's control. If you think something isn't right with your friend, ask questions and don't judge. This may just happen to you someday.

I still live every day knowing this man can come and kill me or my sons anytime and will probably get away with it. Until you live it, you never know what it's like. I lived this hell, day in and day out for thirteen years. I was forced to live with this man for more than five years after I knew his bodily fluids could kill me.

I didn't even get much of a break when he was in jail. He wrote the threats to me daily. I kept the letters. If I'm not around when they get a court date, I hope the letters and my taped testimony help to put him away. Ike told me that he was the one that got his wife hooked on drugs. He was an adult when they married. I think he said she was fifteen.

He also said on their wedding night she spent the night with the best man, and he spent the night with her cousin. Those little girls must have really lived through hell. I check on them all the time on the website they emailed me on. They are all beautiful little girls. They seem happy and healthy. They are all cheerleaders.

Ike said flat out that it was his fault that all of his girls are crack babies. I still think it is so sad that he has no higher expectations for those girls than him saying they were all going to be drug whores and have lots of babies. I just hope they listened to me when I told them to get a good education and never take crap from anyone.

I'm sure I didn't mention the fact that Ike is almost fifty. He was an adult doing this to people. Now he is an adult doing this to children. I honestly can't remember a time that he wasn't coming at me like a rabid pit bull. The physical attacks were very brutal. The verbal, mental and emotional abuse was constant.

Ike would tell me he was going to chain me to a tree and strip me down and leave me to the wild animals and storms. He would tell me he knew of a hundred and fifty foot hole that all the drug dealers had been dropped into and that he was going to drop me in it.

He said I would lay there for days all broken up looking at the rotting bones of all these other people, knowing I would never be found. He said he was going to bury me in my own septic tank. He would tell me in detail how he was going to torture and kill my entire family. He has accused me of some of the sickest things I have ever heard. Things I wish I had never heard.

Every holiday that he had threatened to slaughter my family, on the news there would be someone that did do exactly that to their family. This is not love ladies.

I still don't date. Mostly because I am happier that way but a lot because even though I still test negative for everything, in the back of my mind I think what if they just missed it for some reason. Do I really want to kill someone for sex? Send me lots of batteries!

A friend asked me once what I wanted for my birthday. As a joke I said, "A life time supply of batteries." He choked on his drink, then said, "A lot of women think that but no one ever had the nerve to say it" I guess that's part of the reason people keep telling me I have moxie. I'm not afraid to go anywhere or do anything or say what I think.

I still wonder how I missed getting all of his diseases. Ike used to put his hands in his pants and scratch like crazy, then he would try to rub my face.

He would cuss me like a dog when I put my hand up to stop him. This is pure hatred and pure evil! I am going to need a lot of prayers to help me get the people that can stop him, to stop him. I keep remembering something I heard on TV: "Evil triumphs when good men do nothing!"

I realize now that all those times Ike said he was sorry in the beginning he wasn't. He was just trying to keep me from calling the police. After he realized the police wouldn't do anything, he never apologized and never had an inkling of remorse, ever.

He constantly attacked with no provocation. Without even the slightest hesitation, he would hold me down and look me in the eyes while he was trying to choke and smother the very life out of me.

For years he told me every day that he was going to start shooting me up with drugs a little at a time every night in my sleep until I was addicted. He taunted me everyday saying he was going to do this. I would try to check when I showered to make sure he didn't do it. He didn't want to waste his drugs I guess.

He would walk past me in the hall way smiling and suddenly slam my head against the wall.

Then he would tell me to shut up and take it like a man. If I asked him why he did it, he would tell me since there was no blood or brains splattered that it didn't hurt anyway.

He took and took and took and not once did anything to help in return. He tried to push out my eyes, and he beat my teeth out of my head. He tore ligaments, broke bones, and caused nerve damage that will never heal.

Every time I went out to feed my cats he would scream that I was just out there to get men's attention as they drove by. This was out in the country. Most people passed the house doing sixty miles an hour.

The emotional and mental pain he brought me my sons and many others will never heal. Chris and I both still have night mares, although they are becoming less often.

When Ike worked at that store, he would come in telling me about all the great meals he had every day knowing he had stranded me at home with no money, no food, and no transportation.

He never once even brought me a soda or even a bag of chips. He called me a few times and told me what they were serving that day and asked if I wanted him to bring me something. Then he would come in and laugh and say he forgot it. Knowing I waited all day for this meal.

He would call everyday to tell me about the roasts and hams and pork chops they made to serve in the attached restaurant. He would describe how great all the side dishes were and desserts he just ate.

He would brag about all of this to everyone. As they say, to pour salt in the wound. He would purposely waste the food I bought for the month so I would have to wait in line for hours in the rain and snow and freezing cold to get a box of canned vegetables from the church.

This is America people. Why are we worrying so much about other countries when the people here are starving? I hate to think about anyone going hungry, so it really bothers me that I was forced to be one of those people.

I did without things when my kids were little to make sure they had more. But to be forced to do without by the man I was forced to take care of. Yeah, I think this has made me a little bitter.

I really hope I get over it someday. Slowly I think I am. I really fought hard against letting this make me bitter. I think I need to work on that a little more.

Just think of how you would feel if you came home to find everything you spent your life buying and saving, even keep sakes, just disappeared. He not only did this to me once, but twice. He tried several other times to do the same thing but failed.

I was locked out of my own home while other women slept in my bed and wore my clothes and stole my things. Women that left blood and other fluids behind that could have given me diseases that would kill me very slowly and very painfully.

I raised my sons to respect people and their belongings. When I lived in California and someone had a hard time, I let people move into my living room until they could get on their feet. I try to give people a hand up when they need it. These people kick people down and just keep kicking.

Ike constantly called my sons and a lot of other guys faggots. This was his favorite word for a while. He would cuss me because my sons weren't out trying to jump on every woman that walked by. Outside of having wives and girlfriends, they all have female friends. Ike can't seem to comprehend this. Ike has no idea what being a gentleman even means.

Before my mother died, she called me to tell me she loved how I raised my sons to be such sweet down to earth, caring men. It meant a lot to me to hear that from her. She didn't hand out compliments very often. I couldn't even tell Ike what she said. He would have found a reason to try and beat me for it.

He tried to beat me for even speaking to people that he brought in to my home. I told him that the simple solution was to stop bringing them into my home.

If you have a holiday that wasn't exactly the greatest just think of how every year for thirteen years he went out of his way to beat me and threatened to slaughter my entire family for no reason. He meant it every time. Maybe yours won't seem so bad.

By the way, I don't think I specified that my sons never stayed more than a few hours every time they came for the holidays. Brian has his wife's family to see at that time too. So it wasn't like Ike had any big family crisis to ever deal with.

I also forgot to mention that Ike was the only child from a wealthy family. How difficult could his holidays have been actually? Another thing I have thought of is the fact that after he booby trapped my place to burn me alive he sat next door for a month or more waiting for it to happen. My son was with me, and he would have died too.

Ike never once tried to undo it or warn anyone it was going to happen. The electrician said the noise would have scared the whole neighborhood. He had to have sobered up at least one day out of all this time but still wanted this to happen to me.

He couldn't help me paint because he was afraid of heights, but he climbed on top of my roof to put holes in it to vent the fire he was trying to start. Then he stole my ladder when he left. He stole my garden hose and all my gardening and pruning tools. They don't even have grass or any trees where they live next door.

He felt nothing. He never shed a tear when his own mother died. He tried to talk his pregnant daughter into taking someone's life for him. Not once caring what this would do to her or her unborn child. She has two little girls now.

Because he put me so far in debt and kept stealing my money and all my things to sell to get more money for his and all his drug whores drugs, I was homeless for over two straight years.

He tried for years to talk hundreds of other people into beating or killing me. When that didn't work, he tried to pay people drugs to do it. Think about it, most drug addicts will do anything for drugs.

Having sex with little children is sick enough but doing it knowing they will die slow and painful deaths as a result of it. And the fact that these girls are now killing everyone they sleep with after that for the rest of their lives and don't even know it. Ike knows it and doesn't care.

Using a condom could have possibly saved their lives but even that was too much to ask of this man. That's beyond sick. It's pure evil!

Ike had already admitted to Billy some time back that he stole my mailbox, the same mailbox that Harry Dawson threatened me over, saying Ike had never done anything to me.

I found out from Billy that Ike admitted to him recently that he was the one that took down and smashed all the plug ins, light fixtures and light switches at my place a year after I left. Ike said he purposely left everything he smashed so I would find it and know it was him.

Ike already knew his buddies at the Sheriff's department wouldn't do anything. He ripped out all the ceiling and pulled the wires through the paneling. A friend of Ike's later tore down the rest of the paneling and stole the copper wire and sold it to the salvage place in Sun, Tennessee. I'm sure Ike told him to do it.

The salvage place was going to mail me the receipt where he paid for the wire, but he said when he mentioned it to the police, they told him he couldn't do that. They told him he could only give it to them and only if they ask for it. The guy is bragging about taking the wire.

Billy said Ike Wrench never got back to him about Ike having pictures of his thirteen year old daughter with no clothes on or the fact she said Ike molested her and her mother knew about it.

After the case was dropped where Ike beat Billy in the head with a metal baseball bat, Billy said he became Ike's friend again for their children's sake. Even after the judge told him to never let the girls near Ike or Shellie again. This must have been torture for Brittany to see these people in her home again. I can't comprehend this at all.

Ike hit my son in the face with the door, and I wanted to rip him apart. Ike tried to beat this man to death. He gave his wife and possibly his daughter fatal diseases and probably killed him too when they exchanged all that blood in their fight, and he wants to be friends! Ike must have a lot of good drugs right now or he is cooking again.

Billy said Ike asked his girlfriend Gene to come over to have sex with him. Billy told her to get Ike over to their place. Billy said he hid in the closet to shoot Ike when he came in, but Ike never showed. I guess they aren't friends anymore.

Billy said he was going to kill Ike somehow in the near future. As I told Mr. Kamar, if he does the crooked cops will try to frame me for it because they have protected Billy and his brother for many years.

I have left my number several times for an attorney through the investigators office to call me to get a court date. No one has called yet. I don't understand this either.

This man is killing people daily, even children, and no one other than me seems to be concerned with getting him off the streets.

Chapter 16

The electric company suddenly sent me my deposit. The letter said it was because I had been a loyal customer for over seven years with no cut offs. I didn't think anything else of it.

I stopped by my land when I took Pete to pay his monthly bills and noticed my meter was gone. I was then told by a neighbor that my security light had not been on for a while either. I went to the electric company and asked what was going on. They told me that when they went to read the meter the month before, it was gone, so they cut everything off.

I told them I had nothing to do with it and I want it all put back on. They said that whoever took the meter also tore up the wires on the pole and I would have to pay for repairs. They said I would have to pay for re-inspection and buy a new, more expensive meter in order for them to do that.

They also said that I had to be living back on the land first so I could protect their meter. They said that since it was not my fault that they would work with me when I do get that done.

I have called everyday for over a week now to get an officer to go out and see the damage and file the report I need to do something about finding my meter. As usual no one called me back.

I love my land and want to move back there, but with these people still living there and still getting away with everything, what would be the point? All of this is getting to hard to bare.

Billy said Ike has put hidden camera's all over the house to tape people that come there, without their permission, especially in the bathroom. Billy said he has more than one camera in the bathroom. I am hoping Ike is stupid enough to keep all the tapes.

That will prove everything I have said. I hope he taped his and the sheriff's deals too.

Angel said she was there when Ike got calls from women on the internet to pay him to sleep with them and put it on his porno site. Maybe he taped those conversations too. She said Ike said he wasn't going to see any of these women. I said, "I guarantee the second you got out the door, he called them right back."

I finally drove out to the sheriff's department and was told that they were too busy to go so far out in the county to check out my stolen meter, but if I told them about it, they would file a report. I got a copy of the report right then and took it to the electric company. They said they would try to find my meter.

When I got to my place to take more pictures of the new damage, I noticed the same rusty screws Ike had used many times to barricade me in screwed back into my doors. I then saw the same sheriff that just told me he was too busy to go that far out, just a half a block from my place. I told him that when I got there I discovered that Ike had barricaded me out of my own house.

He just said okay and said he would discuss it at another time. I know he will be too busy again if I go out there. I also told him to put on my other report that Ike admitted to Billy that he had in fact done the damage I had reported before. He said he would do that right away. What a surprise, I checked and it was never done. A report of Ike screwing my doors to the frames was never filed either.

Harry Dawson knows I have all these witnesses to the things Ike has done. Does he really think this won't come out in court someday? I guess he counts on me not having the money to press it.

I took the screws out of the front door and couldn't even kick it open from the inside. I don't know what he has done to it. I had told some people that I considered sitting there one night to see who keeps doing this so I know for sure. So Ike may have screwed the doors to the frames thinking that I was in there.

Billy tried to tell me the electric box that was left on the pole was his. Funny he never mentioned this all the years I had that box. I scratched my initials in the electric box so if someone takes it maybe they can find it. If they even bother to look for it.

I went to Billy's before I left out there. He said that Ike and Shellie have a warrant out for them for not coming to court on their case with Billy and Rick. He said that Judge Mavis told him that they have some extremely serious charges on Ike that they need him in court for.

Billy said Judge Mavis said that one of the charges was meth related and the other was so serious that he couldn't discuss it. The judge said this a few months ago and no one has been arrested yet as usual.

Billy told me that Ike's oldest daughter, the one Ike bragged was going to kill someone for him, was going to move in with her dad at first. Now she won't even speak to him. Then he turned to me and said, "I think he was molesting his girls, too."

Then he said, "You won't believe all the things he is doing now. He is getting out of control!" He started to tell me, but then his girlfriend said they had to go somewhere. He said he would talk to me about it later and they left. If Billy can say this with all he has done, it has to be pretty bad.

Maybe Feather just agreed to kill someone long enough to get away from him. I always prayed she would turn out to be a better person. I hope she saw that look in his eye when he talks about killing people and has the good sense to never come back around him. I hope she keeps her sisters away, too.

I keep wondering why he keeps beating up my trailer. It makes no sense this long after I have moved and he knows I gave it away already. What does he think he is proving? Does he think this proves he is still in control?

After Ike moved in with Shellie, he over dosed on a bunch of pills and he took something that is supposed to help people get off drugs at the same time. You can say it, he is an idiot. Rick had to revive him when he turned blue. I asked Rick why he would do that.

That was before he was forced to move to save himself from this man. I am sure it is a decision he is regretting now. Ike is a threat to himself and everyone around him.

It proves to me that he is getting more and more out of control than ever. I wish the sheriff would finally see it. I truly hope they see it before he kills someone else. Ike has escalated to the point that he is now openly doing these things to people. He doesn't care that there are witnesses anymore. He knows no one will do anything to him. He does what he wants right in front of people now.

I realized the other day that I have started to relax and not look over my shoulder at every sound. I realized one morning that I didn't wake up balled up in the fetal position with my hands and arms around my face and neck for protection.

At first I was happy about that. Then I realized that is what Ike is waiting for. When I, Chris, and the police stop looking, that is when he will strike, without pause and without remorse.

I know in my heart without any doubt that when he gets high and convinces himself the police won't suspect him, he will kill us so brutally that it will be talked about for a long time. I am telling you now that all this could have been prevented, but no one will do anything until it is too late for my family.

I will repeat, EVIL TRIUMPS WHEN GOOD MEN DO NOTHING!

I said to my friend just the other day that for thirteen years I was this man's only conscience, and now he is with someone that has no conscience. That is a very scary thought to me and should be to everyone around him.

I flashed back to all those years that Ike told all those people how his father would get on his knees to beat him for hours while he hid under the bed and how I and all those people felt sorry for him. One day after telling me about it again, he laughed and said, "Maybe I shouldn't have raped my little step sister." He was always evil, and the drugs just made him worse.

When Jed helped Ike steal all my things it took a while to move it all next door to Shellie's place. Jed said he fell asleep in my trailer. When he woke up Ike was screwing the doors to the frame and sealing him inside until he got back from court. I wonder how he talked Ike into letting him out. Once Ike starts something, he doesn't just change his mind.

Ike had told him the night before that he was going to do that and the guy told him no he wasn't. To Ike that was a dare. I still keep thinking that if I hadn't realized Ike had booby trapped my place, Chris and I would already be dead or at the least permanently injured. Ike still probably wouldn't have been arrested. What is it going to take with these people?

I am sitting here so frustrated and so infuriated over the fact that this cruel, evil man is still out there killing young girls, ruining people's lives and still planning on destroying mine and my sons' lives.

No one will do anything because I don't have five thousand to pay them to get off their asses! This is not right. When did we bury justice under money?

As I had said before, Pete helped me and Chris through a lot. He has no car right now, so I still go out once a month and take him to pay his bills and buy food.

On the way home, I stop to see Bea. Bea said to me one day that Billy had to be hiding something because why else would he not do anything about what Ike did to his daughter. Bea's daughter then asked from the next room if we were talking about Brittany Todson.

She said that Brittany goes to school with her and that she has became a lesbian because of what Ike did to her. She told her that after Ike molested her that she would never trust another man ever again. She is not the only thirteen year old to say this about Ike. These girls call him out by his name, not just some guy.

These girls saying he molested them is the nice way of saying he raped them. A whole school knows what happened to this child, but the police can't find anything, or do anything?

This child is screaming for help with this, and no one is listening, and I guarantee no one will even try to help. I would go try to talk to her if I didn't think I would have to fight her parents to do so.

I am sorry, but this is not just rolling off my back so easily. Someone has to help this girl.

If she is freaked out over the fact that it happened, how is she going to deal with the fact that this man just killed her with HIV and Hepatitis C?

If they catch it early, medications can help, but if they don't take her to the doctors now, she doesn't stand a chance to control it later. Not only will they die slow and painful deaths, they will give it to everyone they are with.

The Hepatitis C will easily spread to their families without them knowing it. It is becoming an epidemic because no one wants to talk about it or do anything about it. I have asked so many people for help and nothing has been done. This is supposed to be what we pay them to do. This is supposed to be their job. I truly don't know what else to do.

I told Bea that I had seen a pen sized camera that I thought about getting. She looked at me and said, "Get that thought out of your head. I have seen that look before. You are thinking about confronting Ike and getting him to confess everything he has done, aren't you?" I said that it was a thought. She said, "Well, did you think about the fact that it will be your last breath because you know he will kill you when he sees you?"

I said I was thinking about taking an officer with me to wait outside, and I could tell Ike I wanted to move back to my land and wanted to set a few rules with an officer present for peace. Ike will automatically start bragging to me about everything he has done.

Then she said, "Like these officers have protected you so well so far?" She was right. Plus the fact that I really don't think I could keep from beating the man. I truly do not ever want to see his face or hear his voice ever again.

I don't ever want to give him the chance to say he is sorry because I know he won't mean it. I sure as hell am not giving him the chance to say things to hurt me again.

God gave me the strength not to beat him all those years, but after I have had all this time to really think about all he did to me and my family, I would probably lose it and he is not worth it.

Now that I know this is a fact with these girls and not hear say I sent anonymous letters to Judge Mavis and Child Services. I told the Health Department and the Sheriff's department. Nothing was done. I sent it anonymously hoping they would take it more seriously.

TBI and both this child's parents know Ike did this to this little girl. Even her school knows. This isn't right. Ike watched this girl grow up. He always knew she was underage. If this happened a year ago, she was only twelve at the time. All of Ike's daughters are older than this girl.

I went out to my land again to find that an old air conditioner that was built into the wall has been stolen now. I really didn't think there was anything else they could do to the place or anything left they could steal. I guess they just had to prove me wrong.

I boarded up the hole and nailed the doors shut. I used bricks I found laying there to pound the nails. Both my palms were badly bruised from it, but I was so angry I didn't care. Enough is enough.

Pete was finally able to move the trailer down to his place. He can use it for storage. I am glad to be rid of the bad memories. If Ike were gone, I could start rebuilding my life out there.

I am hopeful that Ike will get all he has coming to him. I asked the church out there if they could at least help me build a bathroom out there eventually.

If I had a bathroom, I wouldn't feel like I am camping again when I move back. I have already proved to myself that I can survive with very little.

I met another woman at Pete's while I was out there this time. She said she wanted to talk to my investigator and tell him all she knows about all of this going on with Ike and the fact that the police never do anything.

She said she has many more facts about the sheriff's department. I told her how to reach him, but I guarantee nothing will be done as usual. I wonder exactly how many people will have to die first.

I was just told that Sheriff Redletter and another guy just cornered the new guy running for sheriff in a store and told him if he didn't stop running for office that they would put a bullet in his head. The guy being threatened taped the whole thing and made lots of copies.

I was also told recently that a girl at the high school told Brittany that she had a headache. Brittany gave the girl a pill and said it was like Tylenol. They found the girl passed out in the bathroom. She almost died. The pill was half Oxycontin and half Morphine.

Brittany said she got it from her dad, Billy. Then I was told that the only thing that had saved Brittany and her sister all these years is the fact that their parents stayed messed up most of the time.

How sad is this? I hate knowing that any child has to go though life like this let alone someone I actually know. I don't even want to think about what this child is going through.

I am very upset right now. It has been two years since all of this happened to me and Chris. Mr. Kamar called and said it was time to finish out my case. I was really happy for about a second. He told me that he couldn't finish my case for the five hundred he was already paid. He says he already has five thousand dollars worth of work already put into it.

If I want to take this to court, I have to pay more than five thousand more. He hasn't even gotten my witnesses' statements yet. As I said, it may as well be a million.

I understand that he needs money to work but this should have been said a year ago when I was busting my ass to get this done. All I can hope for now is that the one guy gets voted sheriff and cleans the town up. I guess we really did bury justice under money!

When I had a dental appointment in Knoxville, I went to the FBI office building. I told them all about Ike and Shellie and what they did to these girls. I also told them about the police doing nothing to help anyone.

They said they would check it out and get back to me. I really hope they mean it. When I left there, I saw people from the local news at the courthouse, so I gave the reporter a copy of the first rough draft. All I can do is get it out there. They have to run with it.

I called the man that was told to drop out of the sheriff re-election. I wanted to let him know that I talked to the FBI and that they may call him. He said that was fine and that he would tell them everything. He also told me that he has already dropped out of the race. He said that he found out that the other guy's circle of friends reaches too high and there are too many for him to fight.

He said that it may even go into federal levels and may include the FBI. Isn't that great?

I went to the FBI to protect those girls from being raped again and to help all the people in that county get rid of the crooked cops.

My hopes were that they could get someone in there that would actually try to do their job. Instead I now realize that I may have just drawn a bull's-eye on my back for the cops. No good deed goes unpunished, huh.

I will try my best to get a copy of this to the President before something happens to me. They may not help either but I have to try. I need a lot of Prayers. Maybe the President's wife would be the better one to send this to. A women would definitely better understand this problem.

A friend emailed me and said that years ago him and a bunch of other people got busted for cooking meth. He said Ike went out to talk to the cops and everyone was told to just go home. He said that Ike showed him how he did the iodine for the cook. He said that he didn't know how Ike was still alive because he had seen the man sweat iodine. Evil doesn't die, I guess.

I was just thinking about how even after I got away from Ike all he has done is threaten me and continued to destroy my property. Wouldn't you think that he had figured out by now that this behavior is exactly why I left?

He even threatened me in the court room while we were waiting for our hearing. I know the judge heard all this and the judge still treated me like I was the bad guy in this deal. How can this be right?

I asked Ike one time if he really thought that threatening and beating us was going to somehow force us to love and respect him. His answer was, "Well that's what my dad did." I then reminded him that he hates his dad so badly that he hasn't spoke to him since he was about ten.

It still didn't sink in.

I just found out that Billy kicked Brittany out because he found out she is now a lesbian. If she went to her mother's, then she is right back with the two that molested her.

The FBI finally called me back today. They say they are now investigating Ike and Shellie. They said they want an airtight case first so they will never have a chance to get out of jail. Their exact words were that they had to dot all their I's and cross all their T's. Maybe they will actually end up doing something.

The FBI thanked me repeatedly. He said most people do nothing and say it isn't their problem. He said that is why so many people get away with it.

Every time I hear on the news about a woman that was shot, beaten to death or burned alive by her ex, I know deep in my heart that she spent years asking the police to help her. For whatever excuse they gave, the truth is they just looked the other way and ignored her until it was too late.

If the laws don't change to force the police to protect us, this is going to keep on happening. Is this the kind of life we are leaving to our daughters and granddaughters? There has to be a change and it has to change now.

I will go to Nashville and bitch until someone listens. Please pray I meet the right one to complain to. One person can make a difference but a thousand will make them sit up and listen. A million woman march on Washington would be so much better. A mob of angry women would definitely get their attention.

I am still haunted by how Ike was so excited by watching people being torn apart in the movie, Hostile. He giggled like a school girl and talked for days about how he wished he had enough money to pay someone to let him have a day to do whatever he wanted to another person.

This still gives me shivers. Just as much as the memories of what he said and did to me all these years.

Chris's and my symptoms are getting worse from the ash spill. They just announced that they are not even going to try to clean all this toxic waste up. They have decided to spread it out and just cover it over. When it rains, we both get really sick from all the toxins kicked up in the air.

Chris still has to go over there to make deliveries. Chris has to drink energy drinks as soon as he wakes up for energy enough to go to work. He chews aspirin like candy for what he calls blinding headaches and drinks Alka-seltzer Plus cold medicine for the body aches every four hours.

TVA still says this stuff is at safe levels. If it were safe, we wouldn't still be getting this sick.

If the heavy metals are still shrinking our brains and muscles, then we will end up with Dementia or Alzheimer's. One of our neighbors says he is eaten up with cancer from living next to this for so many years. He says he only has months to live now, We are essentially trapped in yet another life or death situation.

As soon as my mind is awake every morning, I have to instantly remember to take my right foot and push up my left foot before it cramps up.

It is supposed to rain every day this week, so we will be getting an even higher dose of these toxins than usual. I wish I could afford to move from this. I could afford to move back to my land, a safe distance away, but Ike still lives next door. So my choice is to stay here and die or move back home and die.

Chris is talking about getting married. Whitney moved in with us. I want to move and give them their space. Moving back home alone would definitely make Ike think he could start his terrorizing all over again. I hope a change is coming soon.

Mick Lamby told me the other day that Child protective services talked to Ike Wrench about what Ike did to Brittany. FBI promised they would investigate. All this time has passed and still no arrests.

I was just told that the one cop that never bothered to write that report on the theft and damages or go to court with me when he was subpoenaed, never actually left More County Sheriff's office.

They sent Johnny to the next town over to get him out of the way so I couldn't make him go to court. That is still part of More County. They basically lied to me. They hid him in plain sight. Just like they did Landon Bagley when he was trying to help me. I imagine this is what happened to Officer Dawn too when he was going to arrest Ike when he got out of jail that last time.

I was also told that recently Johnny got high and drunk and hit a woman head on. She was in intensive care, in critical condition, with many broken bones including her ribs. She also has laceration to a few internal organs.

Johnny was not arrested on any charges. He was told to quit his job in Sun and go back to work in Wartville. All of these men are so sure nothing will ever happen to them that no one is even trying to hide any of this anymore.

I sincerely hope I am not the only person having trouble taking this.

A guy on the sheriff's department, Donnie ran for sheriff and said he was going to fire everyone if he won. When I asked to talk to him when I was there last time, I was told he suddenly quit.

A new sheriff was elected. Once he gets settled in, I plan on going over to talk to him. I will tell him my story. That's the only way I know how to see if he is as crooked as the rest or not. If nothing is done, then I will have my answer. Redletter has cancer I heard. That's the only reason he isn't back in office. He was too sick.

The news said that the FBI is investigating the Mayor of Crossburg. They said they are seeing that the corruption is going much deeper than just his office. I imagine it will all be swept under the rug as usual. Maybe when my book is made into a movie someone will get so embarrassed that they will finally stop all this. I can only hope.

As I said, without the money to fight these people all I can do is put the facts out there. Like I keep saying, Evil triumphs when good men do nothing!

Brian and Sara just had their second little girl. I get to meet her this week. Adam moved to California. I told you he was always angry at me for moving him away from there. I told him it isn't like he remembered it but that he had to go see for himself or he would always regret it. I really hate one of my babies being that far away from me.

He is having a real hard time getting a job with the economy as bad as it is right now. He said he still wants to stay and check things out for a while anyway. When Chris gets married, I may go out there and help Adam get on his feet.

If my book is published by then I can look up old friends to get all the gory details put into a movie. Being around this evil Meth addict was truly a roller coaster ride from hell. If you have nightmares from the movie don't blame me. I did warn you.

Adam wants to get into acting. Maybe my friends can help him too. It really is "Who you know." I figured that one out years ago.

Chapter 17

Three years have passed, and Ike still hasn't been arrested. He still lives next door to my land. When I went out to take Pete grocery shopping, I was told that Ike had burned down Shellie's barn. It was burnt to the ground.

Either he was cooking meth again or he was proving one of his stupid points to her. Glad it is her and not me. Sorry, but very sadly true.

I got to spend two weeks with my new granddaughter. When I got back, I had to rush around to get a few last minute details done for Chris and Whitney's wedding. It turned out beautifully. They still live with me but want to get their own place after he gets his taxes back.

Adam moved in too. He had to come back for his disability hearing. He has to wait for their decision. It kind of pisses me off. His attorney is supposed to get twenty five percent of his money, yet in two years they hadn't even sent for his medical records to take to court with him.

They didn't mention that this was a nineteen year old case. Or that the state of Tennessee declared him disabled nineteen years ago. They said they didn't think it was relevant to this case. They are asking for only six months back pay.

Adam said the judge wasn't even there. He was on a big screen TV via satellite from South Carolina. He was screwed over by yet another government agency that he spent the last nineteen years working and paying into.

By the way the court date for the TVA ash spill doesn't even start untill September of next year.

They sent some of the ash to an underground mine in Alabama. Even putting it miles underground, in sealed containers, all the people around there are already starting to get sick. But TVA still insists it is safe.

They said on the news this summer that all the tourist should come back and go swimming in the water again. The next sentence was for them to shower thoroughly afterwards. My new daughter-in-law miscarried with my grandchild shortly after moving in here. I know it was because of the toxins from the ash spill.

I am sure that everyone that is suing TVA has already realized like I have, that we will never get a dime for our future and past sufferings from their mistake. Personally since they knew it was going to happen and chose to do nothing to prevent it, I think they should all go to prison for attempted murder. Especially since they chose to waste the money they had that could have fixed the problem on personal toys.

Since I no longer drink the tap water, I don't get dizzy anymore. I can tell the toxins are still in the air especially on rainy days because we all still get tired and have all the symptoms of a bad cold. Since I still take allergy medications, my symptoms are a little less than theirs are. I still get the bad leg cramps all the time. Some days are worse than others.

I saw a doctor last week that stuck needles in my legs to shoot electricity through my legs to check the damage. It was really painful but maybe they can come up with a way to stop the cramps and the pain.

They did a similar test to Adam. He is still waiting to hear from disability. We could use a few prayers for that too. I love having both my sons here, even my new daughter-in-law. I just wished we could afford a little bigger place to live. One bathroom isn't cutting it.

As I said before, my having to pull myself with my arms and push myself with my legs on my belly all those times Ike refused to help me did damage to the sciatic nerve that has never healed.

Most of the time I just have minor pain and I can barely feel my little toe on my left foot. Some days when I get up I have a lot of back pain from the back surgery. I walk bent over for a few minutes, but then it eases up. I always tell myself that it still could have been much worse.

I just remembered when Billy shot his gun at our trailer and all the sheriff did was call him on the phone and tell him he needed to quit. I have the report where they say they didn't bother to go out there, they just called.

I was told that I had to change the names of the bad guys in here. They want to protect the guilty I guess.

When Ike would get mad enough that I could see he was going to hurt one of the girls, I would get his attention on me. Now I can't even do my gardening very often because my knee pops out and I roll around in pain until I can pop it back in. Saving those girls from that terror was still worth it to me. Maybe they won't be as scared.

When the boys were little, I would spend all day Sunday cooking meals. I would freeze them right away. After work, I would put something in the oven, and we had a nice home cooked meal even on very exhausting days.

When Ike stole all my cookware and mixers and food processors and rotisserie ovens, he took all this away from us. Now I have one skillet, one pan and the microwave Brian bought us to try to cook our meals on.

It's like taking a chef's tools away and telling him to go cook your meals. It doesn't work. I don't have another lifetime or enough money to replace everything he took from me, especially my time and my health. He almost succeeded in killing me more times than I could try to count. How do you come back from that? "OOOPS just doesn't do it."

I guarantee that he still thinks he has done nothing wrong. He still thinks we have to be punished because I am no longer paying his way and taking his crap. He has probably convinced himself that I deserted him for no reason and he will make me pay and pay dearly.

All Ike ever talked about and all he cared about was his next lay and his next high. He didn't care who he had to hurt or who he had to kill to get it. He said he never had to pay for sex, but the only women that slept with him were the ones that would sleep with anyone for drugs. He ended up paying for it with all his money, and because of the diseases, he will eventually pay for it with his life.

This man decided the day he met me that he was going to do everything he could to terrorize me and my family. From day one he did everything he could think of to destroy my family and our entire way of life. How twisted can this be?

He tried over and over to kill me for an acre and a quarter of land he said he didn't even want to live on. He had almost five acres a few lots up from mine that he has done nothing with. He kept trying to force me to fix up his land with my money.

Picture this. You are peacefully sitting in your home. Out of nowhere a six foot tall, two hundred and fifty pound rabid pit-bull bursts in and traps you in the corner, chomping, snarling, foam from his frothing mouth going everywhere.

You can see in his eyes that he wants to kill you. You know you have to fight him to save your life. After you think you have defeated him, you relax again. An hour later he is in your face again trying to rip you apart.

Think how you would feel after thirteen straight years of having to deal with this, with no help from the police that are getting paid to protect you. When the police have every reason and every right to remove this animal from your home, they refuse to do their job over and over again. Welcome to my life.

I am hoping that with the next book I can tell you I made enough money from this book that I paid Mr. Kamar and finished my case. End results being Ike is in Prison. Help me pray that God helps to end his reign of terror on the world.

I sincerely hope that you never have to feel this terror. If you are in it, do everything you can to get out. Staying is not helping you or your children. Those girls came into my life like little whirlwinds, and they were swept out of my life just as fast.

Wendy called me really upset. She said her friend took food to Ike and Shellie because they said they had nothing to eat. Ike attacked her and tried to rape her. Her friend's face and arms were all cut up from the attack. Pete said he saw at least a four inch cut down the side of her face.

If blood was drawn on either her or Ike during this fight, then he has succeeded in killing again and nothing was done.

Two days later Wendy was beaten to death and another man was found beaten two blocks away. They burned his body. The people there told the More County Sheriff that Ike was after her, and they said the cops said they didn't care because Ike was a good snitch.

Wendy called Pete and told him that Wanda Butt broke her nose when they beat her and that she couldn't breath. Pete heard a knock at the door and she said she had to go because she hoped it was the police. That was the last thing she said to him. She was found face down in the ditch the next morning. The whole truth will have to come out eventually

They listed it as death by natural causes. When Wendy's daughter identified the body, she said she wanted an autopsy. The police said to cremate her to cover their asses. The next call her family got was to pick up her ashes. That family didn't even get to tell her goodbye, and they will never get justice for her.

I went to the DA and told her Victim's Advocate what happened. She told me that I couldn't keep interjecting myself in his cases, no matter what he had done to me. She totally ignored what the police did because she is treating me like a jealous ex.

I still have this uncontrollable urge to just slap the crap out of anyone that thinks I ever cared about this man. I mean so hard their ears would ring for a week. In other states it is the LAW to report any kind of abuse. Why is that not the law here?

These cops are walking around high on drugs, armed and on duty, covering up crimes that their criminal buddies are doing, crimes that they are doing themselves. And collect a paycheck from us. Why do they not make these cops and judges take drug tests? Everyone else has to.

My doctor said all those times Ike slammed my head that it didn't end with just that slam. He said your brain floats on a cushion of air. After that slam, your brain bounces off your skull many more times. Each time causing swelling and bleeding in your head.

That's why an infant will die after being shaken.

Chris went for his TVA deposition. They gave him a hard time and tried to keep him from talking about all of us being so sick all the time. Just afterwards our attorney called to say that the judge decided he was not going to hear about any illnesses because we couldn't prove if it was from the ash spill or if it was from the cleanup.

I can prove that they hadn't even begun the cleanup when we got sick. When I went to that first meeting and they pissed me off enough to make me call Erin Brockovich, they were just starting to tell everyone how they were going to start cleaning up.

The judge decided there would be no jury, only he will decide everything. Those voices in my head telling me how much easier it is to pay off one judge rather than a whole jury started screaming at me again.

Chris got a job at a factory. He really liked this job. It not only paid a great salary, he got lots of overtime, at time and a half. He would also have insurance to cover his now pregnant wife's delivery of their first child.

It rained here for several weeks. So much that many areas flooded. Chris got sick and went to the hospital. He had a serious sinus infection. They gave him one of the strongest antibiotics they could. It is called a z pack. He got sicker a day or two later and went to the hospital, and they said he had an even more serious ear infection. It took two rounds of this z pack to get rid of it.

He was eight minutes late for work after being at the hospital all night and got fired. All again as a direct result of all the toxins TVA put in the air.

Adam woke me up several times that same week and said he couldn't breathe. He said to wait and see if it got better before I took him to the hospital. It got better a couple of times, but soon after, I ended up having to take him to the emergency room.

My sons are not wimps. Just like me they will deal with the pain until they absolutely have to go be treated. They said he had almost a whole lung full of pneumonia.

When he told them he had gotten sick several other times but it had gone away, they told him that he had what they call walking pneumonia. Then they told him that was the one that killed most people before they ever even knew they had it. They gave him a z pack.

When he went to his regular appointment a few weeks later, he still had it. They gave him another z pack of antibiotics.

When I went for my TVA deposition they let me tell them about all of our illnesses, including Adam's. They have nothing to lose now that they think they can't be charged for poisoning us. All we are allowed to do is sue for lose of enjoyment of our home.

I didn't even mention the fact that when Whitney miscarried and found what she thought was a blood clot, it turned out to be her dead child. This is something she is never going to forget. I can't forget how I felt just hearing about it. Now I have to wonder if she will miscarry again or if this child will have birth defects from it.

TVA asked if I had written anything on the computer about this and asked for my Facebook name. I told them I don't blog or tweet.

Two days later Facebook sent me a message that some one in that town was trying to hack my Facebook account to read it.

I was mad already since they held the depositions right next to the ash spill area. It rained that day. When I came home I got really dizzy. I was nauseous and had a pounding headache. I had to go to bed.

When Brian brought his girls for Chris's wedding he was here at a hotel for a few days. His youngest girl's eyes started getting this bright green pus oozing out of them. He doesn't like coming here anymore. He still comes, but he picks us up and we go to a restaurant out of this area to visit.

If this attorney doesn't appeal this judge's decision, then I will find someone that will. I am not going to let them get away with poisoning my family. They killed some and almost killed others. I will fight it all the way to the Supreme Court if I have to. Court is still set for September.

I just realized why Ike beat up my pots and pans so bad. The first time he scratched them up really bad and left them for me to find. They had a lifetime warranty on them so I got them replaced. He beat the bottoms and handles up to void my warranty this time. Like I said, isn't he just the most thoughtful man?

Every time I hear of a flood or tornado or fire I think to myself, how sad. I know exactly how they feel instantly losing everything they spent their whole life working and saving for. They lose all their photos and memories. Sometimes they almost lose their very lives.

I still go to find something I know I should have and quickly realize Ike has it. None of them know how I feel losing everything twice. Not to a natural disaster or act of God. I sit here every day knowing I lost everything to someone I spent years taking care of.

I lost it all to a vengeful, evil man that never had any reason or any right to do this against me and my family. He did it all purely for spite. All of my terror, all of my pain, all of my loss could have been prevented if the police had only done what they got paid to do. There is truly more than one evil man in my story.

People have said to me so many times that I could have just easily walked away that I started wondering if I had missed something in all this. It just hit me what Ike had said to me once. He said he knew me long before I met him.

Ike picked up that AIDS diseased woman in a bar. He said he saw me that same night. He said that when I smiled his knees buckled and he knew I was the one he was going to get. Not only did he sleep with her knowing it would kill him and anyone he was ever with, but he left her with his girls while he stalked me at the bar.

Ike said from day one he started telling horrible lies about me to anyone that would listen just to alienate me from everyone. When he first met me he called my mother to tell her I was on strong psychotropic medications to control my behavior and that I stopped taking my medicine and started beating him.

My mom asked me if he seriously thought that she didn't know her own child better than that. She was well aware of the fact that I smoked pot and never did any other drugs, not even the ones my doctor prescribed.

He called Adam and told him I hated him and never wanted to see him. He said he would beat him if he ever came to see me. Adam knew better but that still had to hurt for someone to say that to you.

So no, there is nothing I could have done any different to change any of this. It played out exactly as it had to play out.

This man was determined to destroy mine and my family's entire way of life and to eventually kill me long before I ever met him. Evil has no conscience.

I also questioned myself about whether or not I should publish this now and write a second one later, after all my court cases are over, or if I should wait to make it one big book. If I do it now, I would have to come up with a good idea for You tube to ask for help with the fees. I decided to ask God for his input to help me decide what to do.

To start my story I need to explain that I never go outside the apartment except to go to Chris's car to go to the store or the Laundromat. I go to the mailbox everyday and straight back to the air-conditioning.

Second of all, since I have lived here most of the bad storms have gone around us. I see all that damage on the news but never around here.

The third point I need to tell you is the fact that in the more than twenty years I have lived in this state, Channel 8 news has only come to this town once. They say that we are barely inside their viewing area. They came here after the ash spill first happened.

They didn't even come here to interview Erin Brockovich when she was here. All the other news stations came.

On July 1st I was watching Channel 8 news and Laura Estrada was on with an interview. Most of the time, she is not on camera. She interviews from behind the camera.

I looked up and said, "God I need a sign. A real act of God miracle so there is no doubt that you are behind me on this. If you think I should publish right now and if Laura Estrada is related to my friend Erik Estrada, get her to my neighborhood. I will get her to call Erik and he will help me get my book published."

Then I said, "If they aren't related then I will just give her a copy of my book and ask her if she knows anyone that can help me. It has to be something really serious to get her here but please make sure no one gets hurt for this to happen."

Then I gave him my list of things I promise to do if he did this for me. This is not just for me, I promised to use this money to help the other people hurt by this man.

On the 4th of July a pretty good storm rolled through and it knocked out our power. Adam opened the door when the air-conditioning went out. I started noticing a lot more traffic going down this little one block street than usual.

I walked up to the corner to see what was going on. A tree limb was in the middle of the road and the police was routing traffic to our road to go around while they cleaned it up.

On my walk back to the apartment, I looked up and jokingly said, "This wasn't our deal God. If she is several blocks away, I won't see her."

"She has to come to my neighborhood." I was not even seriously thinking that this had anything to do with me.

When I got almost to my door I glanced over my shoulder and out of the corner of my eye I saw a news van going by. I said to Adam, "Come on out honey, a news van just pulled up by the other corner. Let's walk up there to see what is going on."

Adam was in the shower, so I walked up there. I kept hearing popping and cracking sounds and I could see smoke billowing up. You could see wires laying on the ground. The neighbors were out there looking.

We watched as the van pulled in the driveway across the street and a tiny blonde woman got out and set up her camera, just up the hill out of our site. I was trying to see which news station it was but couldn't see the logo clearly.

A few of the neighbors tried to get me to go over to see what was going on. I said no because my hair was all frizzy from the rain and I was still in my pajamas. I wasn't about to get caught on the evening news looking like that.

After an hour I see her putting her camera away so I went over to see what had happened. As I passed the woman sitting in her car, she kind of waved like she was trying to get my attention. I waved and said, "How you doing?" and went on up the hill.

When I got up the hill the guy that lives there says, "This was a real act of God. Lightning struck this tree and it fell over. Then the lightning skipped across the driveway and hit that pole with the transformer on it. The pole fell across the tree."

When he said, "Thank God the tree fell that way and not this way because we were all in the living room, we would have all been killed." It hit me that I had just passed by Laura Estrada. When I turned to go talk to her, I could see the van rolling out of sight.

I have kicked myself for days now realizing that God had given me the exact miracle I had asked for and I was too late and too stupid to see it.

Adam says that means that God sent me the sign to publish now but he is telling me that I don't need her to help me do it. Chris agreed and said I should just email her. I am a face to face kind of person. That is why I asked to get her to my neighborhood in the first place.

I still can't believe I let this opportunity slip through my fingers. The odds of all this falling so perfectly into place like that are probably a billion to one and will definitely never happen again.

The number one thing I promised is to pay the investigator to prosecute Ike and everyone that has protected him. Number two is to force the laws to change and make the police protect the women and children of this state. I hope that forces them to protect women and children everywhere. Then I will help all my sons to get on their feet. I will definitely keep my promises.

I still get really angry when someone says, "Why would you take that from that man." I didn't take anything. I fought back every step of the way. That is why for so long I didn't feel I was a victim. Even though he tried so hard to make everyone believe he was the victim.

I said so many times that I didn't let him intimidate me. I didn't let him break me, but in reality I lived in fear for my and my son's very lives everyday for thirteen years. I never knew from one minute to the next what this evil man was going to do to us.

Like I said unless you lived it, you will never understand the constant hell I lived through. I sincerely hope you never have to.

When the window broke the day Ike had me arrested, Louise had a tiny, tiny scratch on her face where she had wiped her face after putting her hand near some of the glass. Tiffany came in and stepped on a small piece of glass and had a very small cut.

This town held me in jail and screamed that they were going to put me in prison for twenty to thirty years when he said I did this. Ike did nothing for the next twelve years to help me out of this. He just talked about what idiots he thought they were for believing him to begin with. I know there is nothing I could have done to stop any of this. You cannot break those bonds when evil sets it's site on you.

I saw on Oprah the other day a show about a six year old boy whose father and stepmother left him chained in a small closet. At the end of the show they gave the child abuse hotline number to report if you knew of something like this happening to someone. I decided to try one last time to get someone to help Brittany Todson.

I haven't been out by my land for a while since Pete got a car and found different people to drive him to pay bills and shop. So I hadn't heard anymore stories about Ike for a while. I still knew in my heart that things hadn't gotten any better for this girl. Knowing Ike as well as I do I figured it had only gotten worse.

I told the hotline the whole story again. They said again that they would investigate just like every other time. I decided to call Bea to see if she had heard anything.

When I told her that I tried one last time to get these people to help, she said, "Oh thank God. I have been hearing for months now that all

Brittany talks to her friends about anymore is how she is going to buy a gun and blow all these people away."

She saw Brittany in a store recently and told her she had heard about what she was going to do.

She said she begged her to think about it. She told her that this act would destroy her life and that none of those people were worth that. She said Brittany just walked away.

If she is still that stressed about this years after it happened, then my gut tells me it is still going on. She may be having to see her younger sister going through the same thing by now. As I said before, Evil Triumphs When Good Men Do Nothing. This could have been over with long ago if the police had just done their job. All these lives could have been spared.

I keep praying that somewhere, someone will at the very least see that this girl gets the help she needs to deal with this. She is a child. She shouldn't have to deal with this alone.

I just found out that when they took Brittany out of her home to investigate last year that it was Brittany herself that reported the abuse. So if she told them what these people did to her then why was nothing done?

No wonder she wants to blow these people away. After reporting abuse over and over and you see that they are not willing to do their job, you start to believe that the only way to end it is to take it into your own hands.

I told Chris what I had heard about Brittany when he dropped me off from Church tonight. He told me that ever since we had left out there, he felt like he had just left someone else to deal with Ike. I told him that I thought about that every time I packed a bag to leave.

First thing I thought was that Ike would go after my family. Then I always thought, "What if the next woman doesn't see it coming? What if the next girl doesn't know how to fight? How many more lives is he going to destroy if I'm not there to stop him?"

Then I told him that I had gotten to the point that I knew I couldn't handle it anymore. I knew it was down to being me or him to die. He was not worth going to prison for and definitely not worth dying over.

Chris mentioned that he still can't play Magic with anyone anymore. He said he tried, but it would always remind him of the thousands of dollars worth of Magic cards Ike stole from him the first time he took everything.

He had a box the size of a card table top filled with full decks of these cards. He sold cards for his living. It wasn't just the game Ike stole from him, but his livelihood.

Chris and Whitney found an apartment and moved about a month ago. Their son should be born in about six weeks. I miss them both so much. They both work a lot, so I only see Chris when he picks me up on Sunday. But at least he stays to talk for a while after church. It does my heart good.

I just thought back to when I was fifteen. My parents didn't want me to marry my boyfriend so they bought a restaurant in Alabama and moved me there. There was a two lane highway between us and a huge lake.

The place had five cabins at the side and a gas pump out front. My parents sold live bait and tackle, and they put in a little general store up front. I only had to work during the afternoon rush and clean the cabins.

My dad built a boat dock and rented out fishing boats. He built a big floating pier and floated it out on the lake. He burned down the floating pier when a boy got killed out there. It turns out that snakes decided to use it to breed under.

My parents moving me to this beautiful lake to keep me away from my boyfriend was torture back then. I can't begin to comprehend what Brittany is feeling toward her parents right now. By the way legal age to get married in Alabama was sixteen back then, so it turned out my parents made it easier for me to get married.

I regret getting married so young, but five years later I had my first bundle of joy, Adam. He was the one good thing that came out of that marriage.

As many people found out the hard way, I will fight tooth and nail against anyone that tries to hurt one of my babies. I won't even tolerate anyone talking down to them. That is why I truly cannot understand why these people are letting this happen to their children. Especially finding out her own mother was part of it. Parents are supposed to protect their children from harm, not cause it.

I was also just thinking about the time I went to San Francisco. My sons didn't want to go with me, so I drove all night to get there. I saw all the sites but missed my boys so much that I started back home with no sleep. I drove till I couldn't stay awake any longer.

I pulled to the side of the road and fell asleep before I turned the car off. I had work done on my car before I left. The guy didn't tighten something down and my car burst into flames. Two truck drivers said they saw the flames miles away. By the time they got to me the front of my car was engulfed.

They pulled me out of my car and put out the fire. Even my brand new tires had melted. I was still in shock when the two truck drivers dropped me off at my house hours later. The purple coat I had used for a pillow was stained yellow from the smoke that had filled my car before the truck drivers could get to me.

I remember looking up and saying, "Okay God, I know I said that I wanted to be cremated and let my sons split my ashes and take me with them, but I didn't know that I had to specify that I want to be dead, FIRST."

Wendy's family didn't get to make that choice when she was murdered. I still feel so badly that they will never get justice for her.

When Ike constantly told me that God hated me, he talked me into second guessing myself. I kept wondering what I had done to piss God off. My pastor said in church recently that if you have the Mulley Grubs and go around complaining about what is happening in your life that God will stop listening.

He said that you have to praise God for the good things in your life. Then you can tell him what is going wrong and ask for his help to get you through it.

My sons decided a few weeks ago to tell me that since I didn't take David Soul up on his offer of making me a star that it was all my fault that we weren't rich and living in a mansion.

This really upset me that my grown sons were still blaming me that their lives aren't perfect. Then I thought back through my life. I didn't blame my parents for not making me rich, but every time something happened in my life that I didn't like, I blamed God.

As soon as something happened to me I would look up and say, "What did I do? Why are you letting this happen to me?"

We all do it and now I can see how this would hurt God that we all blame him for our problems. I would like to think he can take it, but it doesn't make it right. I promised right then to make a conscious effort to stop doing that. See, everything does happen for a reason.

I wanted to put in a picture of the girls. I can't find a picture of them when I first met him. I think the pictures were destroyed by Debney back when they stole everything the first time.

Tell me ladies, could you have walked away from these beautiful little girls and left them to fight for themselves? This state did exactly that. That is why I had to do this myself, no one else would.

I can't put in the photo of me and my sons either. I wanted to show you how happy we all were before Ike. Ike couldn't stand that we were happy. He had to destroy that.

In closing, I want to tell every woman that is going through this, to hang in there and start telling the people around you what is going on. You CAN get through it and move on with your life.

Chris wanted to edit this for me and add his comments about how he felt about all of it as it was happening. He got through about half of the book and got too upset to finish.

He told his wife, "Much more had happened than I even realized and I was living there." And like I said that was even without all the gory details.

I don't think any of my sons should go to see the movie. Like I also said, don't blame me for the nightmares.

I hope to hear from you all when I get my website up and running. Now I see that men need a place to vent too, not just the women. I will try to get both on line soon.

Michelle Obama wrote me back. She said to stay passionate and keep up the good work. I don't think she actually had time to read it though. I would like to think that if she had read it, that she would make someone do something about what he is doing to these girls.

I sent a letter to the President too and asked him to read the book. I told him that I know he can't help Adam but to please hire someone to find out how all these government agencies that are supposed to help people are getting away with stealing everyone's money and screwing them over. I hope he listens.

I still think that a million woman march is a good idea. Maybe someday soon we can get that in motion. I'm up for it. How about you?

OPRAH magazine just wrote back to say that my book was too long for the magazine and too short for a book. None of the other places even answered back. It isn't a big enough story until I am dead I guess.

I wish I could give you all a warm sincere hug and take all your problems away. I can assure you that the proceeds from this book will go to getting the websites on line so I can help as many of you out there as I can. For the ladies website the motif was Fairies on all the forums. The saying was "Believe in Yourself." Just being able to vent your problems will be a big help to many of you.

Please get out as soon as you can if you are in this situation. It never gets any better. You deserve a better life. I can tell you ladies that there really can be life after complete terror. God will help you heal.

Most people feel happy when they see a smile on someone's face, especially if you know you put it there. A smile only makes Ike angry. He will say and do anything to take it away from you. He is only happy when someone is running away, screaming in terror. This is what makes him truly happy.

I heard something on a soap opera today that I want to pass along. After they said, "Evil triumphs when good men do nothing." They said, "When people fight back the forces of evil can be conquered."

That's what I have been saying all along, only no one is fighting back for me or these little girls. Somewhere out there someone will have to take up that sword and strike down this evil man. I hope I am still alive to see it. God bless you all.